IMAGES
of America

UNION COUNTY
1970–2003

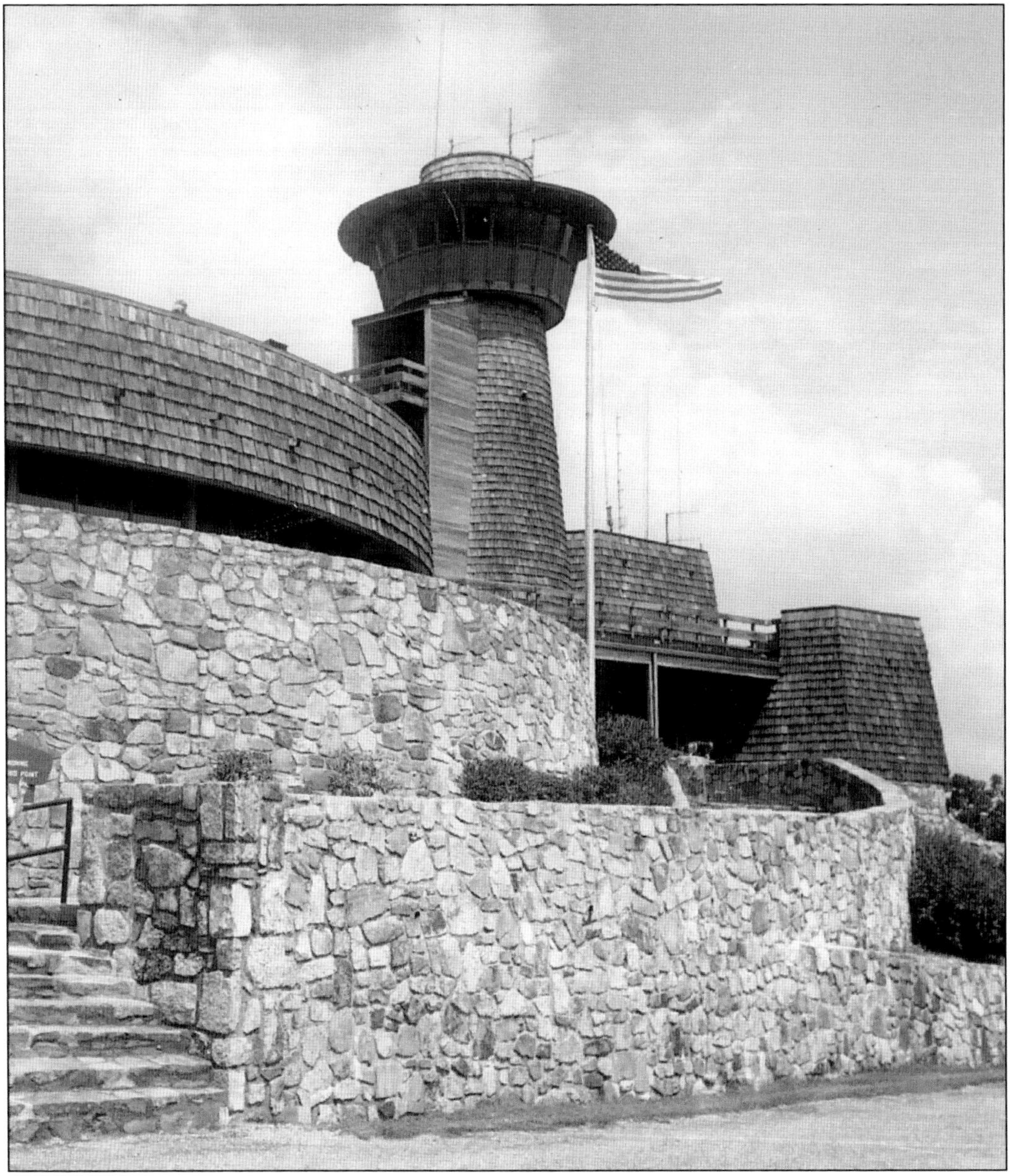

Brasstown Bald is Georgia's tallest spot. (Photo by Martyne Jokela.)

IMAGES
of America

UNION COUNTY 1970–2003

Norman Cooper

ARCADIA
PUBLISHING

ISBN 978-0-7385-1637-0

Published by Arcadia Publishing
Charleston, South Carolina

Printed in the United States of America

Library of Congress Catalog Card Number: 2004103211

For all general information contact Arcadia Publishing at:
Telephone 843-853-2070
Fax 843-853-0044
E-mail sales@arcadiapublishing.com
For customer service and orders:
Toll-Free 1-888-313-2665

Visit us on the Internet at www.arcadiapublishing.com

Contents

Acknowledgments

The authors wish to extend their appreciation to the following for their assistance with this publication: Terry Rogers, Allen Conley, Ed Rohrbaugh, Union County Historical Society, Leon Davenport, Wanda West, and Kenneth West.

The authors extend thanks and appreciation to the numerous individuals, organizations, and others who have contributed to the publication of this book. Many people have contributed photographs and information, which have been valuable assets in the book's creation. Individual donors of photographs are acknowledged with the photographs wherever possible.

The authors extend thanks and appreciation to those who purchase this book. We value your interest in the history of Union County, Georgia.

The cover photo is courtesy of Norman Cooper.

Introduction

Formed from the land once inhabited by the Cherokees, Union County was created by the Georgia Legislature on December 3, 1832. John Thomas, chosen as a representative for the new county, when asked to suggest a name, is reported to have said, "Name it Union, for none but union-like men reside in it." Scottish, Irish, and English descendents were the predominant settlers in the area. Many generations of mountain people survived with determination, endurance, resourcefulness, and self-sufficiency.

As the 21st century begins, many who live in the area are descended from those who moved here years ago—some dating back many generations. Many residents of Union County were born here, raised here, and have remained throughout the years. Many who live here now have no roots in the mountain area but were drawn to Union County, the heart of the majestic and beautiful North Georgia mountains. As more than one has said, "I wasn't born here, but I got here as quick as I could." From 1990 to 2000, there was a 44.2 percent increase in population, from 11,993 to 17,297. Union County was the 10th fastest growing county in the state of Georgia in that decade. The growth of the community and the collaboration of residents from various backgrounds present both opportunities and challenges, yet most who live here exhibit the same characteristics as those who were drawn here two centuries ago. Union County residents are resourceful, independent, and willing to work hard. They have a desire for living in a wholesome community with old-fashioned values.

In the years this book covers, 1970 to 2003, more changes have taken place in the county than in any period since the Cherokees were removed. Education, religion, business, military service, community involvement, family life, and recreation have all played a major role in the county's development. This book provides a pictorial history of some of those who have had an impact on the community.

The Union County area is remote and enclosed by mountain peaks and ranges, making access from the south more difficult than from the north and east at the beginning of the 19th century. As Union County enters the 21st century, the area is easily accessible by paved roads, a four-lane highway, and an airport. The early settlers were hardy and self-sufficient, with the skills of many generations of mountain people. They included craftsmen, blacksmiths, wheelwrights, millwrights, gunsmiths, tanners, and carpenters. As the 21st century begins, residents include mechanics, engineers, architects, designers, computer operators, administrators, accountants, retail specialists, and manufacturing specialists. National publications have listed Union County as one of the top places to retire, but businesses and families also enjoy the county.

About half of the county lies in the Chattahoochee National Forest; much of this land has been wilderness for centuries. From the mountain peaks to the lake and along the roadways and wilderness trails, Union County features flowing streams, waterfalls, abundant wildlife, spectacular flora, and magnificent views of abundant forests. The county includes Trackrock Archeological Area, with ancient petroglyphs of unknown origin; Vogel State Park, one of the most popular parks in Georgia; Lake Nottely; Lake Winfield Scott; Brasstown Bald, the highest peak in the state; Suches, the highest town and home to the smallest public school in the state; Brasstown-Russell Scenic Byway, the only National Scenic Byway in Georgia; and a section of the Appalachian Trail, which includes the only spot on the entire 2,100-mile route where the trail passes through a building. Union County is much admired for its scenic qualities, environmental resources, and recreational opportunities.

This book offers a fascinating pictorial glimpse of some of the people, organizations and events that have helped shape the county. With fond memories and a great respect for the past, Union County marches forward into the future while maintaining the Appalachian charm the area has been traditionally known for.

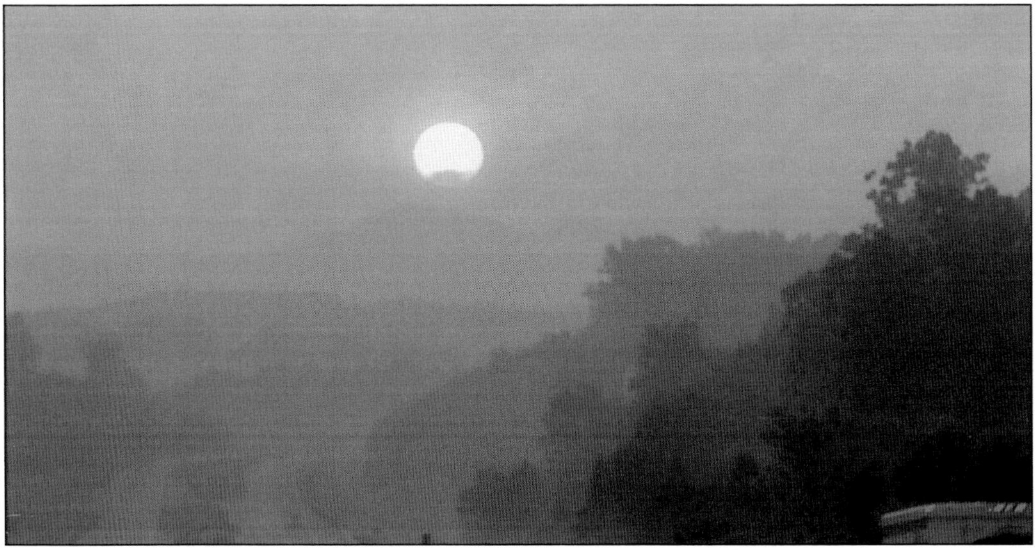

Shown above is sunrise in Union County. (Photo by Norman Cooper.)

Here's sunset in Union County. (Photo by Norman Cooper.)

One

Community Life

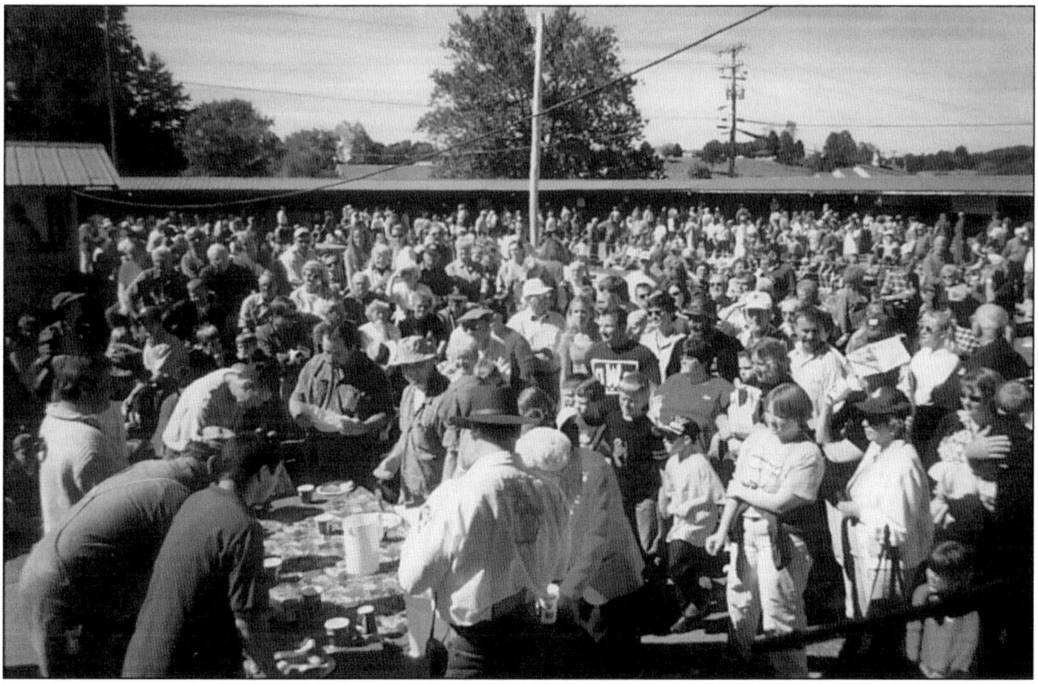

Union County is the definition of community. Union County is a place where you can find fun and fellowship in various venues from parades in downtown Blairsville to picnics along Butternut Creek, from big crowds at the Sorghum Festival to solitude along hiking trails, from music in the old courthouse to spiritual comfort in church. The quality of community life in Union County is unequaled. Above is a typical Saturday morning at the Sorghum Festival, held annually in the fall. (Photo by Norman Cooper.)

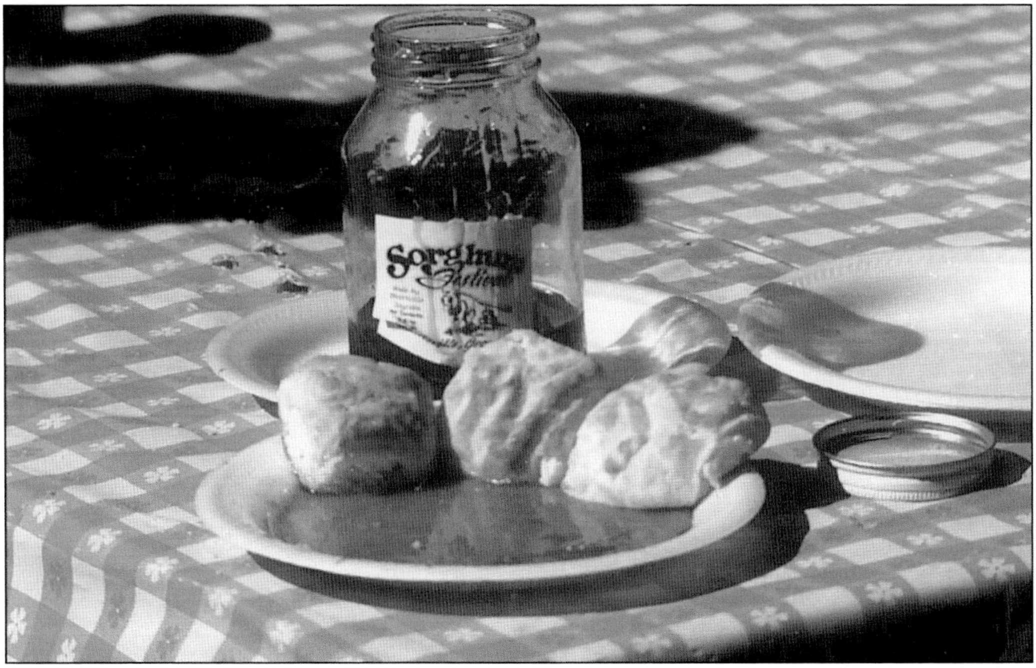

North Georgia's only three-weekend festival has been celebrated for more than 30 years. The Sorghum Festival takes place each year during the second, third, and fourth weekends of October at Fort Sorghum, nestled in the heart of the North Georgia mountains in Blairsville, Georgia. Each weekend features exhibitors with handmade arts and crafts, tasty food, and activities for all ages, including "biskit eatin' " with sorghum syrup, shown above; one highlight of the festival, is watching sorghum syrup being made.

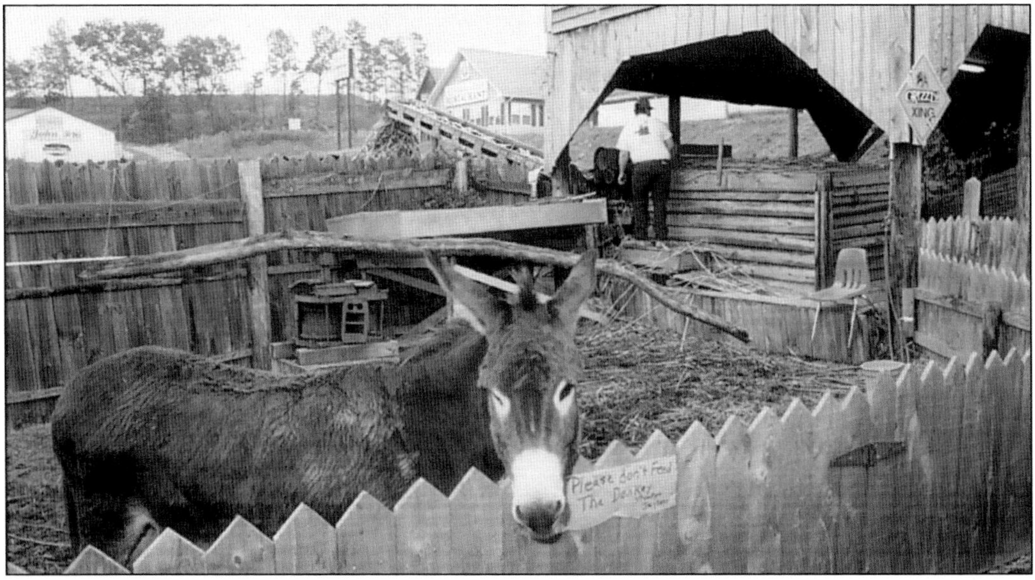

The Sorghum Festival occurs during the time of the year the leaves are changing to brilliant colors on the trees, providing a spectacular view from Fort Sorghum and throughout the mountains. A mule and the old grinder are no longer used in the process of making sorghum, but both can be seen at the Sorghum Festival. (Photo by Norman Cooper.)

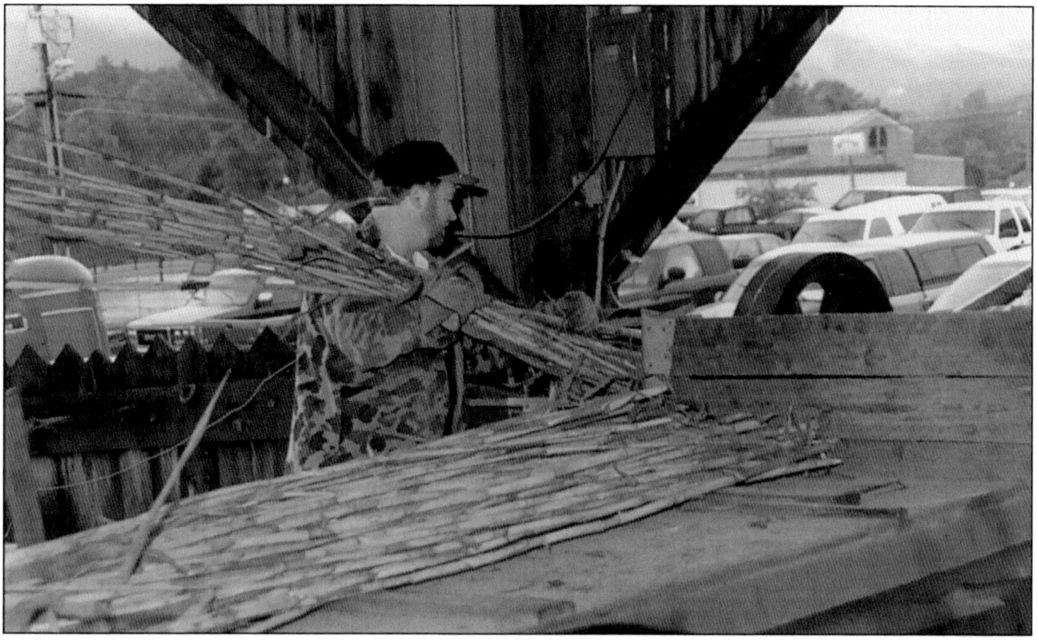

Sorghum made its way to the United States in the mid-1850s, with seeds coming to America from China by way of France. By the 1860s, Georgia was the fourth largest producer of sorghum in the country. Cane is cut in the field and hauled to the place where the syrup will be made. The cane is stripped and put into a grinder. The grinder squeezes out the juice, which is then released toward the pan in which it will cook. After the juice has filled up the pan, a fire is lit. Someone tending the pan uses a skimmer to take the green, slimy-looking substance off the top. Once the golden brown sorghum is done, the thick syrup inches its way down the spout, where it will rest on top of a cloth over a barrel. This is the final filtering process. The sorghum drips into the barrel. From the barrel, the syrup jars are filled and sealed.

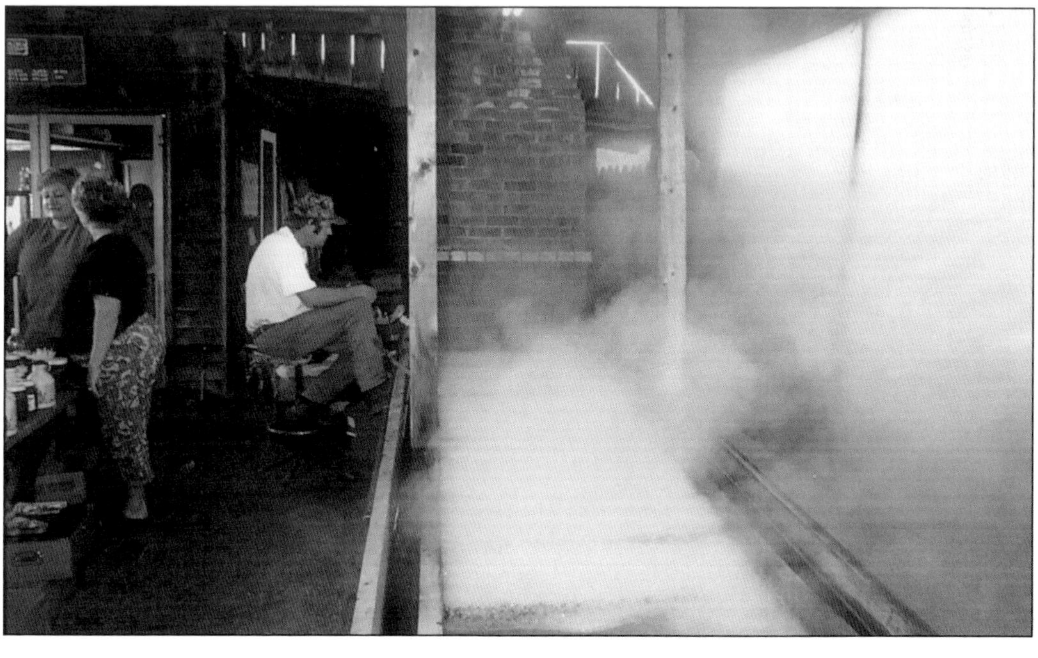

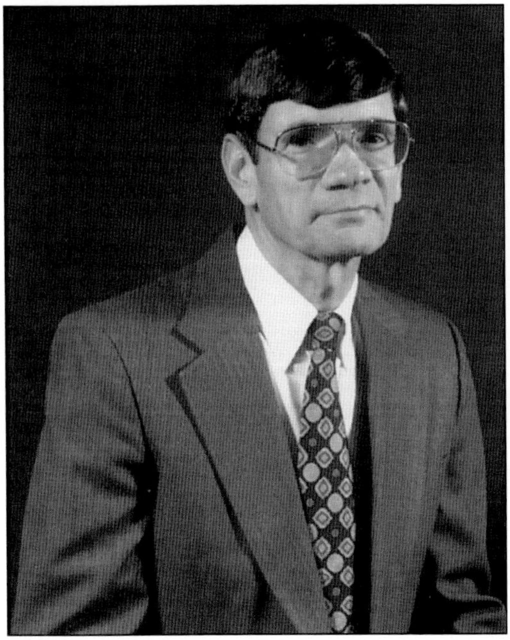

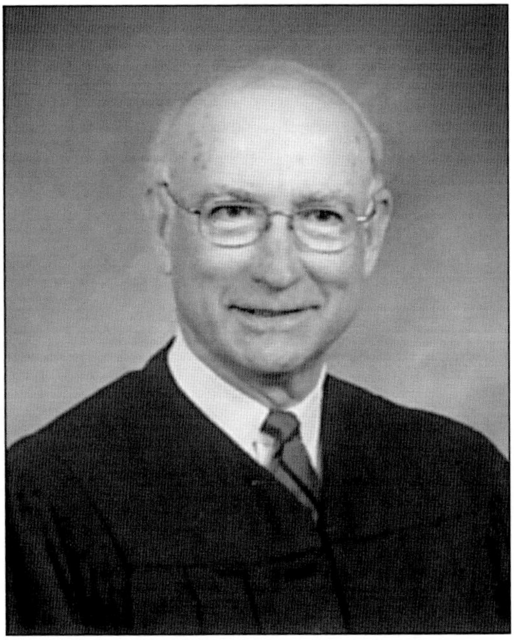

(Above, left) Allen Conley became clerk of Union County Superior Court in January 1985 and has served five consecutive terms. He served as chairman of the Ninth District Clerks for two years. Conley has served on the Union County Chamber of Commerce Board of Directors and the Union County Historical Society Board of Directors. He was a member of the Kiwanis for many years and has been involved with the American Red Cross for several years.

(Above, right) Judge Hugh Stone was appointed by Gov. Zell Miller in 1992 as chief judge of the Enotah Judicial Circuit. Judge Stone was then elected in 1994 and has served in consecutive terms since that time as chief judge.

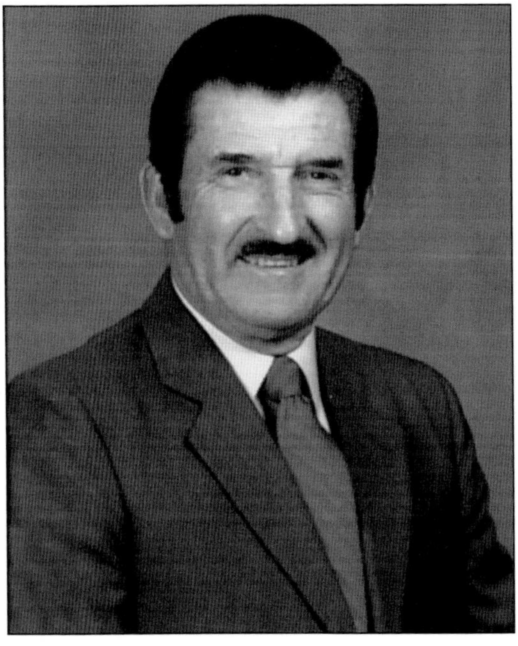

J.W. Payne, Union County tax commissioner, took office in January 1969 and served nine consecutive terms.

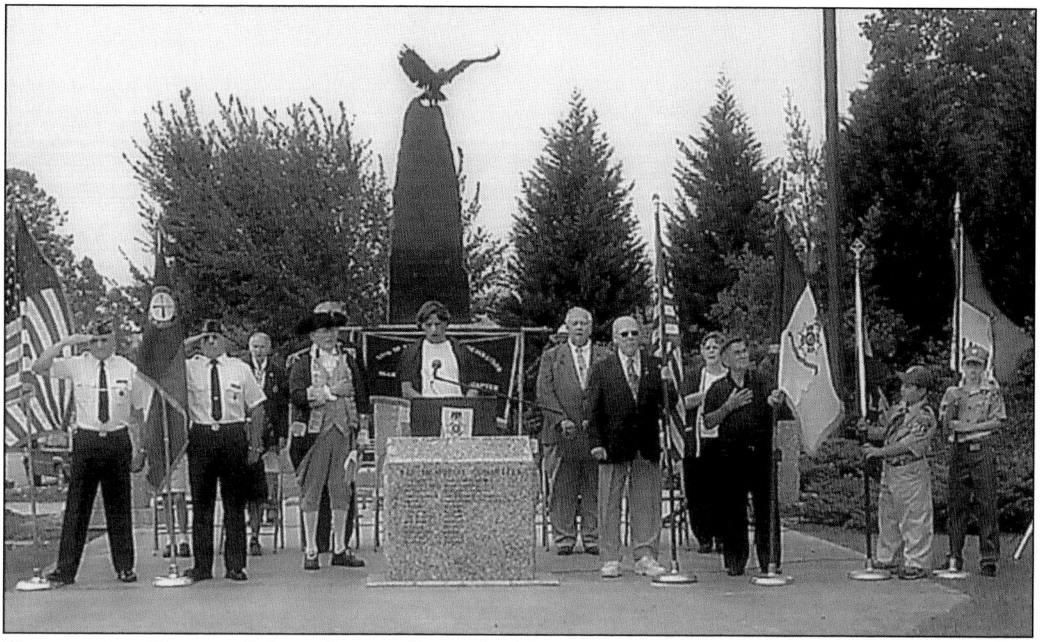

Constitution Day is celebrated annually at the Union County War Memorial. The Sons of the American Revolution and Daughters of the American Revolution organize the event with the help of the North Georgia Honor Guard and the Boys Scouts of America. The event features patriotic songs, reading of the Bill of Rights, speeches, flag-waving, and bell ringing. (Photo by Norman Cooper.)

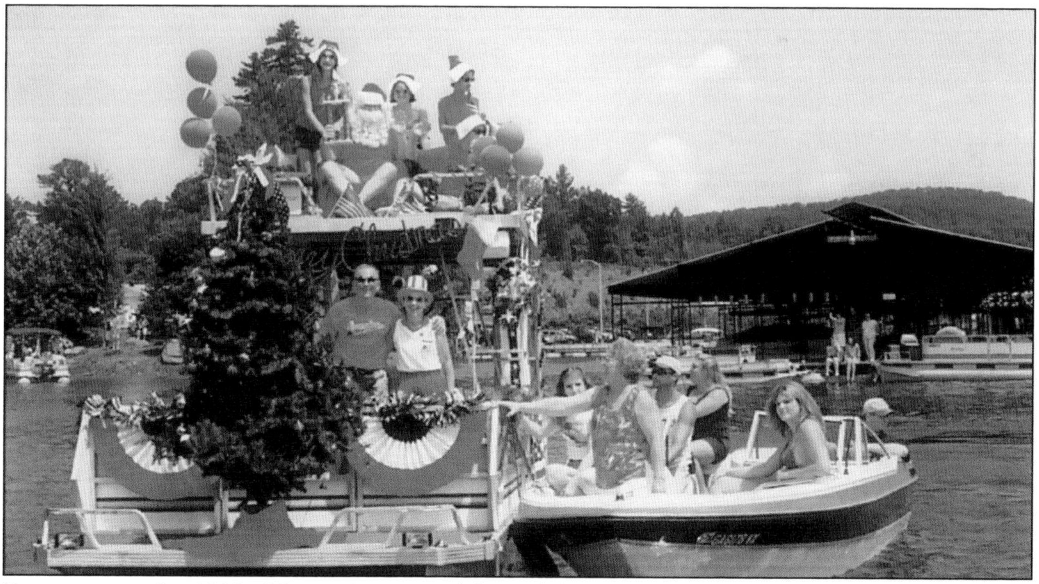

Beginning in the 1990s, Union County celebrated the Fourth of July with an Independence Day Boat Parade. In the beginning all the decorations were strictly patriotic. In recent years, the boats were allowed to use various themes. This boat was decorated with patriotic bunting and a Christmas tree, complete with Santa and the elves sitting on top. Nottely Marina sponsors the parade annually and presents trophies to the top decorated boats. (Photo by Norman Cooper.)

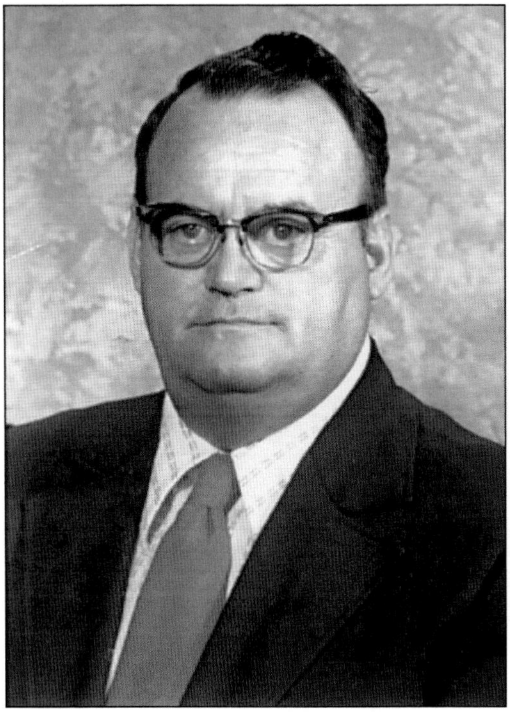

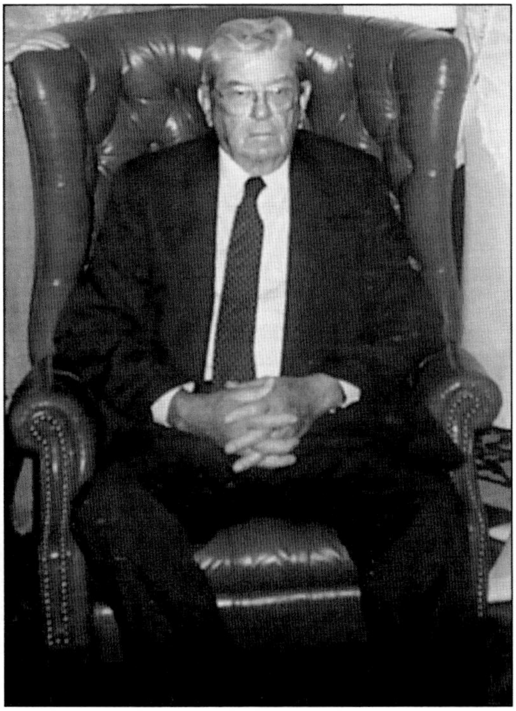

(Above, left) Howard O. Thomas served as mayor of Blairsville from 1971 to 1981.

(Above, right) Charles Allison served as mayor of Blairsville from 1981 to 1995. Allison Park in downtown Blairsville was dedicated to him for his years of service to the city.

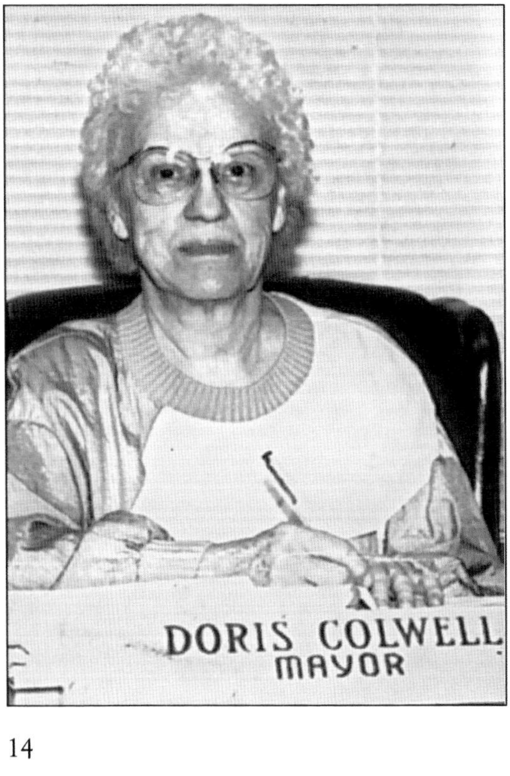

Doris Colwell was appointed to the Blairsville City Council in the mid-1990s and served as mayor of Blairsville from 1996 to 2001.

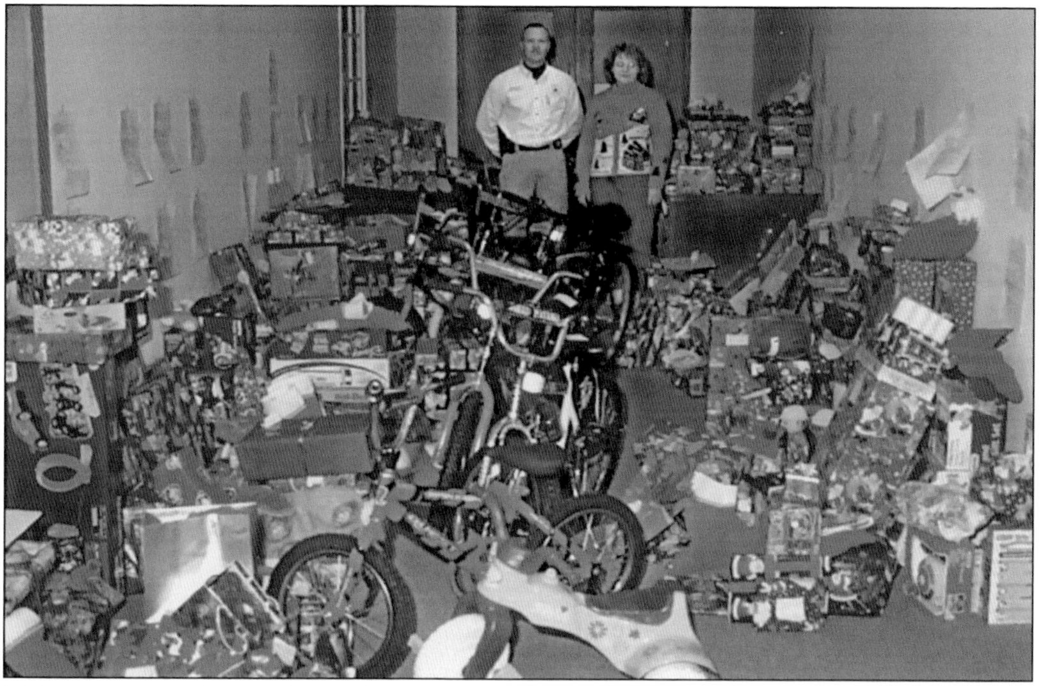

Children are the focus of law enforcement in Union County and the city of Blairsville during the Christmas season. The Union County Sheriff's Office collects and distributes hundreds of toys to children in need, including clothes. Sheriff Scott Stephens and Give-A-Gift coordinator Ginger Carey are seen with a sampling of toys distributed. Police Chief Johnny Carroll, Assistant Chief Michael "Bear" Baxter, and the Blairsville Police Department sponsor an annual Shop With A Cop program. (Photo by Norman Cooper.)

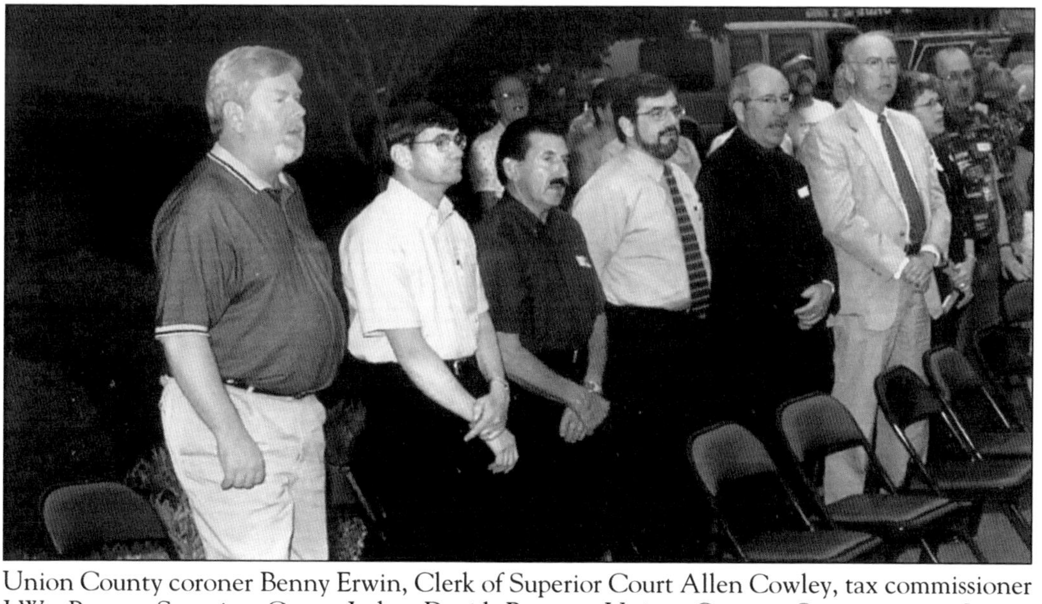

Union County coroner Benny Erwin, Clerk of Superior Court Allen Cowley, tax commissioner J.W. Payne, Superior Court Judge David Barrett, Union County Commissioner Lamar Paris, and Superior Court Judge Hugh Stone attend an event at the courthouse. (Photo by Norman Cooper.)

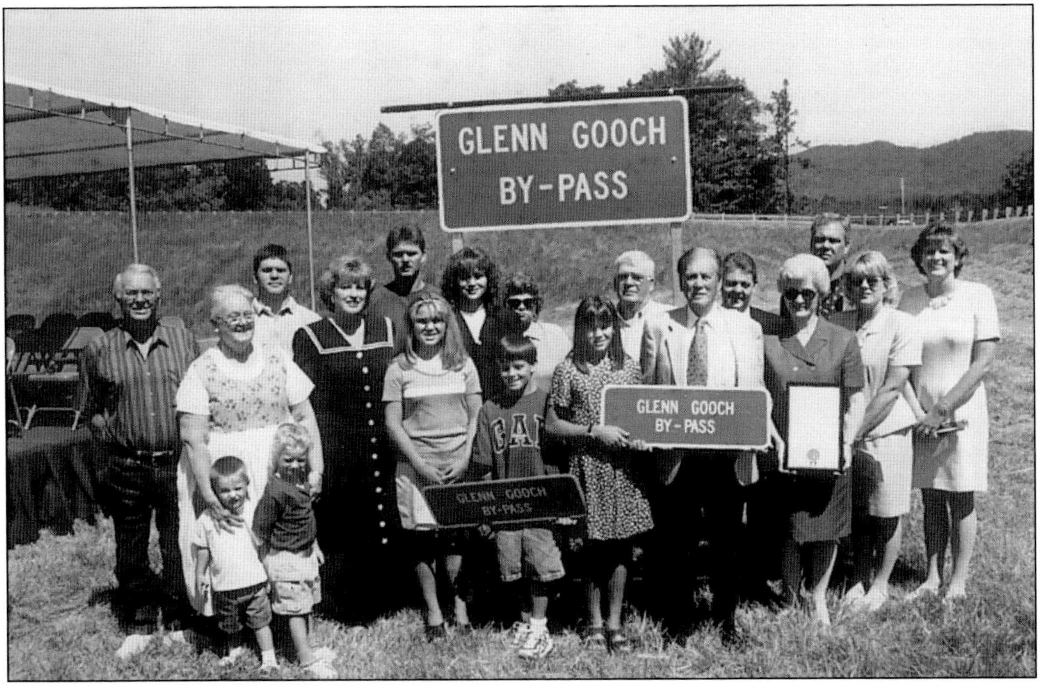

World War II veteran Glenn Gooch served on the Union County School Board from 1961 to 1973, as clerk of the Union County Superior Court from 1973 to 1985, and as Union County commissioner from 1985 to 1997. Because of Gooch's years of dedicated public service, Georgia named the Glenn Gooch Bypass in his honor. Pictured are Gooch, holding the sign, and his family members at the dedication. (Photo by Norman Cooper.)

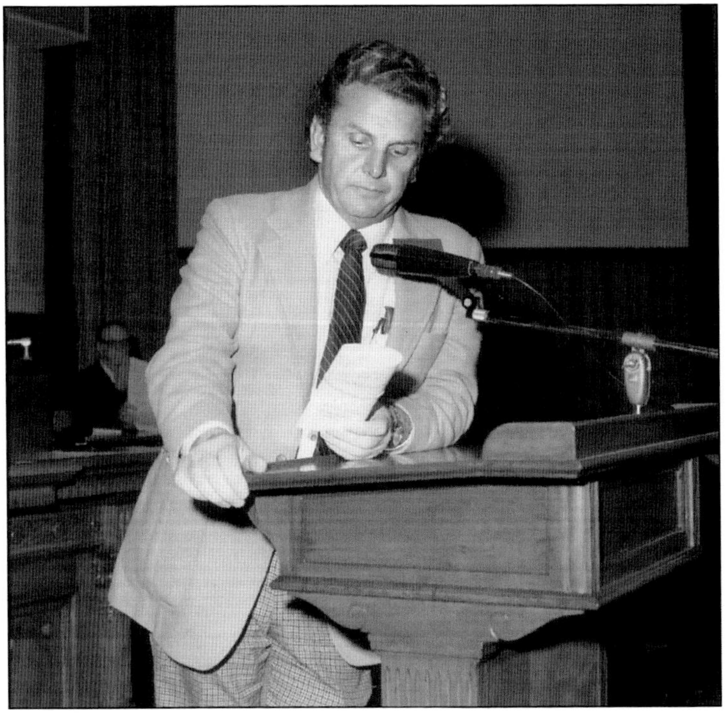

Rep. Carlton Colwell served as a Georgia state representative from 1965 to 1995. He served on the Appropriations Committee for 30 years. He served on the Game and Fish Committee, the Transportation Committee, and the Constitution Revision Committee, and he served as chairman of the State Institution Property Committee. Representative Colwell was Legislator of the Year in 1982, voted by the Recreation and Parks Society of Georgia. A detention center in Blairsville is named in his honor.

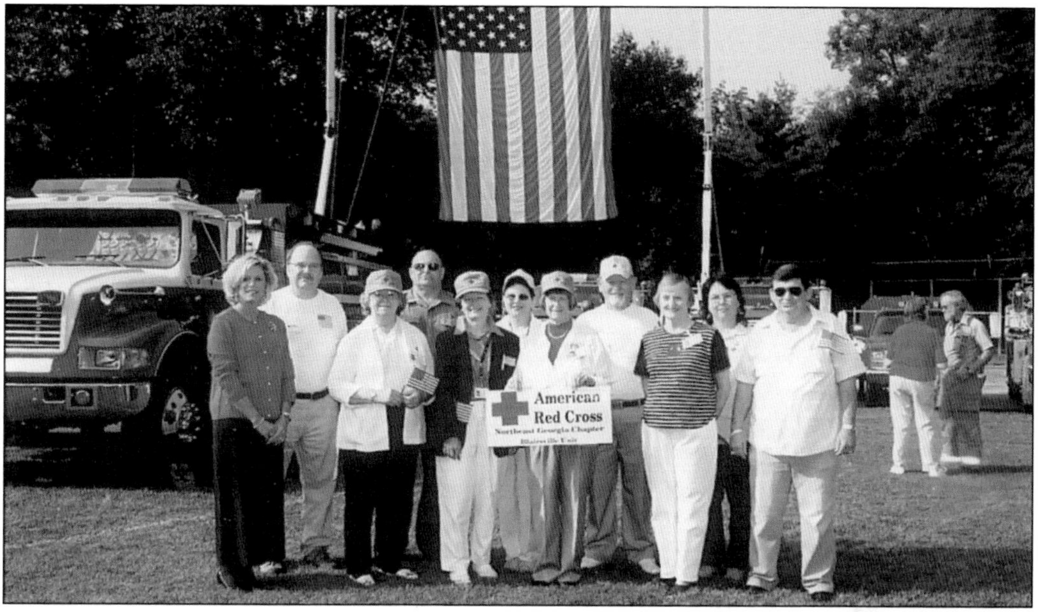

The Union County committee of the American Red Cross joined with members of the Union County Disaster Action Team at the 911 Remembrance at Meeks Park. Shown from left to right are Tracey King, Committee Chairman Norman Cooper, Martyne Jokela, Union County EMA director and fire chief Charles Worden, Charlotte Goebel, Roberta Johnson, Florence Ford, Dave Johnston, unidentified, Cecilia Holland, and unidentified.

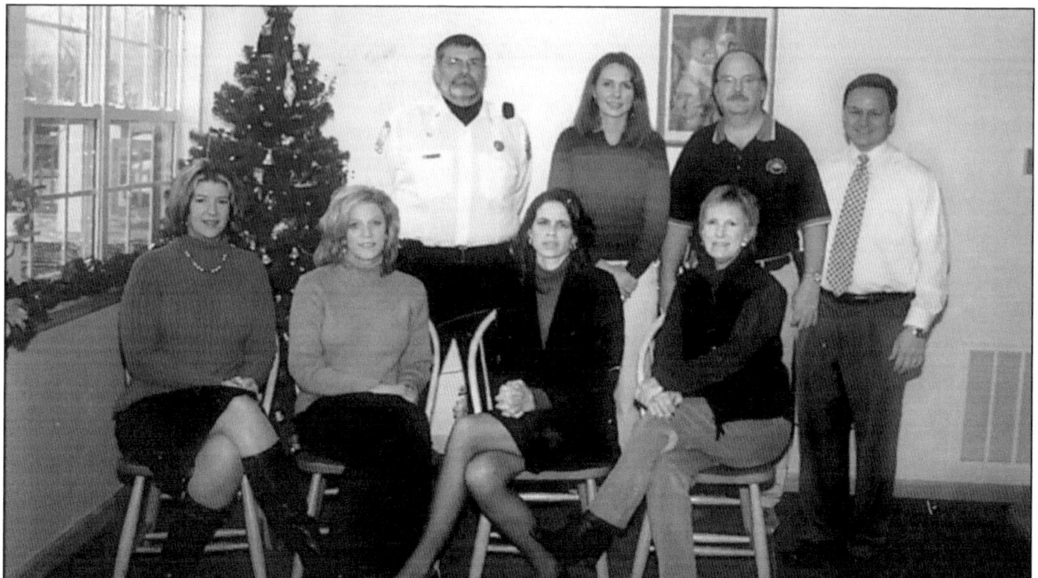

The Union County committee of the American Red Cross is very active. The committee donates one-fourth of its proceeds directly to groups in Union County, with the remainder going to the Red Cross. Seen here are, from left to right, (front row) Teresa Lockaby, Tracey King, Susie Rose, and Karen Roxbury; (back row) Charles Worden, Janeen Junod, Chairman Norman Cooper, and Brandon Grimsley. Pat Hartness and Brenda Burnette (not pictured) coordinated the instruction for the Red Cross annual CPR Saturday in Union County.

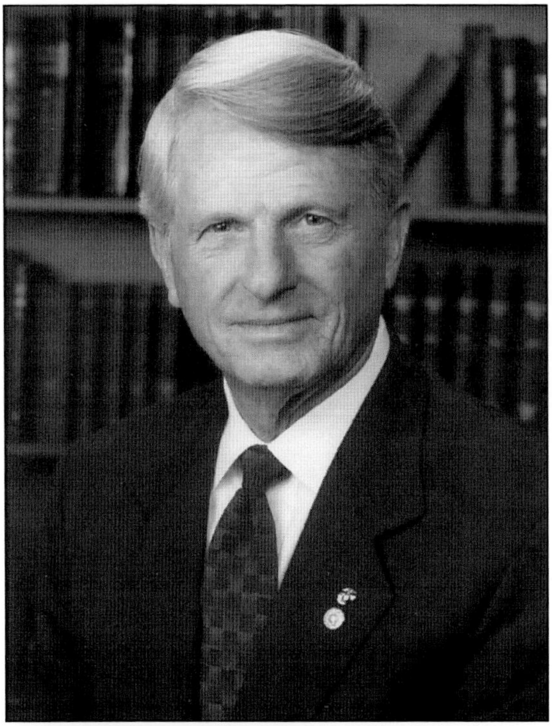

Sen. Zell Miller, who grew up playing ball in Union County, has had a career of public service spanning more than four decades. He served four terms as lieutenant governor and two terms as governor. Governor Miller was one of Georgia's greatest and one of the most recognizable governors in the nation. *Governing* Magazine named him governor of the year in 1998. After two terms, Miller headed back to the college classroom and back home to his beloved North Georgia mountains. His retirement was cut short when he accepted an appointment to the U.S. Senate in July 2000. In November 2000, Miller was elected senator to filled an unexpired term. Miller became only the third Georgian to be elected both governor and senator.

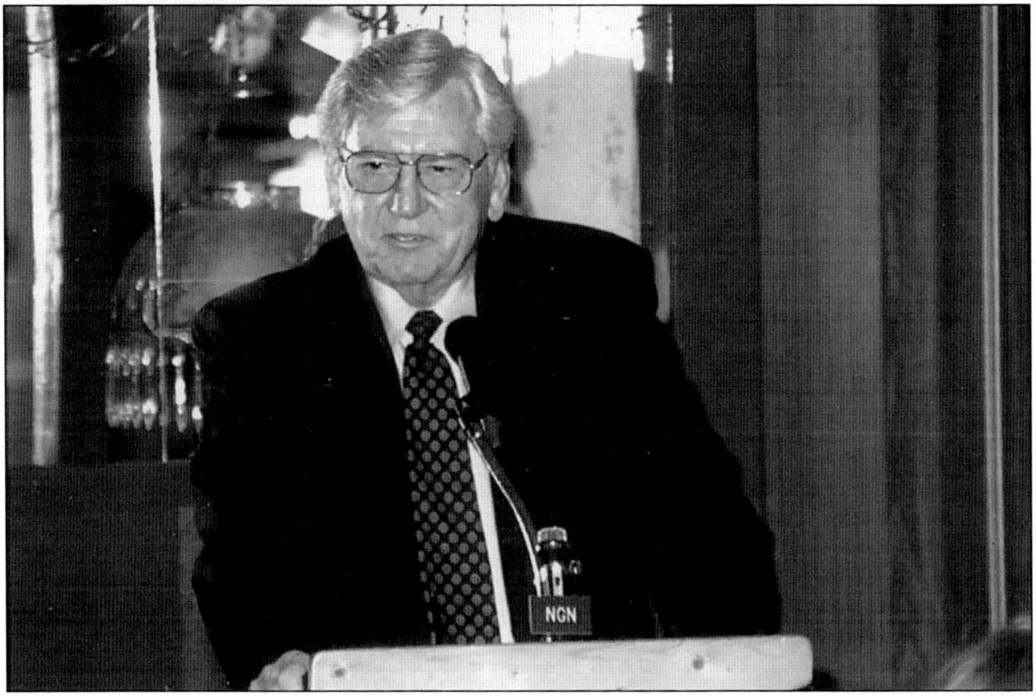

Rep. Ralph Twiggs served as Georgia state representative for nearly three decades until his death in 2002. Representative Twiggs served as chairman of the Transportation Committee and the Public Safety Committee. He also served on the Natural Resources Committee and the Appropriations Committee.

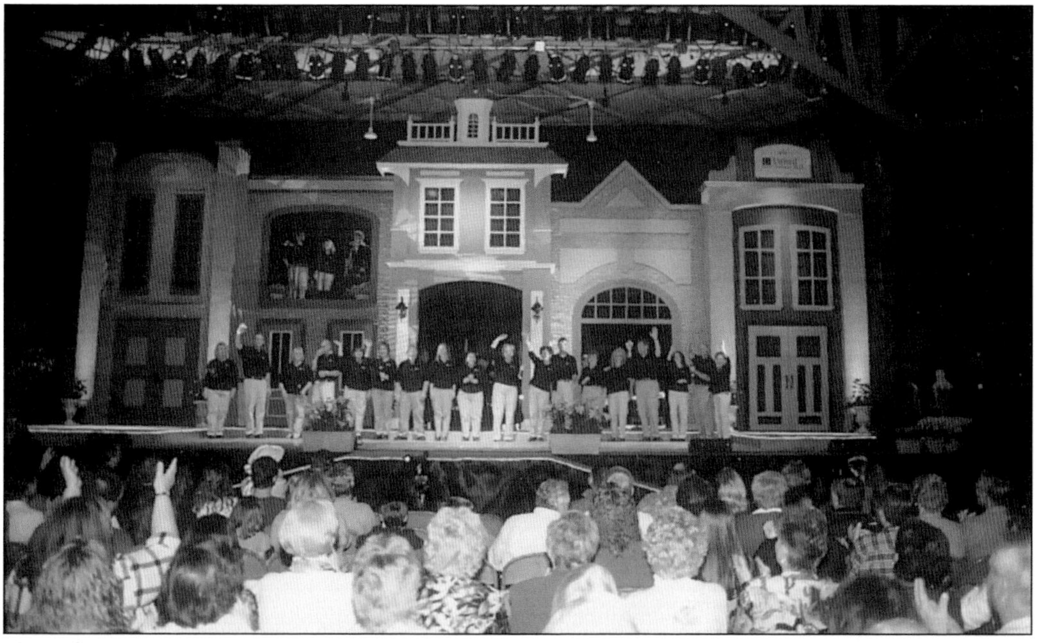

United Community Banks, based in Union County, present a show every year in North Georgia using bank employees and family members. The show draws thousands of spectators every year. Admission is not charged, but donations are distributed to charity organizations. For years the theme was "Hee Haw," based on the popular television show. After several successful years, the theme changed to "The Banker's Hour." (Photo by Norman Cooper.)

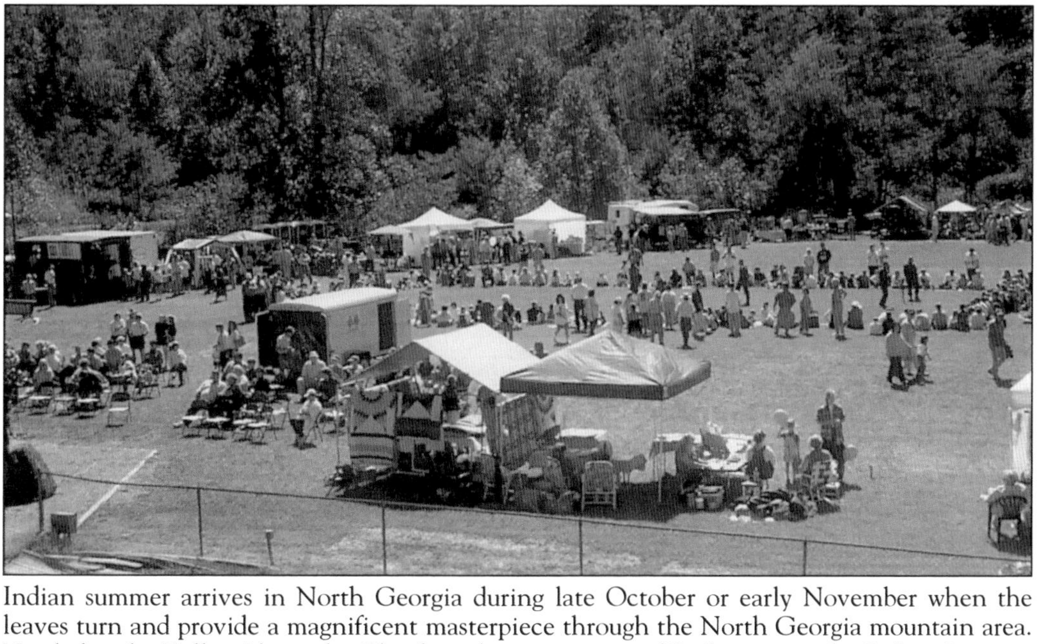

Indian summer arrives in North Georgia during late October or early November when the leaves turn and provide a magnificent masterpiece through the North Georgia mountain area. Nestled in the Valley Above the Clouds in the community of Suches, a two-day Indian Summer Festival is held. Activities range from turkey shoots to military combat demonstrations, arts, crafts, food, and a quilting show. A square dance and a road race are held in conjunction with the festival. (Photo by Norman Cooper.)

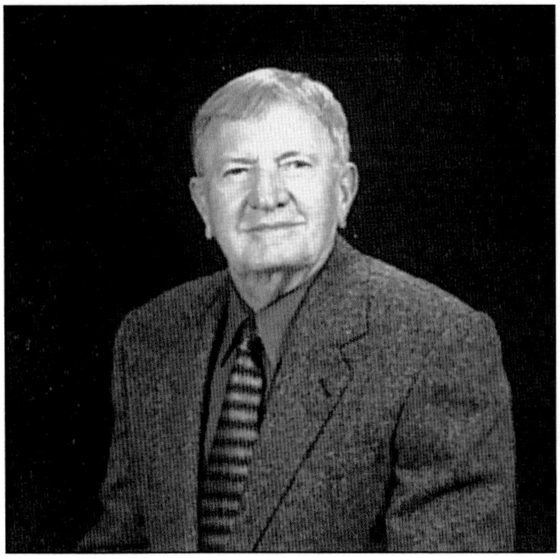

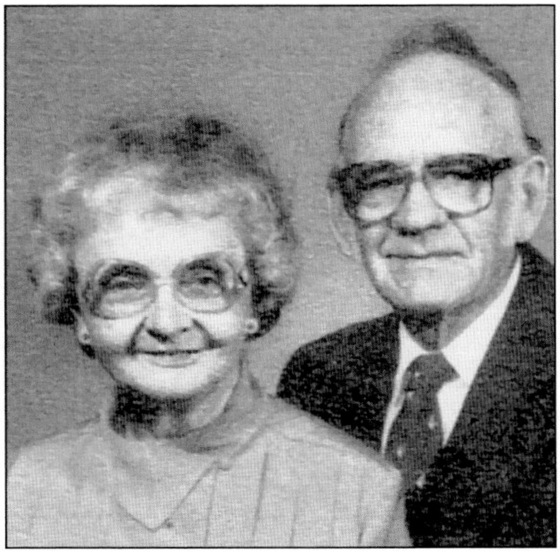

(Above, left) Jim Dobson was research agronomist for the Georgia Mountain Experiment Station for 19 years and superintendent for an additional 19 years until his retirement in 1991. He served as president of the Union County Chamber of Commerce, as chairman of the economic development committee for the Chamber of Commerce, and as chairman of the Georgia Mountain Soil and Water Conservation District. He was president of the Blairsville Kiwanis Club twice and served as Kiwanis lieutenant governor of the 10th Division.

(Above, right) Edwin Cook worked with the U.S. Department of Agriculture for 37 years as county executive director in Union County. He retired in 1982. Edwin and Lucille celebrated their 50th wedding anniversary in 1992.

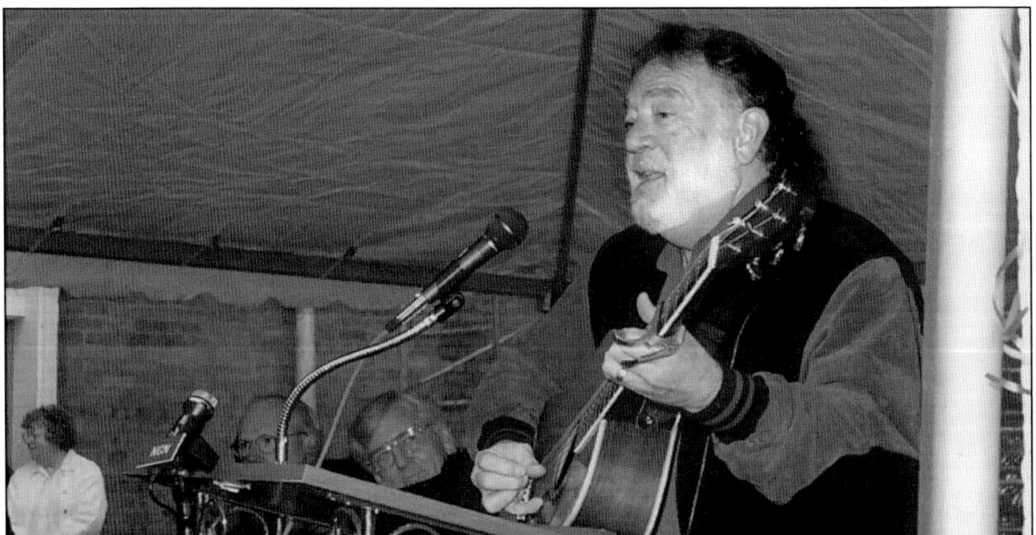

Sam Ensley is a teacher and a musician who taught history at Union County Middle School for many years. He has played with numerous well-known country and bluegrass groups. He has coordinated the musical concerts at the Old Courthouse and other musical events in Union County. He wrote a tribute to the Old Courthouse that he sang at the dedication of the clock and bell tower. Ensley has even performed on local television, most notably in the program *Roots and Branches*. (Photo by Norman Cooper.)

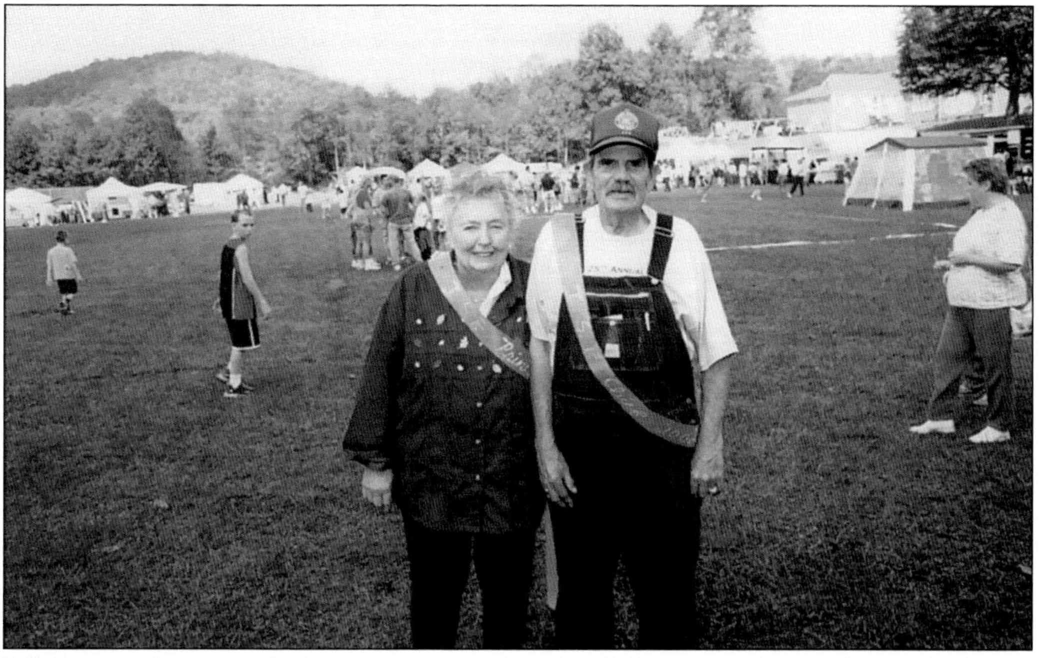

Bill Owens is known as the honorary mayor of Suches. Bill has served as a volunteer firefighter in Suches for many years. He and his wife Peggy were chief and princess of the Indian Summer Festival in 2002. Bill served as commander of the V.F.W. and was a member of the Allegany Lodge and Shrine Club. Bill and Peggy are lifetime honorary members of the Lions Club. Bill was presented the Melvin Jones Award, two International President's Awards, and is in the Lions Club Hall of Fame. Peggy was a Lioness until they merged with the Lions Club; she served as president and received the Presidential Award. (Photo by Norman Cooper.)

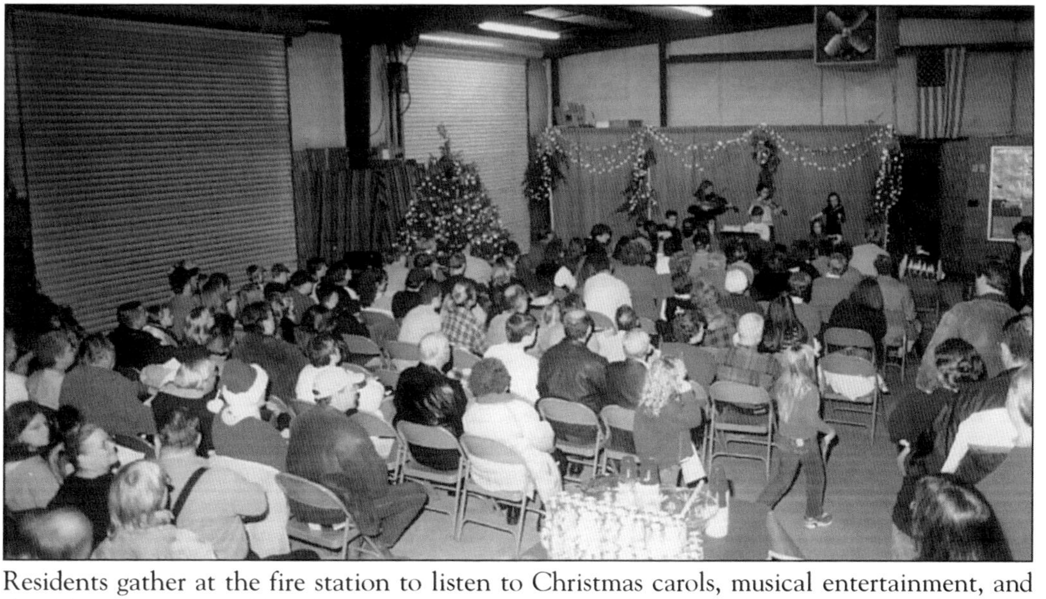

Residents gather at the fire station to listen to Christmas carols, musical entertainment, and the Christmas story. After the program, everyone eats food brought in covered dishes. The Christmas tree outside the fire station serves as the community Christmas tree. (Photo by Norman Cooper.)

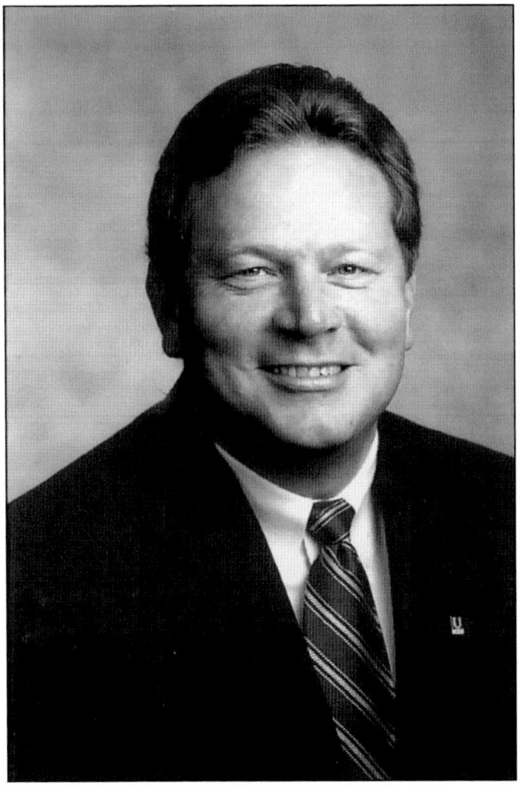

The United Community Banks Holding Company was established in 1985, and Jimmy Tallent, president and CEO of United Community Banks, Inc., built it into Georgia's third largest holding company. The community has benefited beyond measure from the generosity of United Community Bank during Tallent's tenure. The Georgia Economic Developers Association presented its Spirit of Georgia Award to Tallent in 1999 for his "superior ability, originality, potential impact, and courage in business development." Three times named among Georgia's most influential citizens, Tallent is a member of the state board for the Georgia Department of Technical and Adult Education. He was charter president of the Union County Rotary Club and served as president of the Chamber of Commerce. (Photo by Norman Cooper.)

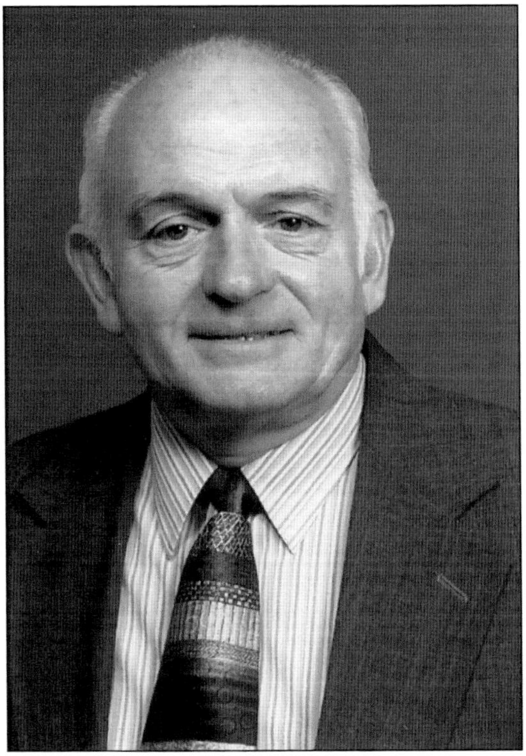

Bob Head is quiet and unassuming, yet he has made an impact on Union County few could ever realize. He serves as chairman of United Community Banks and owns Head Westgate Corporation. Head served with the Georgia Department of Industry, Trade, and Tourism, in the Union County Development Authority, and in the Joint Development Authority. He built the new Union County Jail, renovated the interior of the historic rock building at Woody Gap School in Suches, and constructed the media center and lunchroom at Woody Gap. He also installed the clock and bell tower on the Historic Courthouse in Blairsville and renovated Union County Middle School and the old Union County High School.

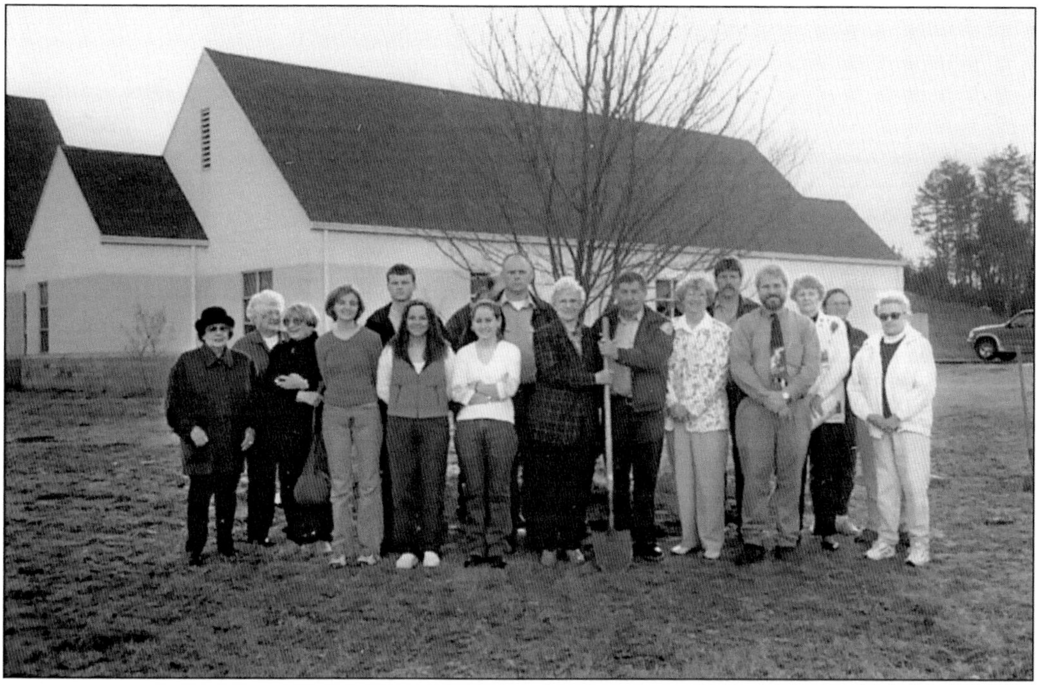

Arbor Day is celebrated annually with the planting of a tree. Blairsville mayor Doris Colwell and Rick Hood of the Georgia Forestry Commission (center, holding shovel) planted this tree at the Union County Senior Center with the help of the Georgia Forestry Commission, the Union County 4-H Club, and the Blairsville Garden Club. (Photo by Norman Cooper.)

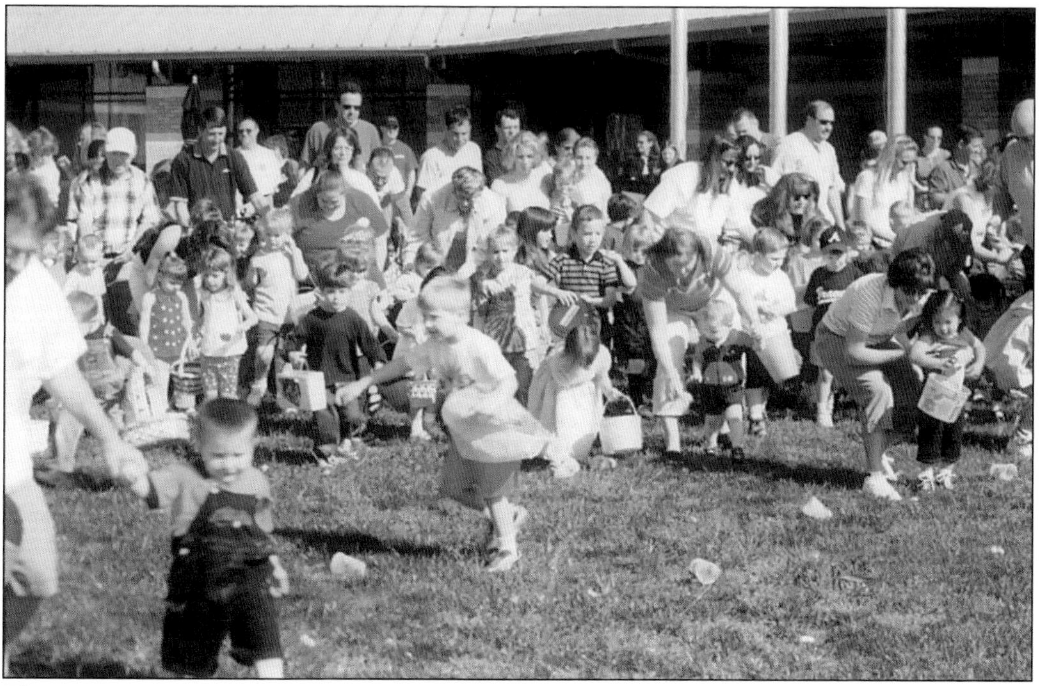

The community Easter egg hunts draw children every year. Hunts have taken place at Meeks Park and at the North Georgia Technical College. (Photo by Norman Cooper.)

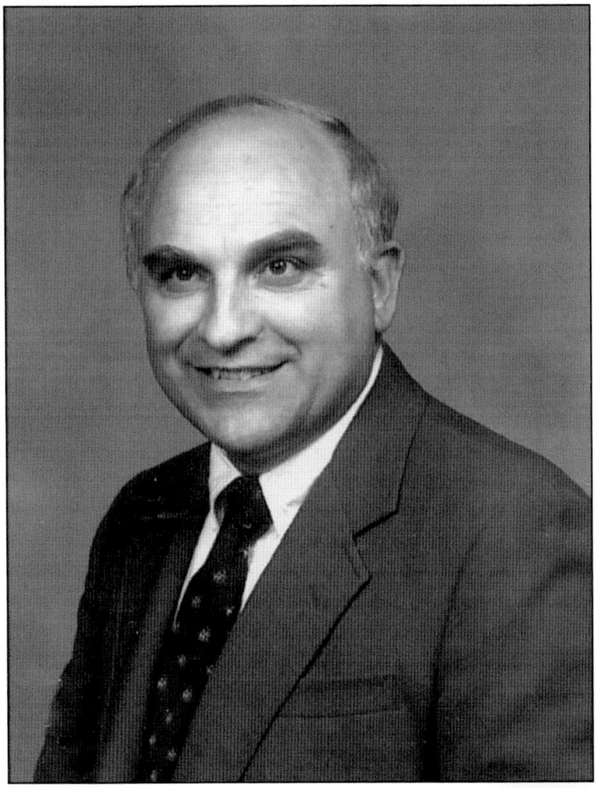

W.C. Nelson has served on the Union County Development Authority since its beginning in 1974. He was elected chairman in the early 1990s, a position he was reelected to in subsequent years for a decade. Nelson was appointed the Regional Resources Stewardship Council of TVA in 2000. He served on the Georgia Department of Community Affairs for six years. Nelson is a member of the Joint Development Authority, having served as chairman, and vice-chairman of United Community Banks, Inc. holding company. He was instrumental in the acquisition of land for the Blairsville Airport and for the Blairsville Airport Regional Industrial Park.

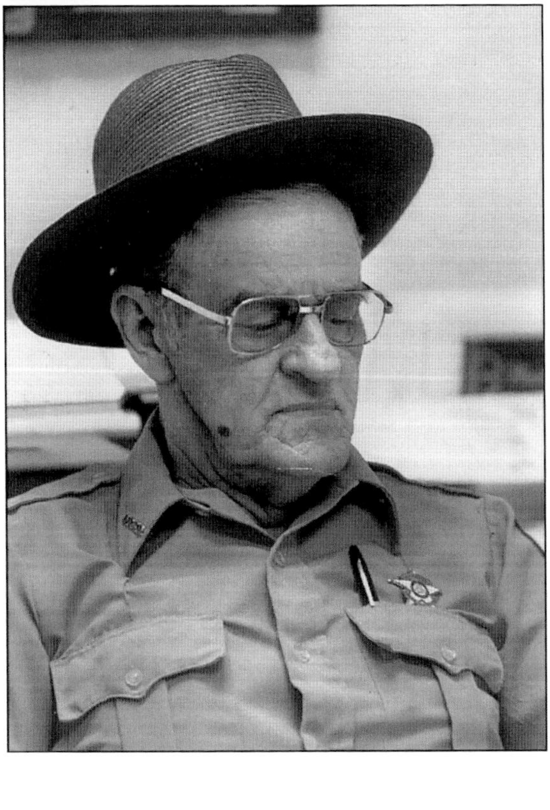

Harlan Duncan served more than 40 years in law enforcement, as a Blairsville policeman, a Georgia State patrol officer, and Union County Sheriff for 21 years. More than 500 residents and law officials paid their respects when he passed away in 1985. The funeral procession included an honor guard riding a white horse and carrying an American flag. Duncan's horse was led in the funeral procession with the sheriff's hat attached to the empty saddle. (Courtesy Union County Historical Society.)

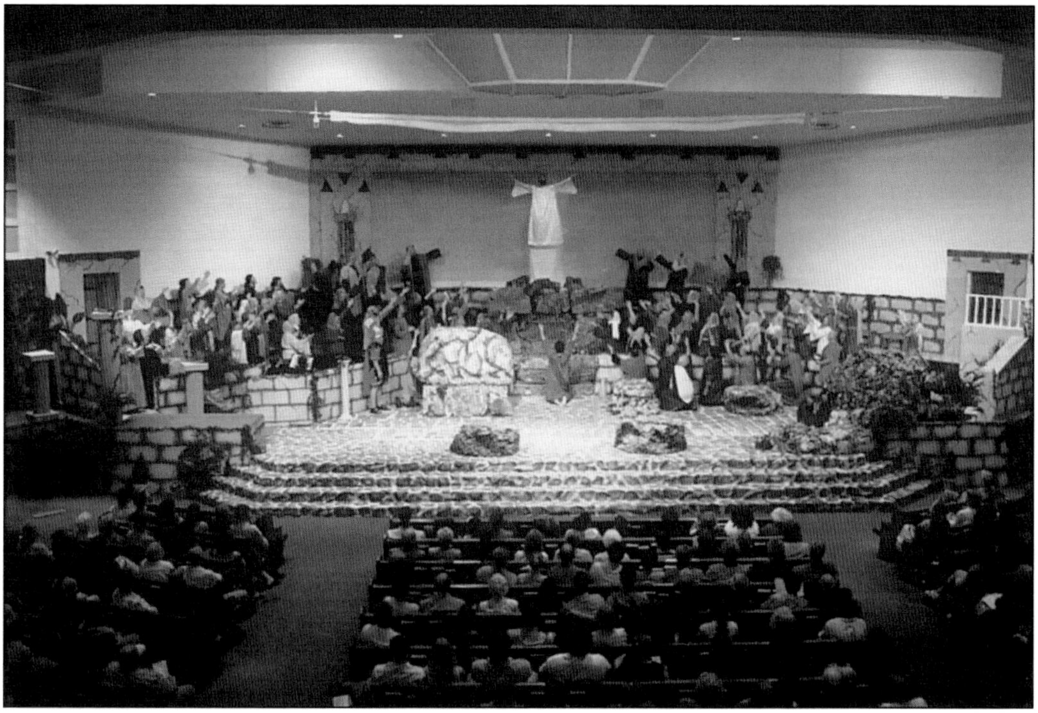

The passion play at the First Baptist Church in Blairsville, the largest production in the county, is seen by thousands of people every year at Easter. The play features live animals, scores of singers, characters dressed in period regalia, and dramatic special effects on a speculator stage creation. (Photo by Norman Cooper.)

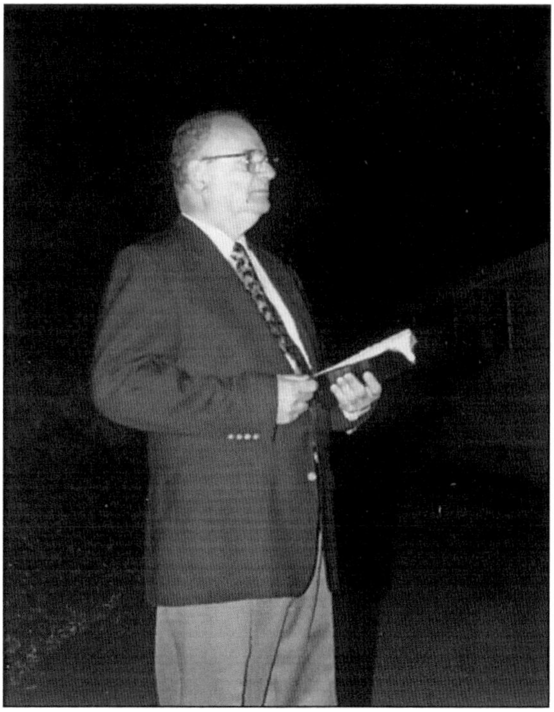

Hughes Chatham served as Union County's civil defense director, was on the Blairsville Police Force, served in the Union County Sheriff's Office, and drove an ambulance. He set up the 911 center for the county and helped start the fire and rescue department. He preached for nearly four decades and was pastor of Zebulon Baptist Church at the time of his death. Chatham, in this photo, conducts an Easter sunrise service. (Photo by Norman Cooper.)

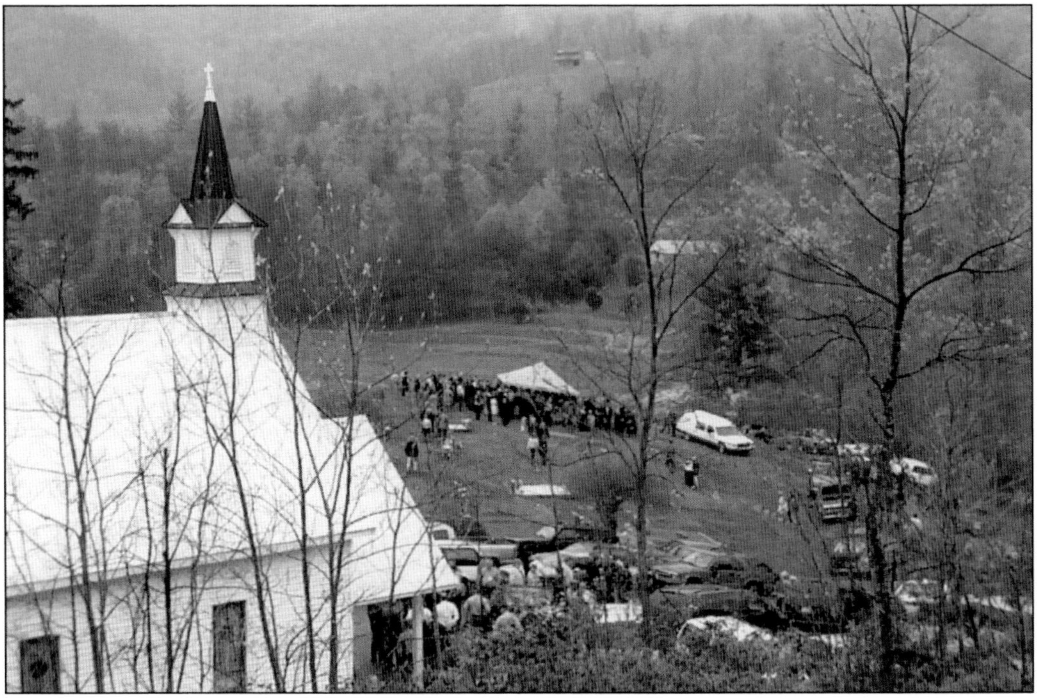

Union County features scores of churches representing numerous denominations and congregations. Churches include Baptist, United Methodist, Assembly of God, Church of God, Lutheran, Church of the Nazarene, Catholic, Church of Christ, Presbyterian, and Interdenominational. Building styles range from modern buildings, small buildings, and storefronts to traditional rectangles with pitched roofs and steeples. Many churches have cemeteries adjacent. (Photo by Norman Cooper.)

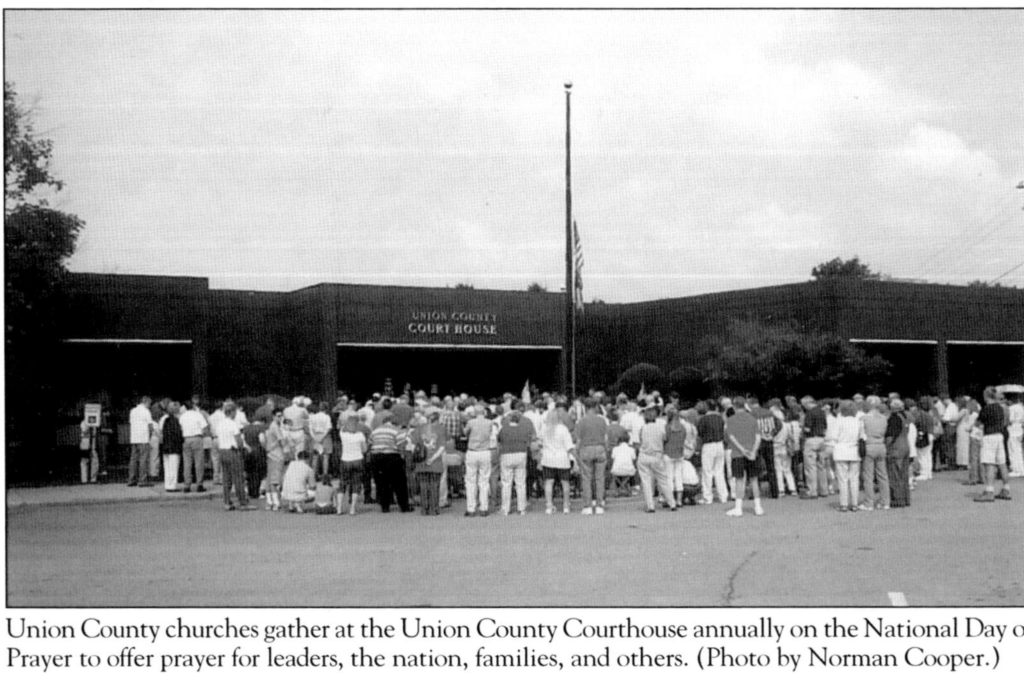

Union County churches gather at the Union County Courthouse annually on the National Day of Prayer to offer prayer for leaders, the nation, families, and others. (Photo by Norman Cooper.)

The old historic church on the Gainesville Highway just south of the square in Blairsville has been home to three churches. Charles Reid, justice of the Georgia Supreme Court, donated the land for the building, and by 1940 the building had been constructed and paid for. Both Methodist and Baptist congregations used the facility until the Baptists built their new church on Blue Ridge Street west of town. The towers were removed when the roof developed problems. By 1988 a new building was constructed by the Methodists on the Appalachian Highway west of town. The old building was purchased that same year by the Blairsville Christian Center, whose facility was located on Blue Ridge Street just west of the square. At the turn of the century the church was pastored by Rev. Wofford Kelley and Sarah Kelley, the founders of the Christian Center.

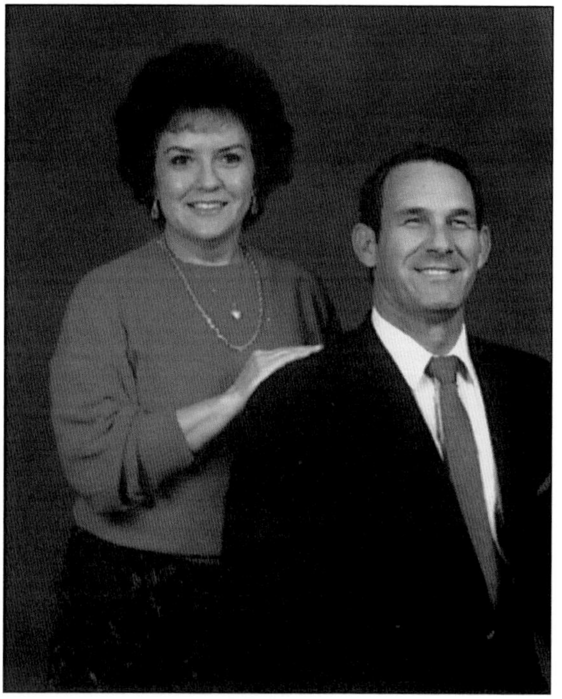

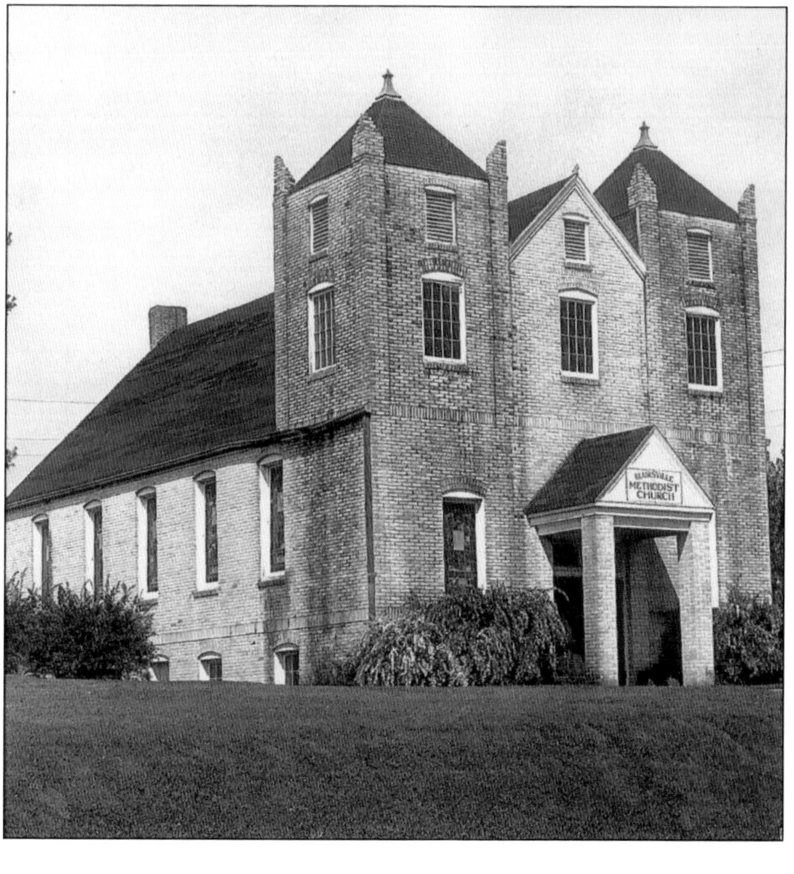

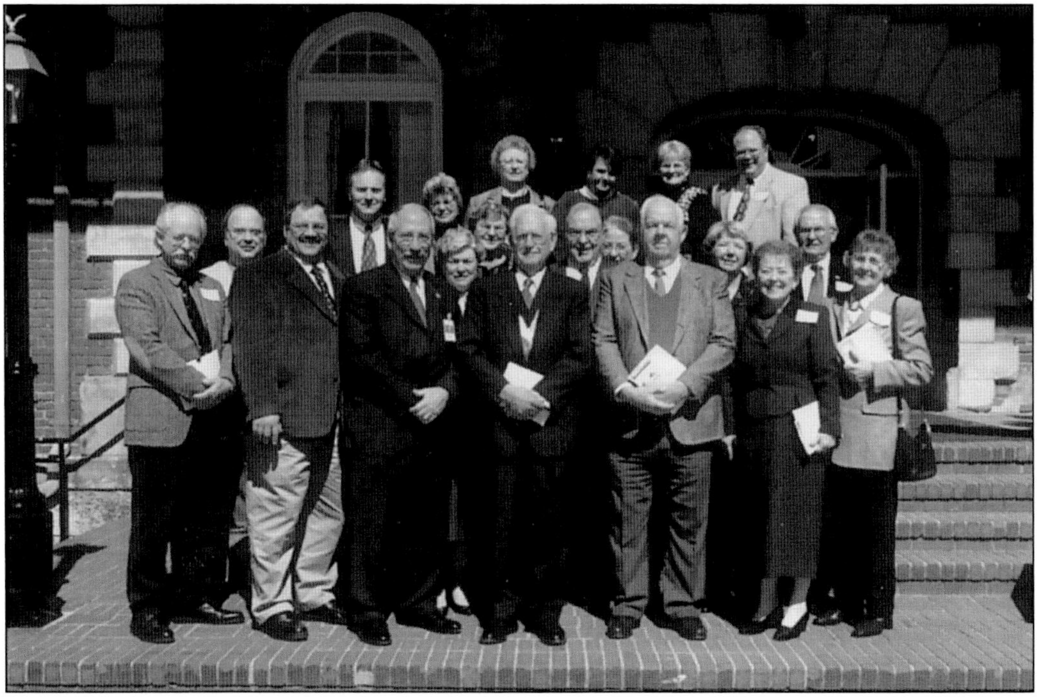

Maurice and Ann Farabee were awarded the Governor's Award for the Humanities for their contributions to Union County. Maurice was the guiding force behind the restoration of the Blairsville courthouse. Ann spearheaded efforts to develop a museum in the courthouse. They were the driving forces in replacing the clock and bell tower and renovating the Candler-Duckworth Courtroom. Maurice (front row, fourth from left) accepted the award for his wife (now deceased) from Gov. Roy Barnes.

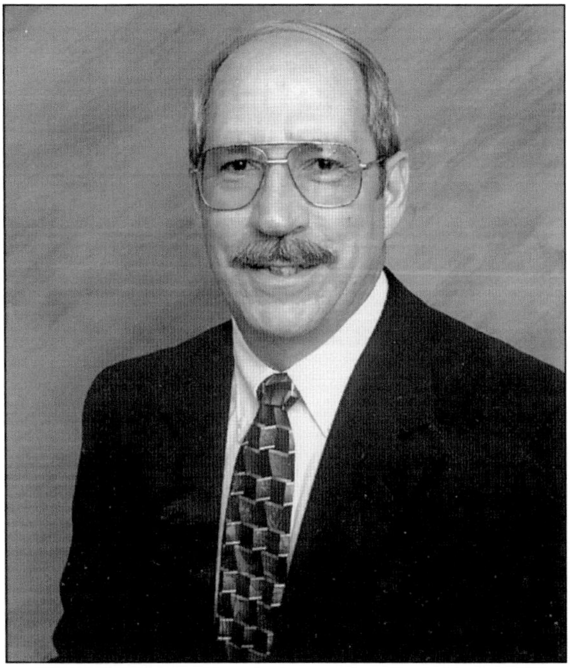

Lamar Paris served on the Union County Recreation Board for 12 years, acting as chairman for eight years. He helped the county acquire property from Bill Meeks. Part of that property was developed into Meeks Park, one of the most prestigious recreation facilities in North Georgia. The golf course expansion from 9 holes to 18 occurred during the years Paris was chairman. Paris, who has owned Paris Finance since the late 1970s, took office as Union County commissioner in January 2001.

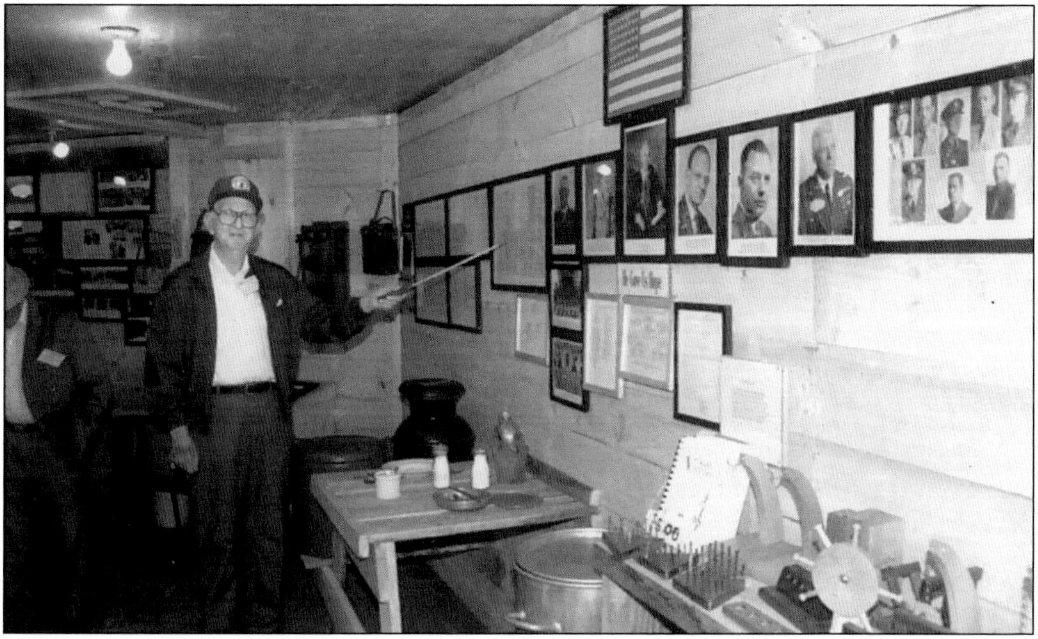

Vogel State Park, in the 2000s, focused on the project of the construction of the new Civilian Conservation Corps (CCC) Museum. The old museum, seen above, located in what once was a snack bar across from the beach, had served its purpose. The snack bar was cold, damp, and drafty, making it a miserable place trying to preserve artifacts of cloth, paper, and metal. The new 1,200-square-foot facility will be climate-controlled, making for an exhibit-friendly environment. At the annual CCC reunion in May 2003, the museum was dedicated to John Derden, above, of Stone Mountain. John, a CCC boy, contributed thousands of hours with his wife Virginia to the development of the museum. The museum will house exhibits that tell the story of the Great Depression and the CCC. (Photo by Norman Cooper.)

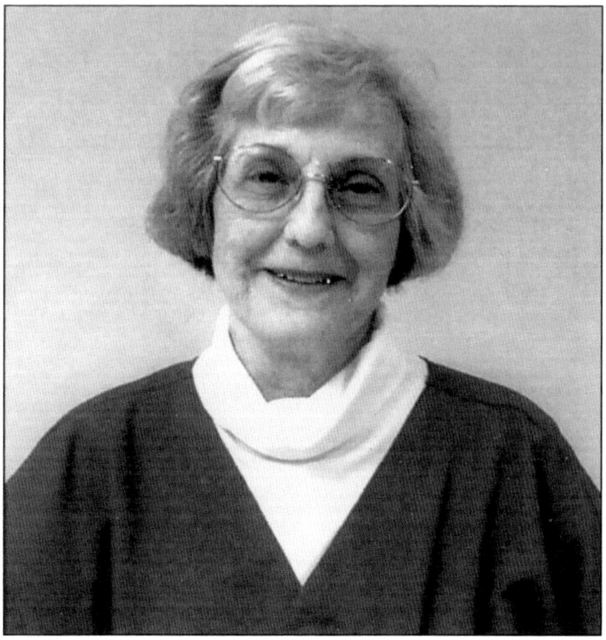

Avis Shaw was the county nurse upon her retirement after 30 years with the Union County Health Department. She joined the county health board after her retirement. During her years, the health department established a dental clinic, women's clinic, and mental health clinic in the early 1970s. She supported and pushed for the flouridation of the city water.

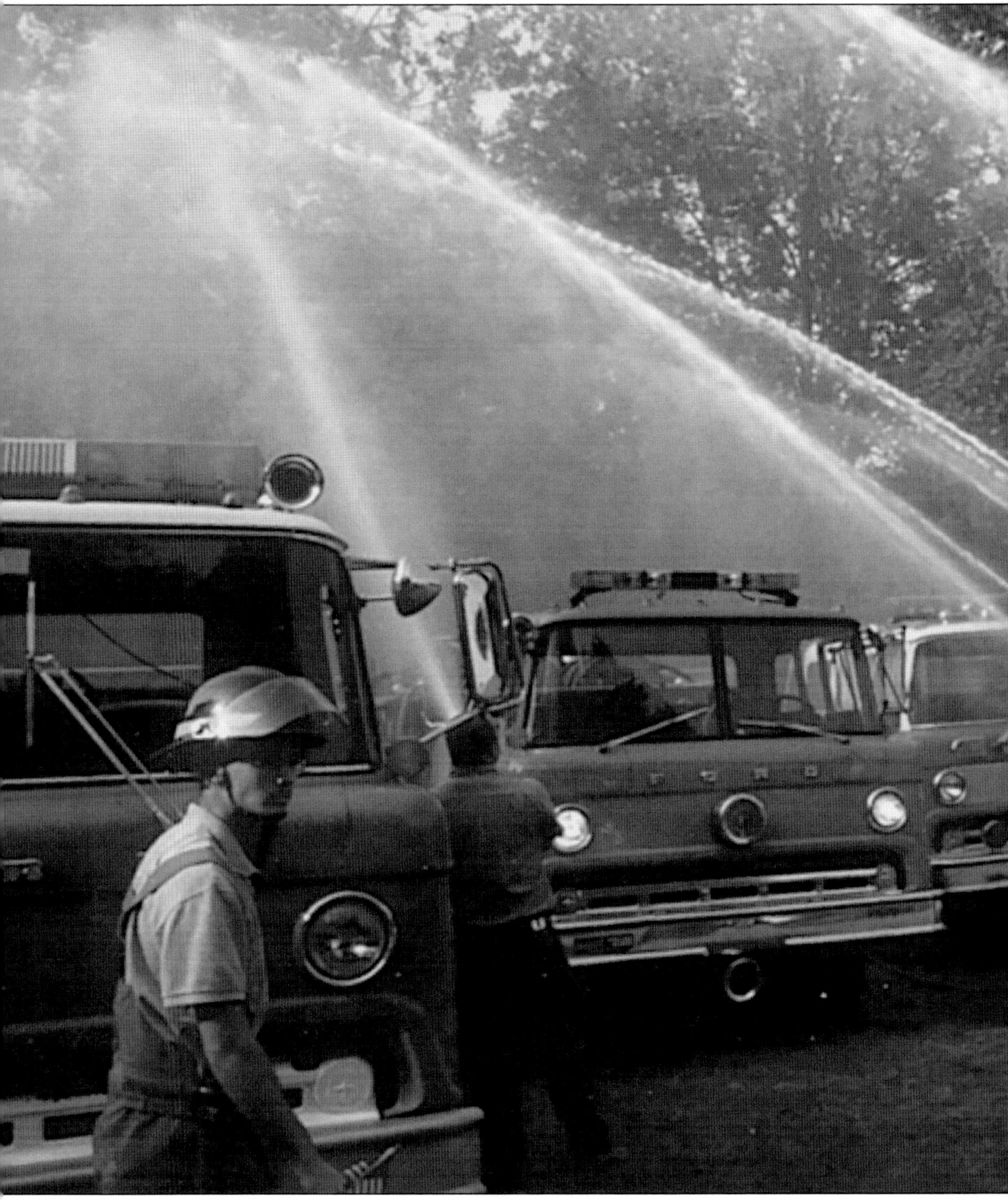

Union County joined the nation in remembrance of the heroes, victims, and victims' families of the September 11 attacks. The event, organized by Union County Commissioner Lamar Paris and held at Meeks Park, paid tribute to those who had suffered a great loss. The Blue Ridge Mountain EMC donated the trucks to hoist high an American flag. The Union County Fire

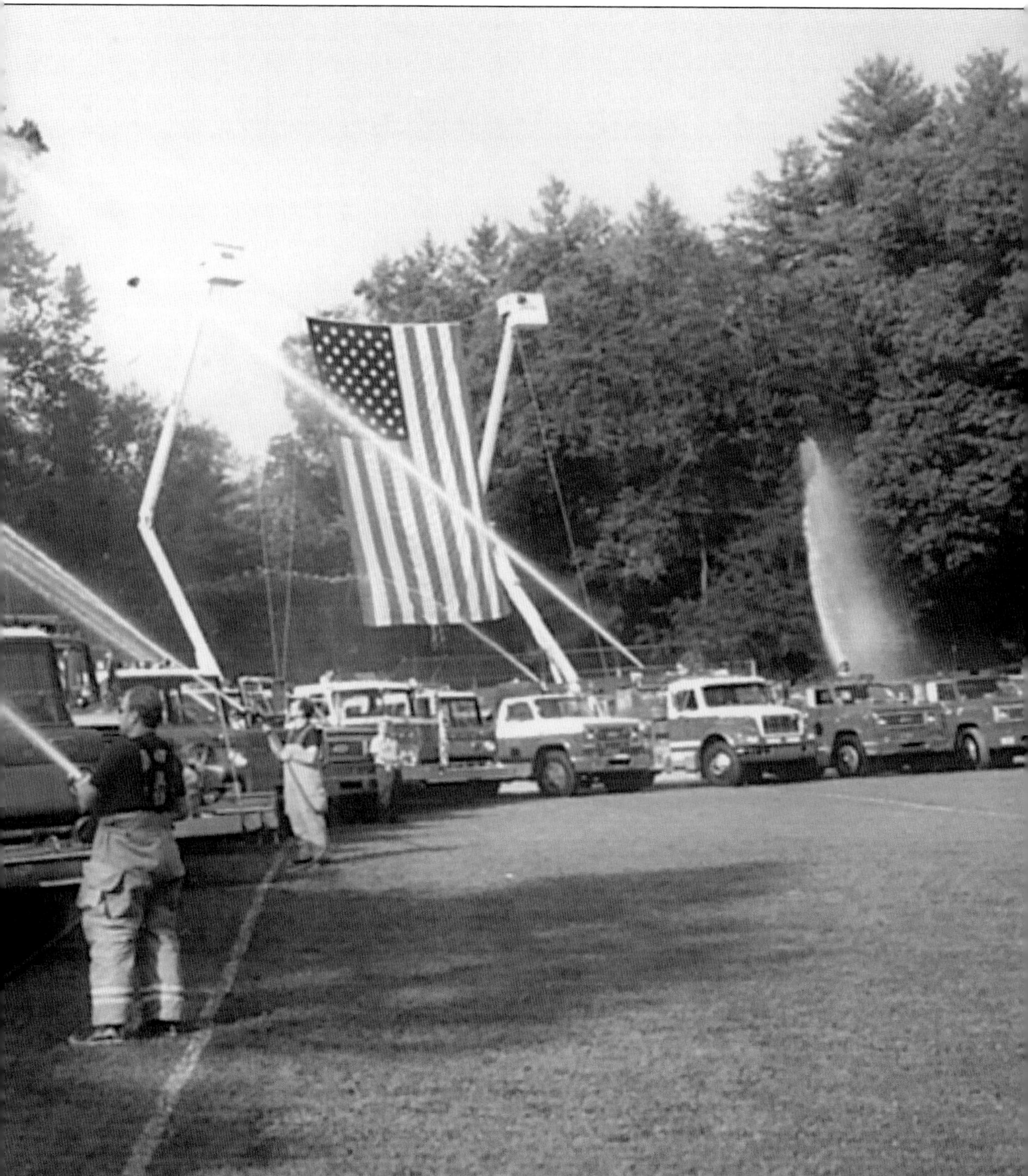

Department, Union County Sheriff's Office, Blairsville Police Department, local American Red Cross volunteers, and others joined in the observance. At the exact time when the first plane crashed into a tower in New York City, one year later, the fire hoses sent streams of water into the air for one minute. (Photo by Norman Cooper.)

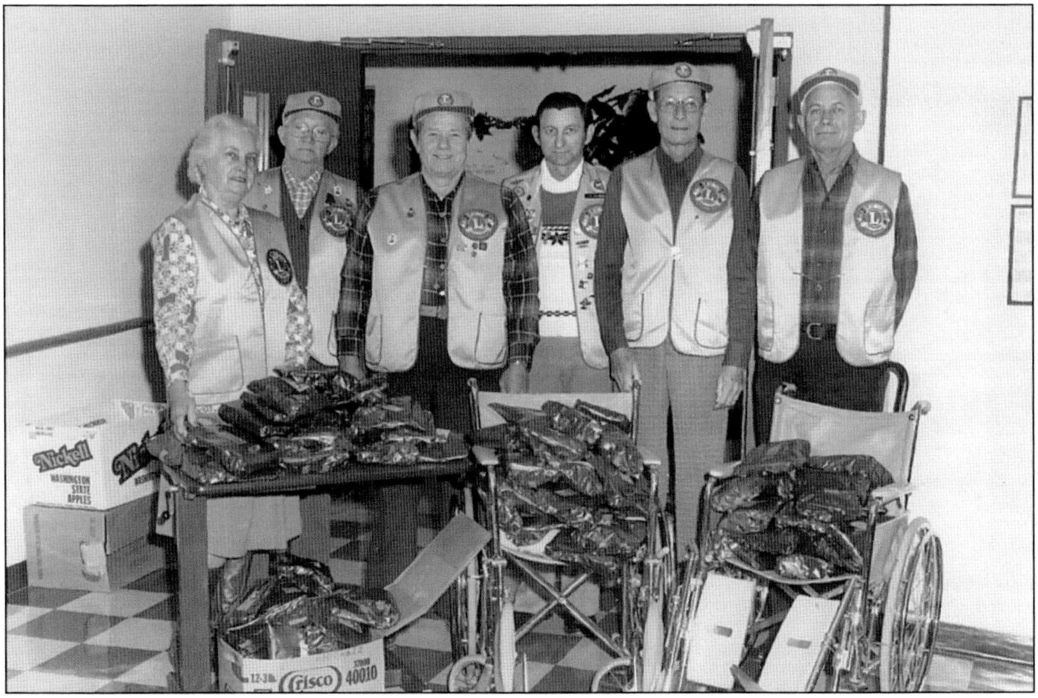

The Lions Club, known for bringing sight to the blind, has always embraced those committed to helping the local community. Thier motto is "We serve."

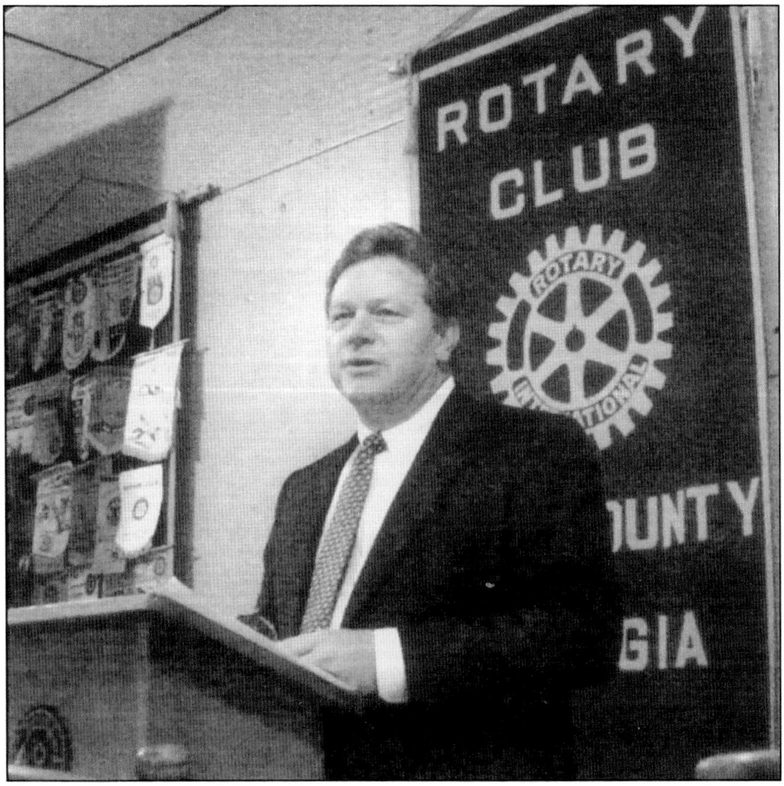

The Rotary Club has served Union County for many years, supporting education programs, youth programs, and international projects all over the world. Jimmy Tallent was the charter president and one of the founding members. (Photo by Norman Cooper.)

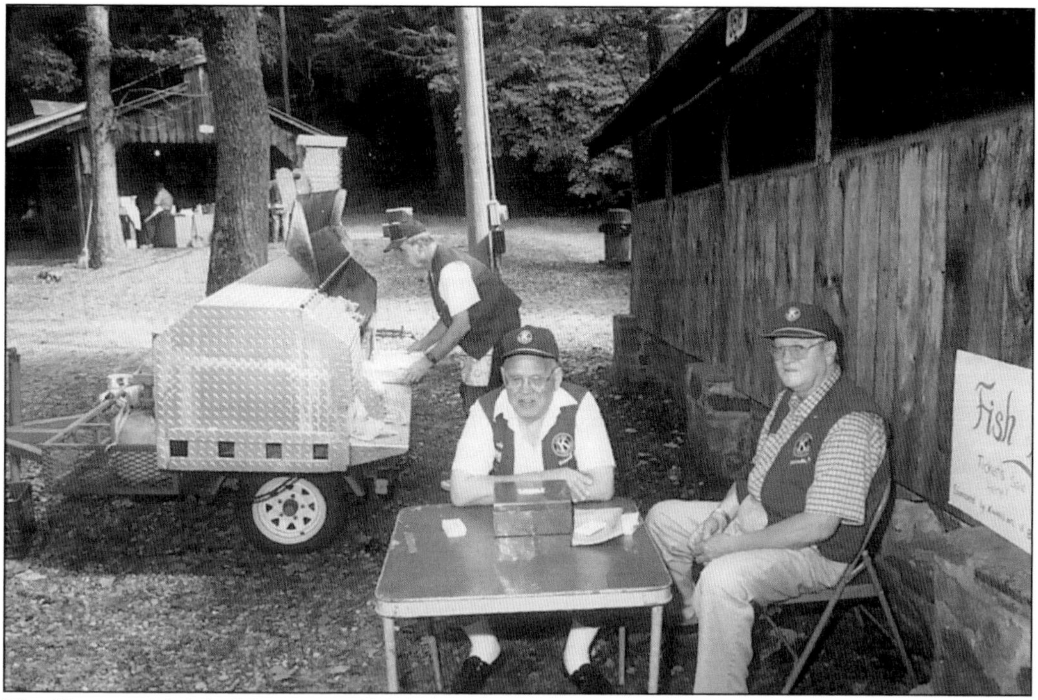

The Kiwanis Club holds an annual fish fry to help raise funds for their many projects throughout the year. (Photo by Norman Cooper.)

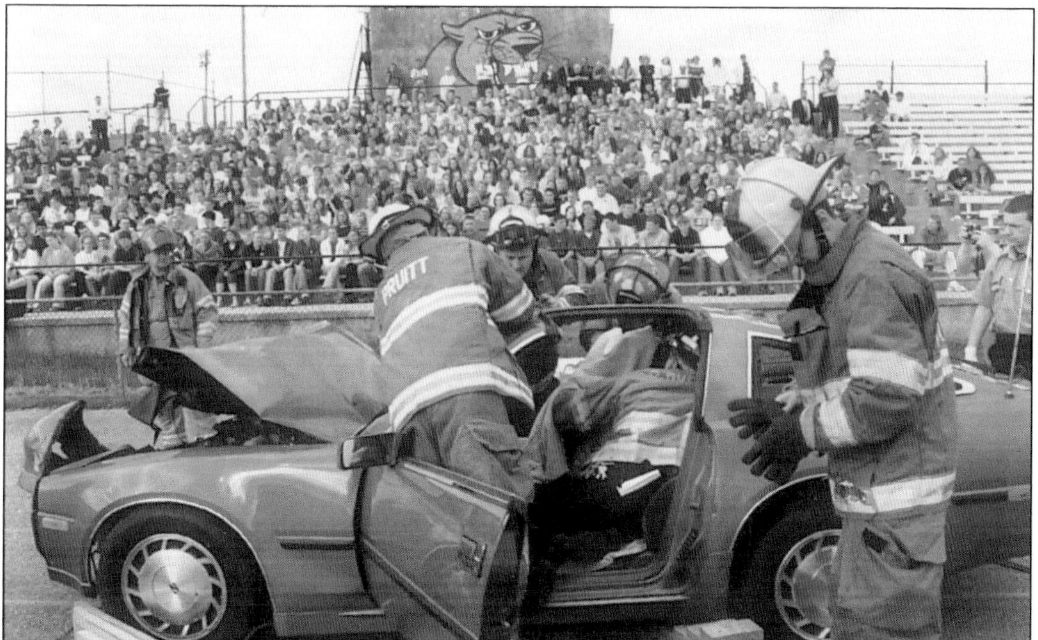

Law enforcement and rescue personnel help Students Against Destructive Decisions at Union County High alert students to the potential dangers of driving under the influence of alcohol and/or drugs. This fatal crash scene demonstration illustrates those dangers. (Photo by Norman Cooper.)

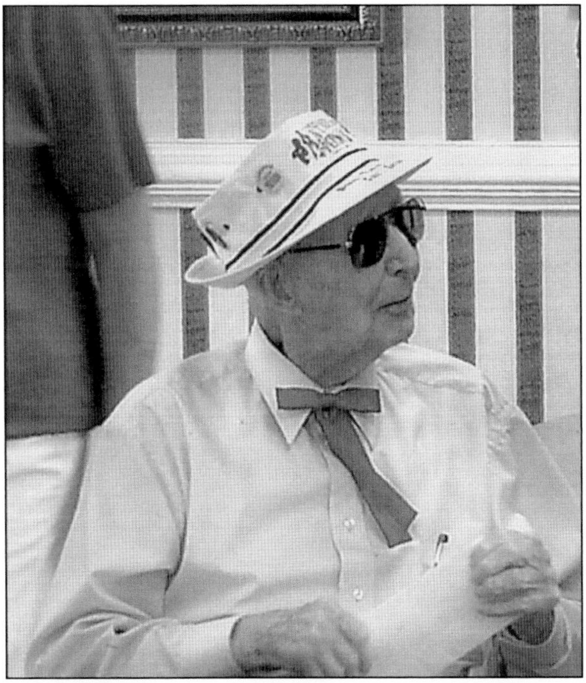

Bud Haines was the oldest living man in Union County at the end of the 20th century. He celebrated his 104th birthday in August 2003 with a huge reception hosted at United Community Bank.

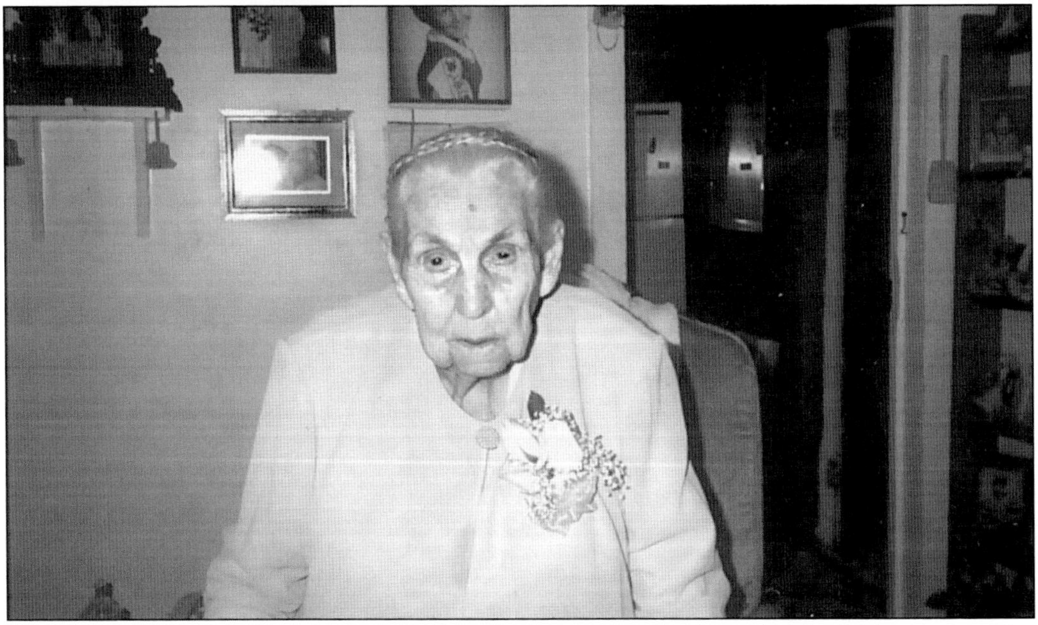

Julia Watkins was the oldest living woman in Union County at the end of the 20th century. The Union County Nursing Home hosted a huge party for her 105th birthday in April 2002. Julie said that she moved into the nursing home "because her kids were getting too old to take care of her." Born in 1897 when President William McKinley was in office, she received a letter from President George W. Bush in 2002; she has lived under 19 different presidents. She married Virgil Watkins in 1918. When asked what kind of advice she would give to others, Julia said, "to try and live right, do the best they can, and not take nothing that didn't belong to them." (Photo by Norman Cooper.)

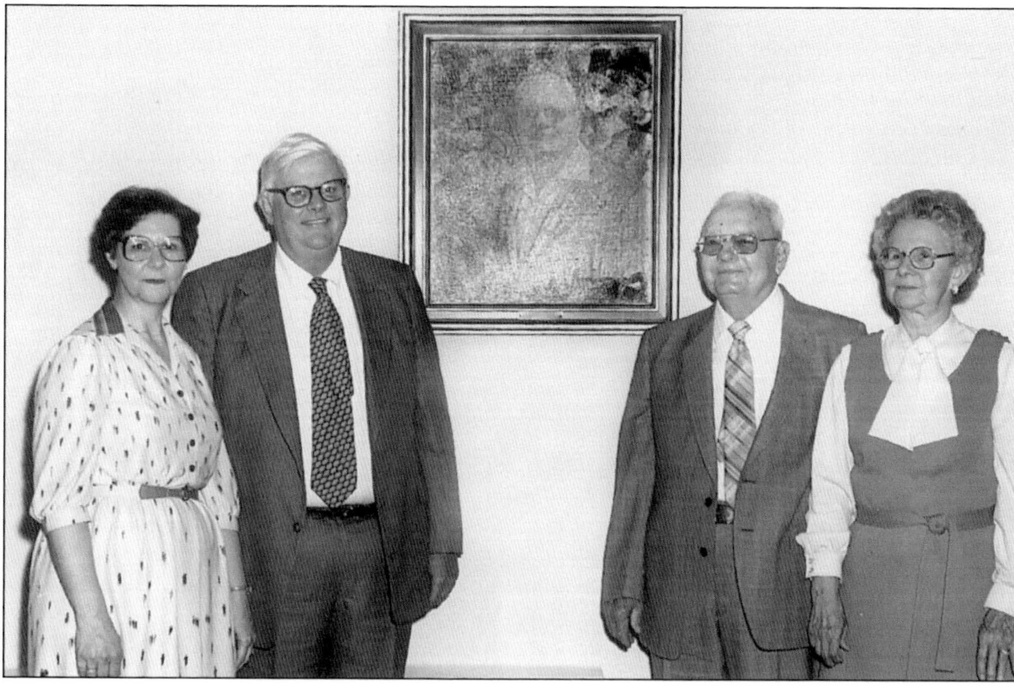

John Bailey (third from left) is shown during his retirement party from the Georgia Mountain Experiment Station. The portrait in the background was presented to him at the event and hangs in the Experiment Station's office. Also in the picture are, from left to right, Catherine Davis Jarrett, unidentified, and Lucille Bailey. (Courtesy Martyne Jokela.)

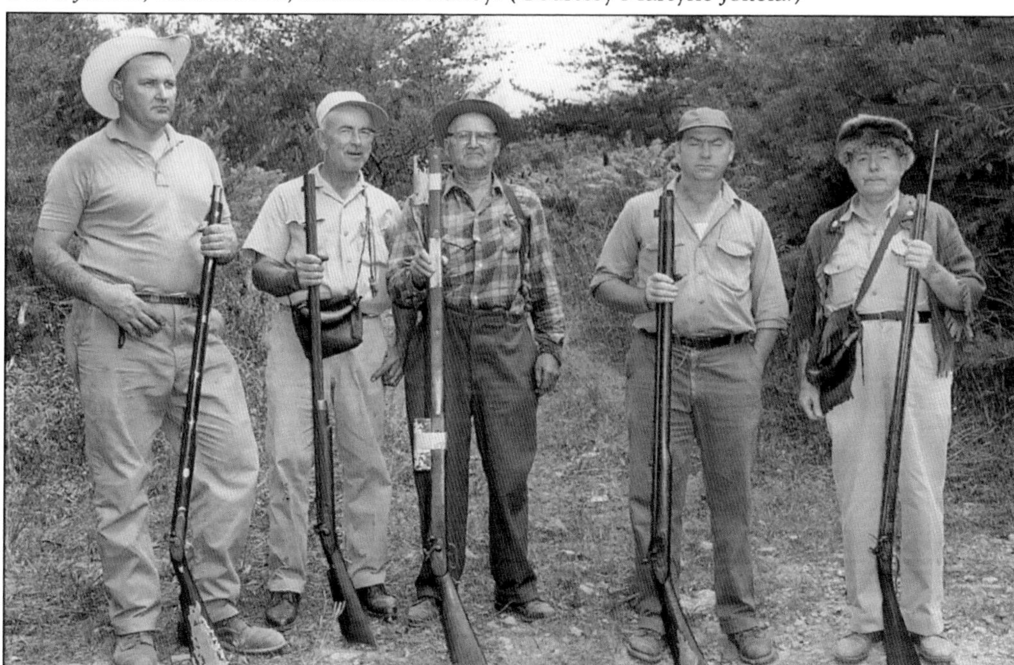

Union County Historian Ed Mauney (far right) joins others in the community displaying their guns used in contests and exhibitions. (Courtesy Martyne Jokela.)

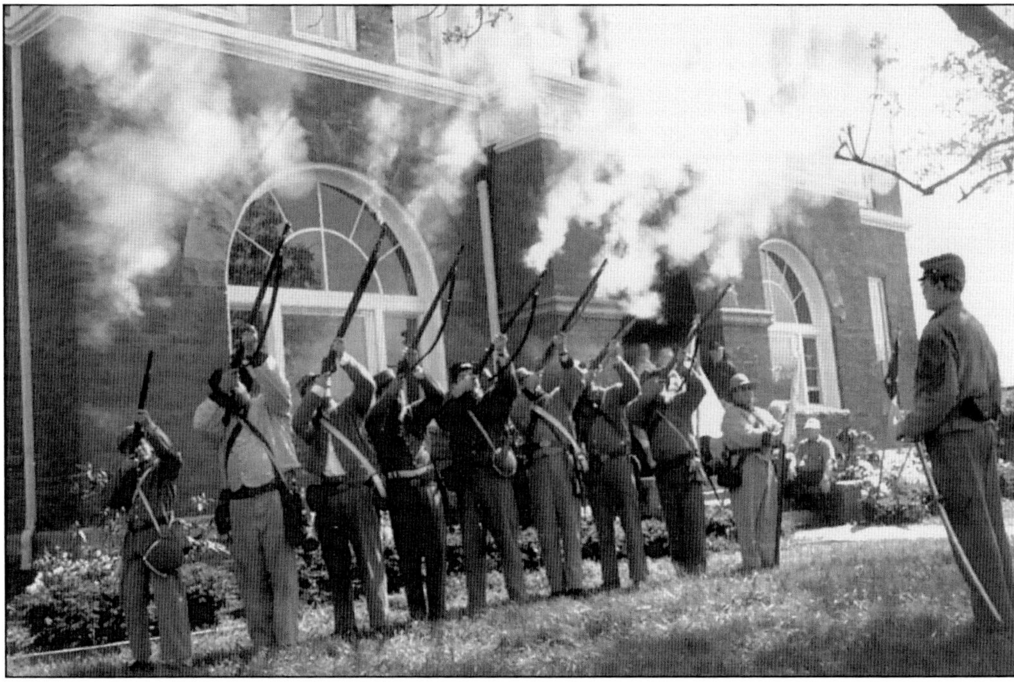

The Sons of Confederate Veterans has an active chapter in Union County. Members participate in various activities, including parades, firing period muzzleloaders, and giving tours of the Payne Cabin. (Photo by Norman Cooper.)

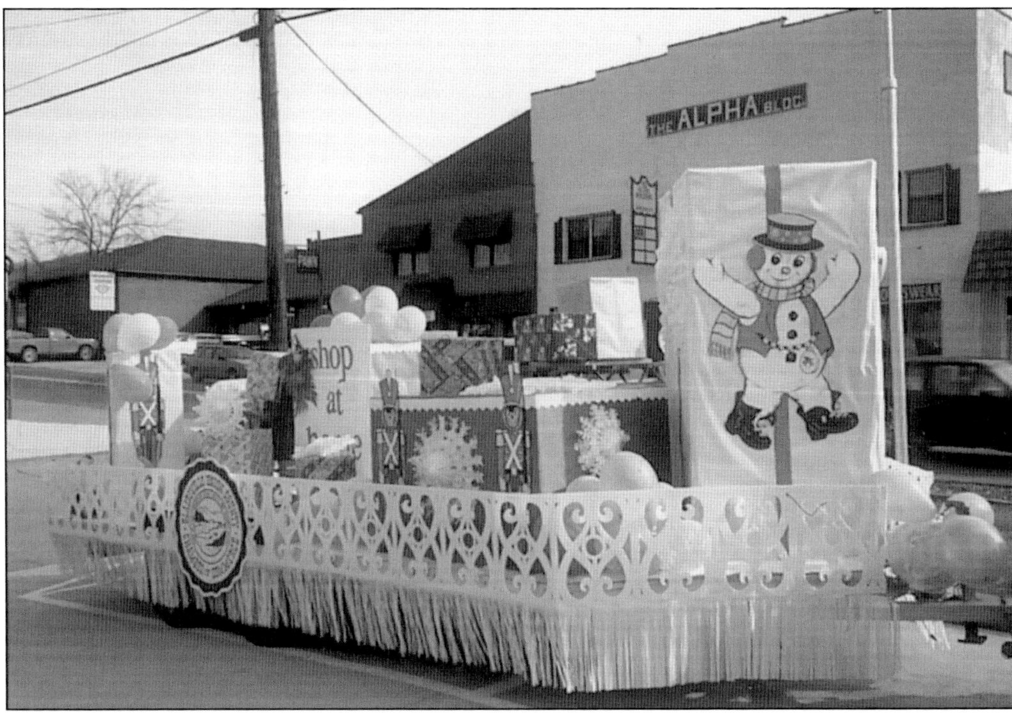

The Chamber of Commerce started a Christmas parade in Blairsville in the 1980s. This is the Chamber of Commerce float in that parade. (Courtesy Martyne Jokela.)

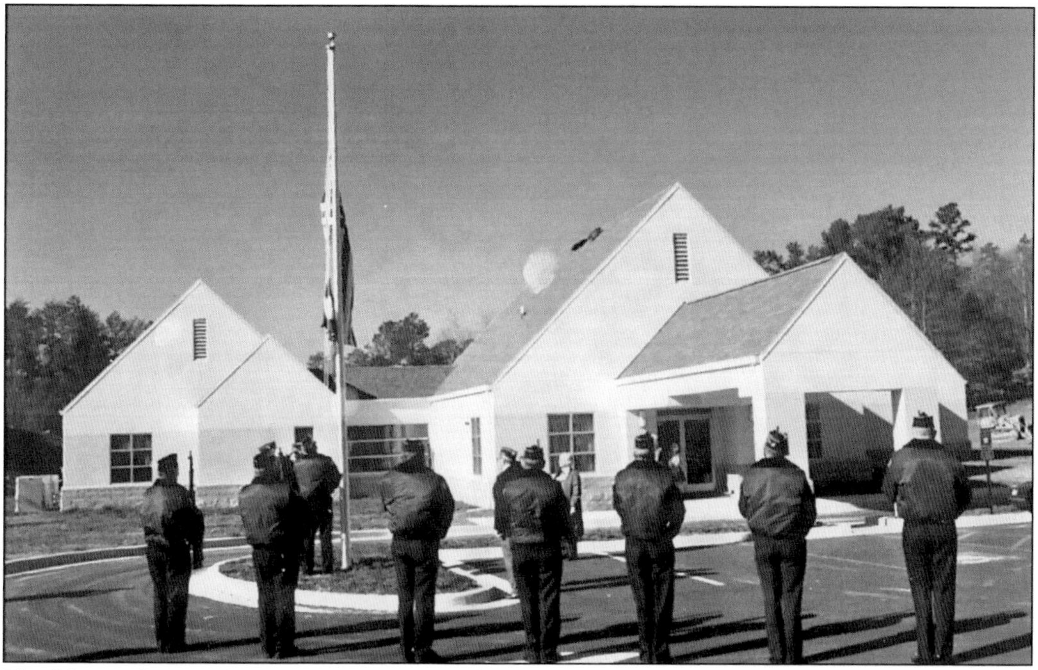

The Union County Senior Center is a social center for elder individuals in the community. It is from this center that the Meals on Wheels program is organized. Seen above is the dedication of the facility. The senior center was formerly located in the Union County Civic Center. Ruth Murrell has served as the director for many years. (Photo by Norman Cooper.)

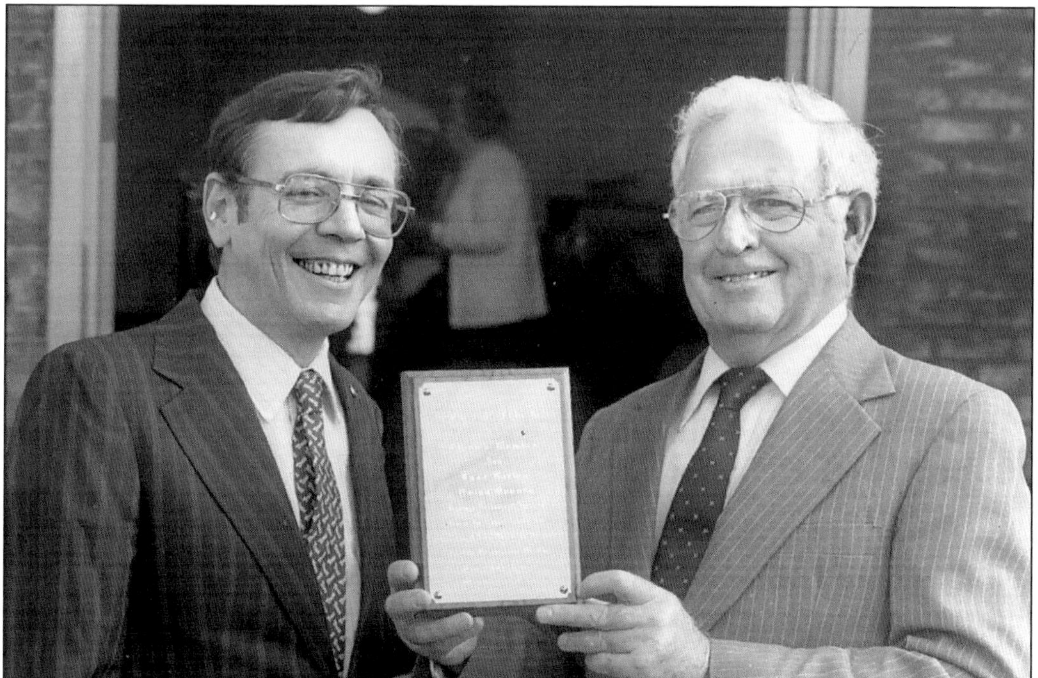

Shown here are Bryan Webb and Maurice Farabee at the rededication of the Old Courthouse, c. 1985. (Courtesy Martyne Jokela.)

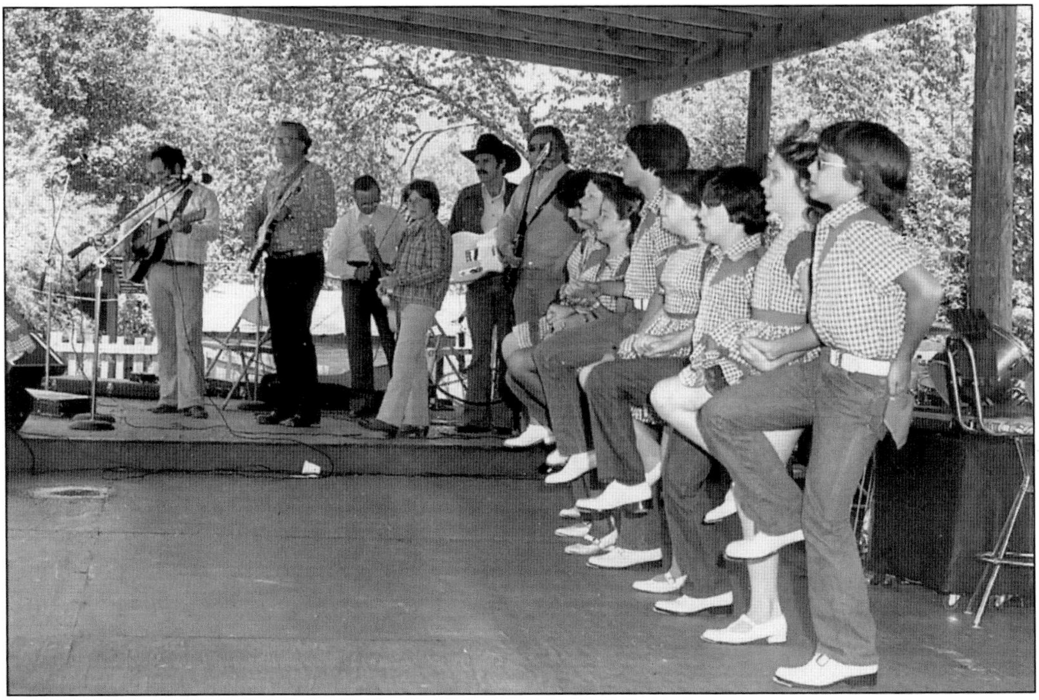

Clogging is a cherished tradition that is part of festivals and special events and is performed both as entertainment and in competitions. (Courtesy Martyne Jokela.)

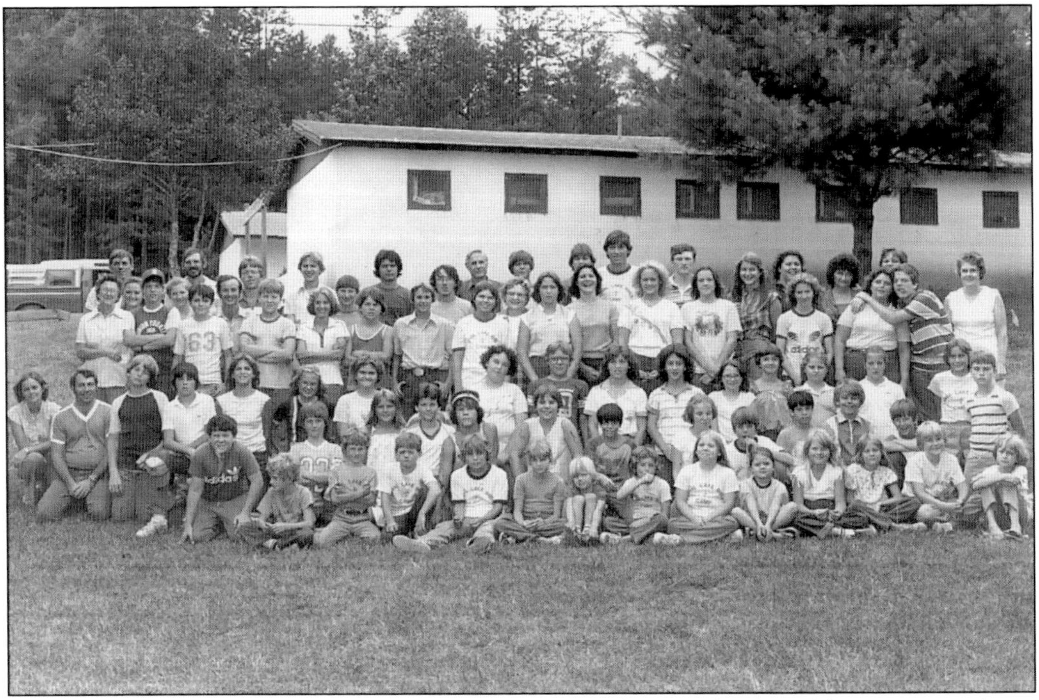

Vacation bible school and other church camps, such as the Canal Lake Bible Camp seen here, are favorites of children during the summer vacation. (Courtesy Martyne Jokela.)

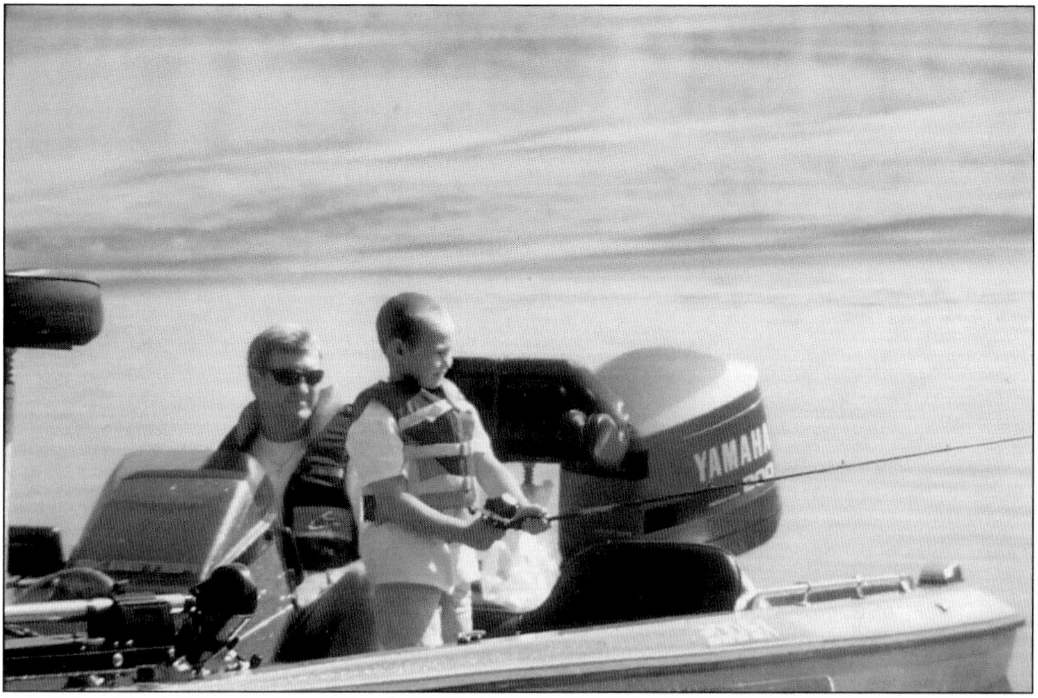

Lake Nottely features some of the finest fishing in the North Georgia mountains. The 4,180-acre body of water has 106 miles of shoreline. Lake Nottely provides recreational opportunities of camping, fishing, swimming, boating, and picnicking. The county also features Lake Winfield Scott, a clear 18-acre lake high in the mountains. (Photo by Norman Cooper.)

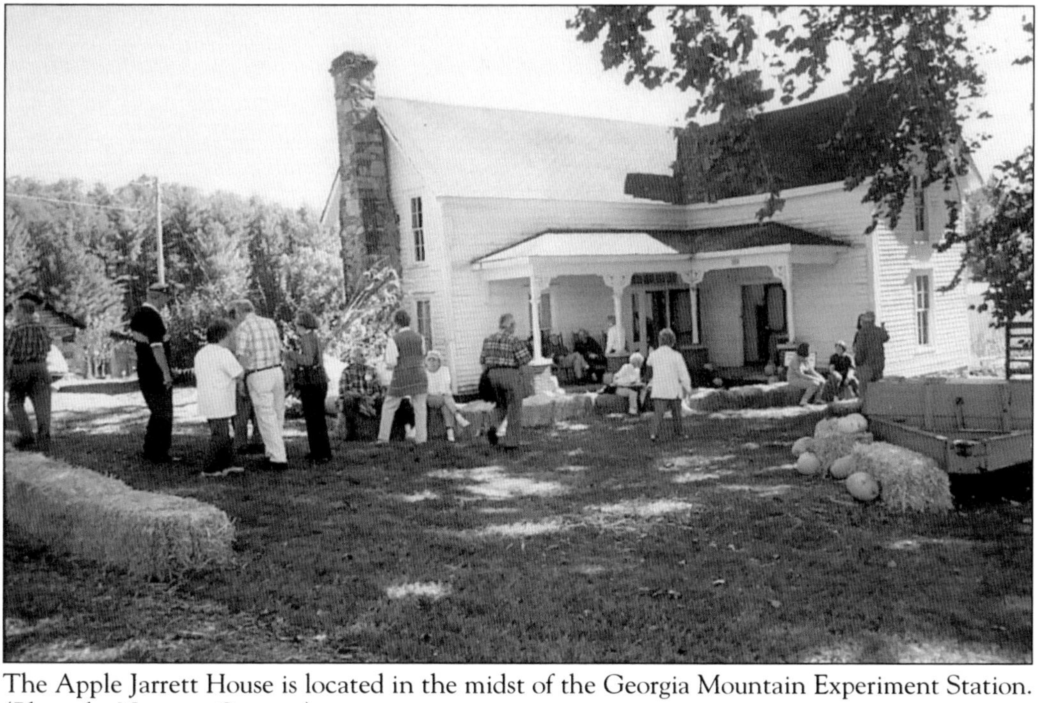

The Apple Jarrett House is located in the midst of the Georgia Mountain Experiment Station. (Photo by Norman Cooper.)

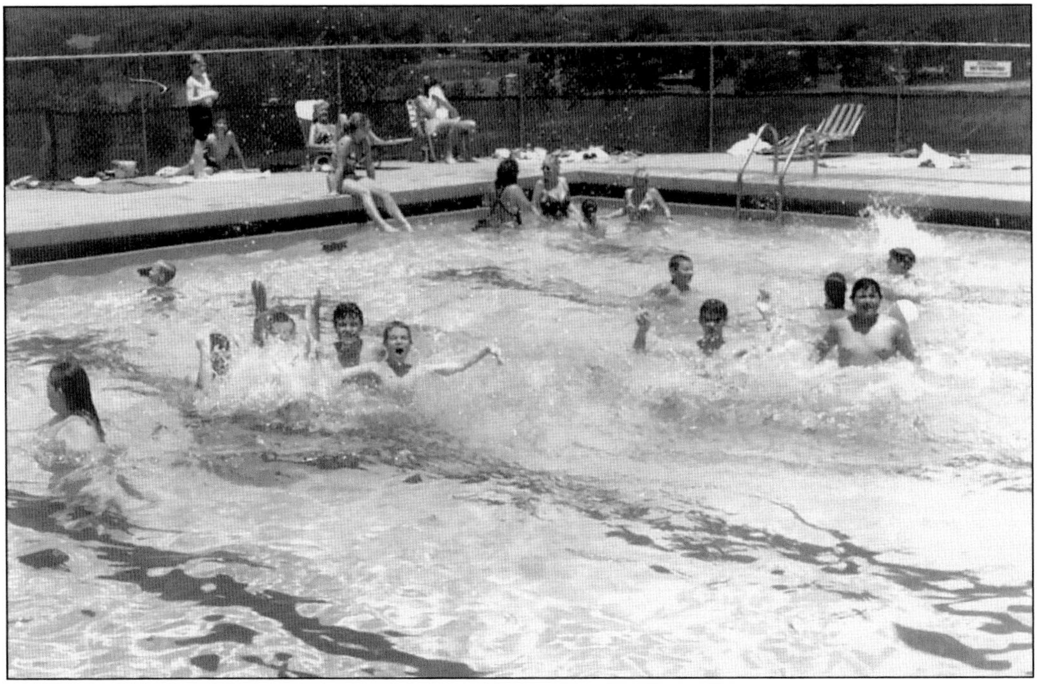

The Meeks Park pool is enjoyed by young and old alike during the summer. (Photo by Norman Cooper.)

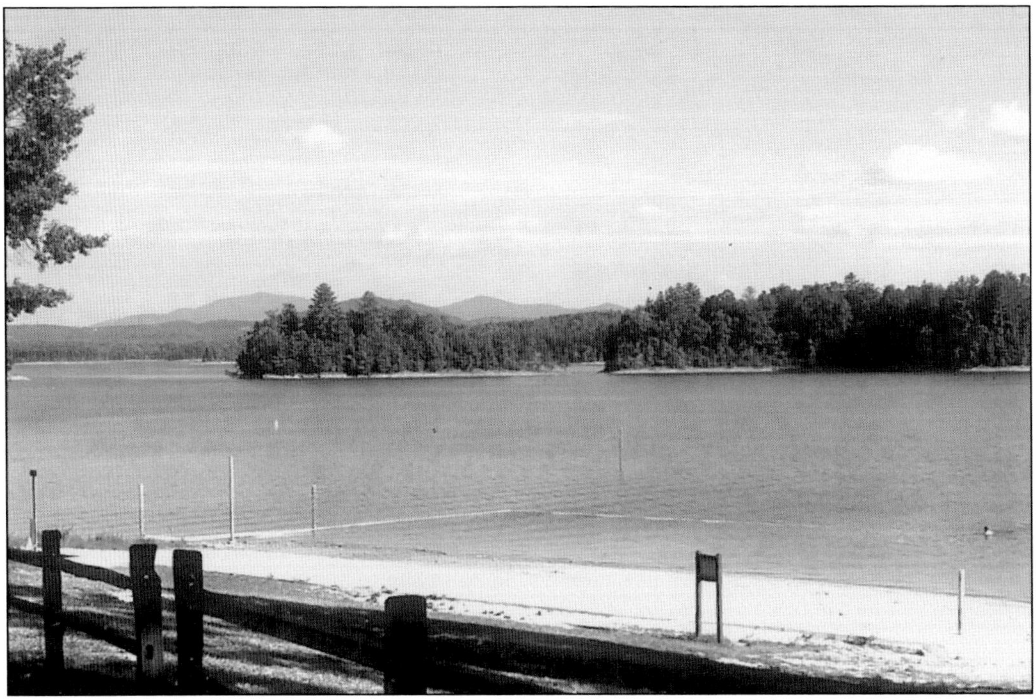

Poteete Creek Campground offers a beach, swimming, picnicking, and the great outdoors during the summer months.

Two

MILITARY

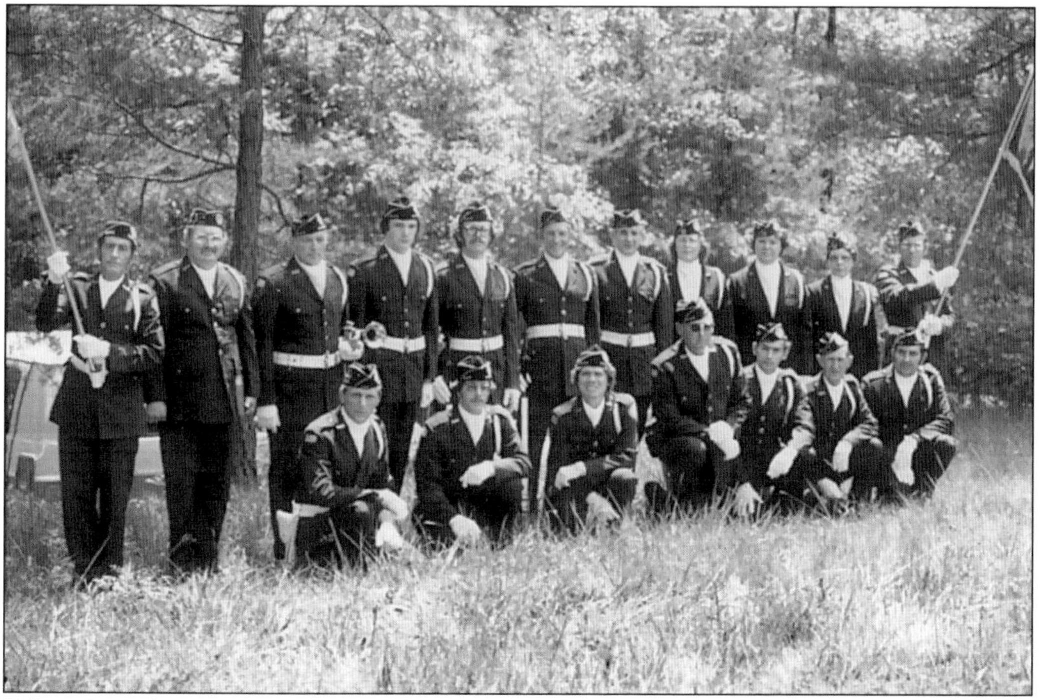

When the military curtailed its participation in funerals for veterans, members of the Disabled American Veterans (D.A.V.) Woodrow Wilson #11 decided to form an honor guard. Their first duty was a flag raising ceremony on July 4, 1980. In later years, other organizations joined the ranks and the group became the North Georgia Honor Guard. In addition to military funerals, the North Georgia Honor Guard performs flag dedications and is involved in various patriotic events. (Photo courtesy of Martyne Jokela.)

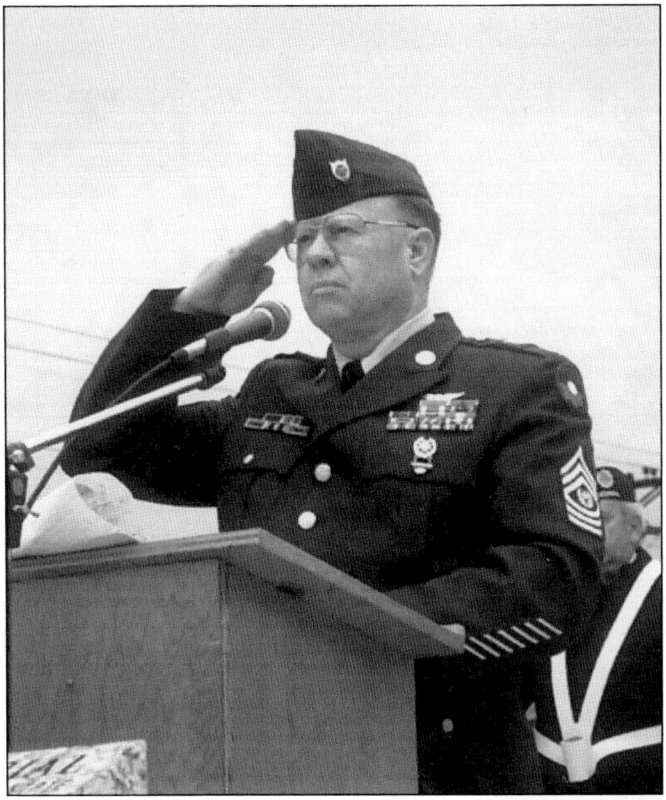

Roy Hamby has helped veterans in numerous ways as manager of the Blairsville Field Office of the Georgia Department of Veterans Service. Hamby, a native of Union County, entered the army in 1958. His major assignments included duty with the Defense Intelligence Agency, two and a half tours in Vietnam, and two tours in the European theater. He completed his military obligations in 1981 with the 9th Infantry Division as a command sergeant major. Hamby's coordination and serving as master of ceremonies of Memorial Day ceremonies, Veterans Day ceremonies, and co-chair of the Memorial Day Parade has championed the community to honor its veterans and military personnel. (Photo by Norman Cooper.)

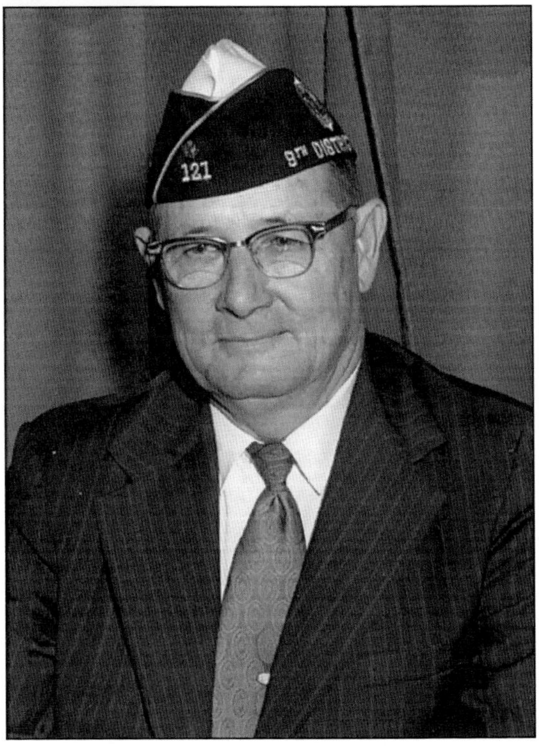

Milford Hamby was a World War II veteran; he was disabled in Korea and left the military after 13 years. Hamby served countless numbers of veterans during his 13 years as Field Office Manager of the Department of Veteran Services, retiring in 1976. Hamby is also known as a photographer, having published numerous photos in the *North Georgia News*. The Union County Historical Society has volumes of negatives and photographs in its Hamby Collection.

Maj. Leon Davenport retired from the army in 1972 after a distinguished military career. Enlisting in the army in 1945, he advanced through the enlisted and officer ranks to his present grade. He is Union County's most decorated officer and has been cited for heroism on five occasions. He was awarded a battlefield commission in Korea as a member of the famed 24th Infantry Division, the first unit to see action in Korea. He has been stationed in the Philippines, Japan, Korea, Germany, and Vietnam. He left the army in 1955 and made his home in Union County until his recall to active duty in 1961. Davenport is noted for his years as administrator of Union General Hospital, from which he retired in 1993.

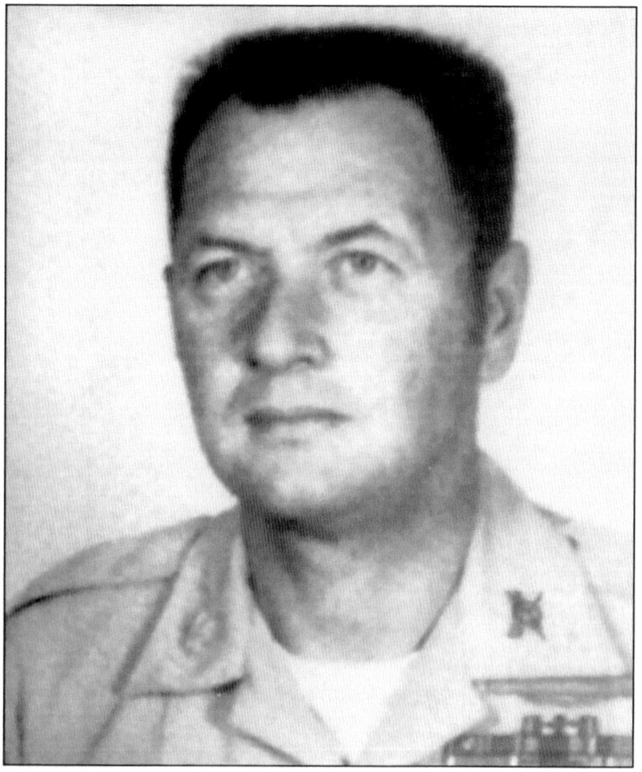

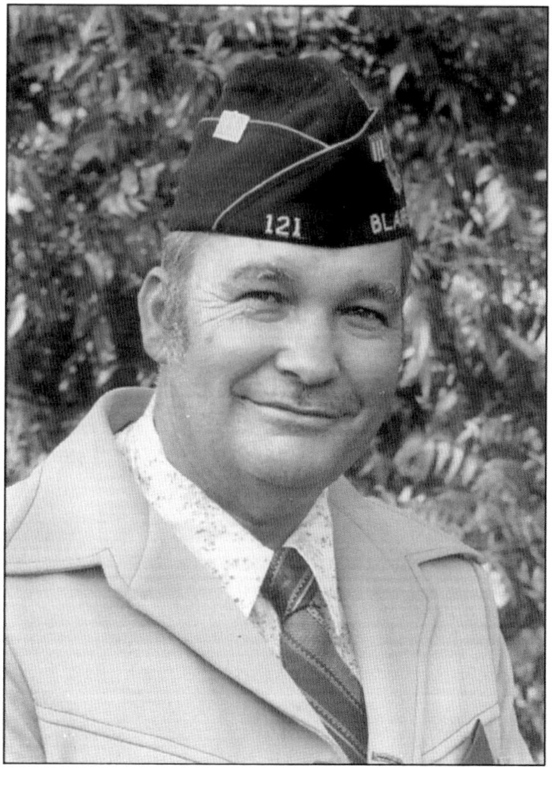

Marshall Kirkland, retired from the U.S. Army, served as post commander of the American Legion. (Courtesy Union County Historical Society.)

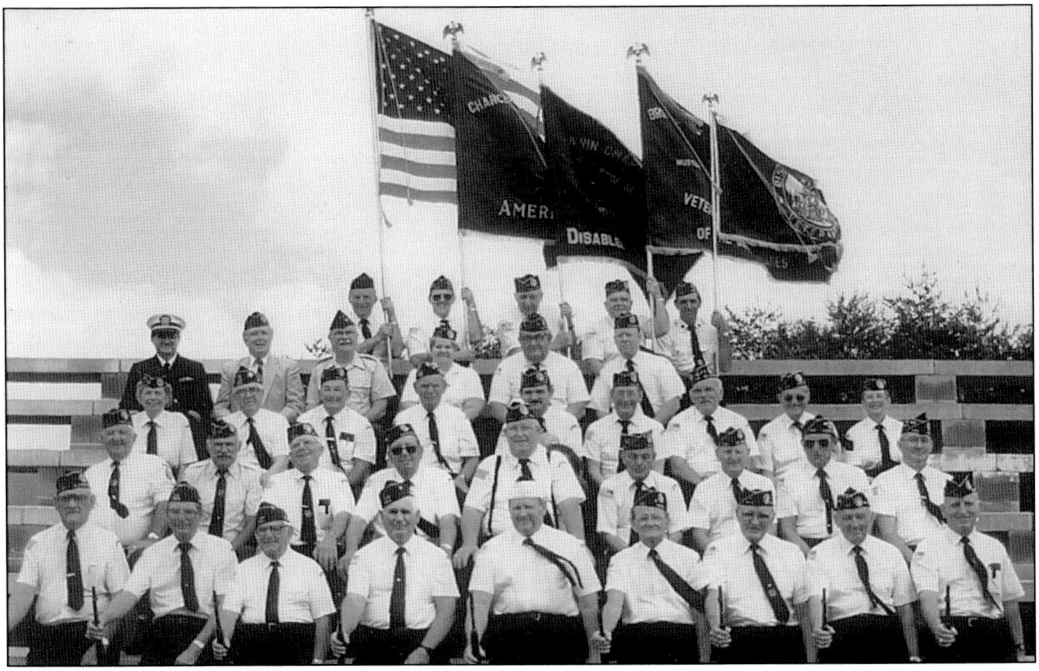

The North Georgia Honor Guard, in this May 27, 1989 photo, are, from left to right, (first row) Earley E. Turner, Jack Reece, William Fry, Robert Keith, J.B. Brendle, Sam Butts, Jim Lewis, Frank Ford, and Hank Hall; (second row) Howard Johnson, Johnny Richardson, Cecil Sisson, Robert Martin, Hank Elrod, Clyde Rhodes, Don Kisseiburg, Weldon Pope, and Charles Galloway; (third row) Lottie Seabolt, Ira T. Harkins, Bobby Flowers, Ernie Holcomb, Mayo Bowers, J.W. Abercrombie, Grady Henson, Jim Gray, and Florence Ford; (fourth row) James Geer, Bob Tackett, Art Estes, Mary Lewis, William Bradley, and Roy Hamby; (fifth row) Marvin Williamson, Earl Leamon Oliver, Floyd Collins, Pete Dobson, and Bud Crisp. (Courtesy Georgia Department of Veteran Services.)

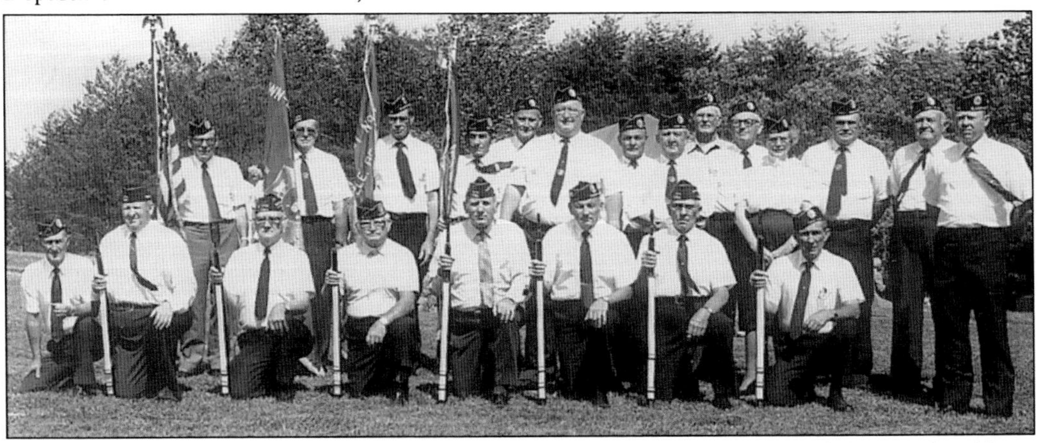

The North Georgia Honor Guard, in this May 3, 1985 photo, are, from left to right, (front row) Bass Henderson, J.B. Brendle, Earley E. Turner, Bob Bryson, Hank Hall, Frank Ford, Fred Weaver, and Bob Henderson; (back row) Alton Brown, James Gray, Homer Nix, Grady Carroll, Elmer Couch, Hank Elrod, Clyde Rhodes, Howard Johnson, Elbert Hutson, Wynn A. Davenport, Elda Brown, Johnny Richardson, Jimmy Mulkey, and Roy Hamby. (Courtesy Georgia Department of Veteran Services.)

The need for an honor guard became evident when the federal government could no longer fulfill all the requests for military funerals. Reino Jokela, at left, commander of Disabled American Veterans Woodrow Wilson #11 and Frank Ford, adjutant, at right, took the initiative to fulfill this need in 1978. Their first steps were the acquiring of uniforms, rifles, a bugler, and the training of veterans in accurate military funeral procedures. (Courtesy Martyne Jokela.)

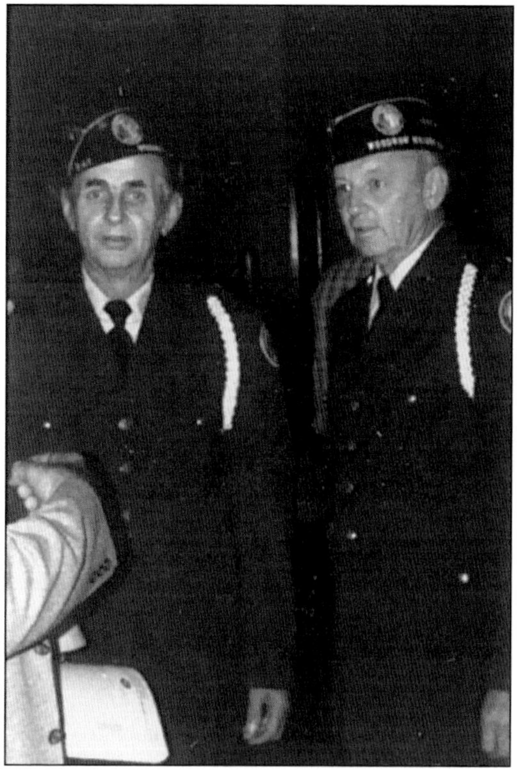

Training was directed by veteran Richard Fleming. Having several ministers in the D.A.V. chapter and Frank Ford as bugler made for a fully trained group from whose ranks a full company could be called on short notice. The Disabled American Veterans Department of Georgia Color Guard, from left to right, Cecil Pruitt, Jay Burle, Bass Henderson, Grady Carroll, Henry Ownbey, and Reino Jokela, presents the colors at opening ceremonies of the state convention in Macon, Georgia. (Courtesy Martyne Jokela.)

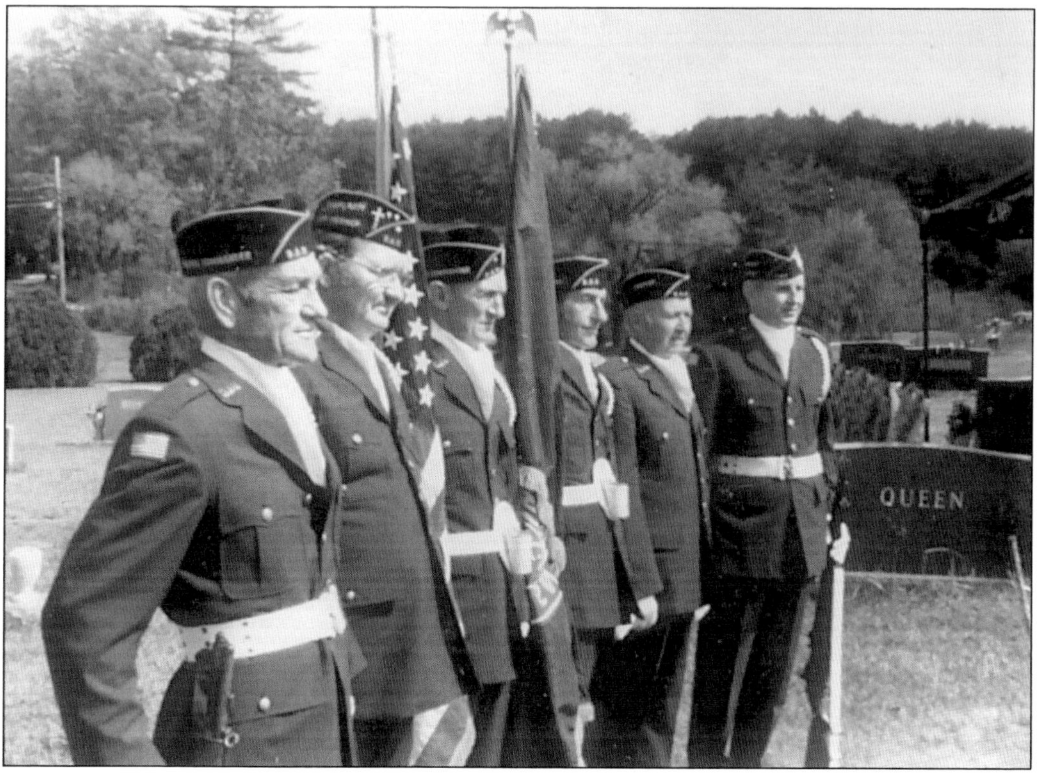

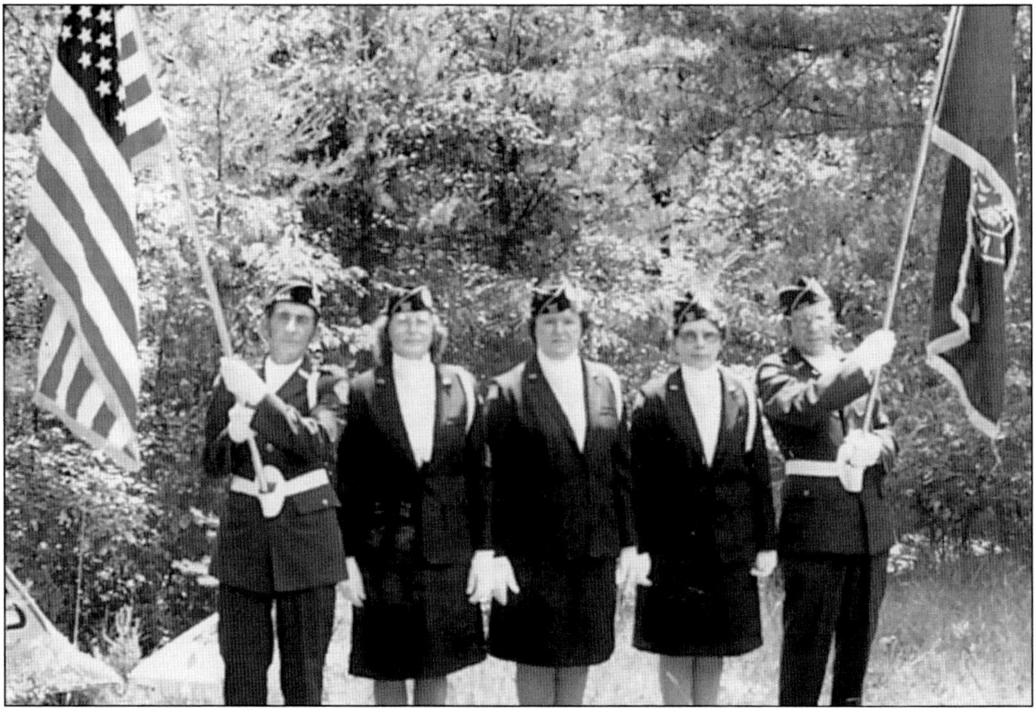

The D.A.V. #11 Auxiliary, women as well as men, participate at military funerals. Among the Color Guard, from left to right, are Grady Carroll; Commander Florence Ford; Adjutant Martyne Jokela; Cecil Pruitt; and Alton Brown. (Courtesy Martyne Jokela.)

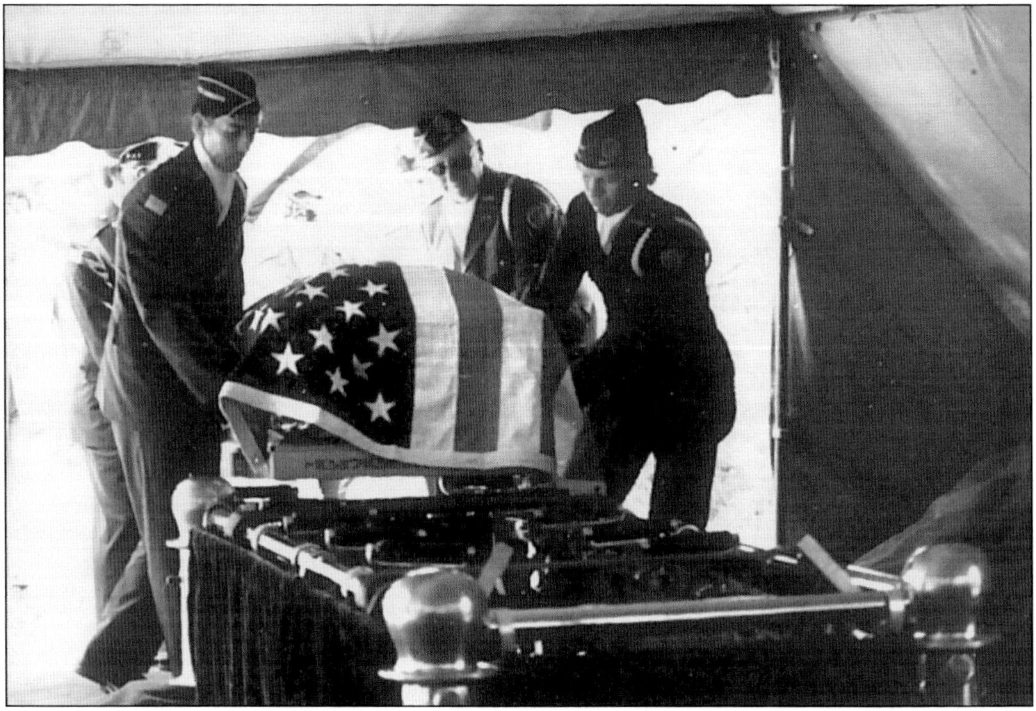

The D.A.V. Honor Guard conducts a military funeral in the 1980s. (Courtesy Martyne Jokela.)

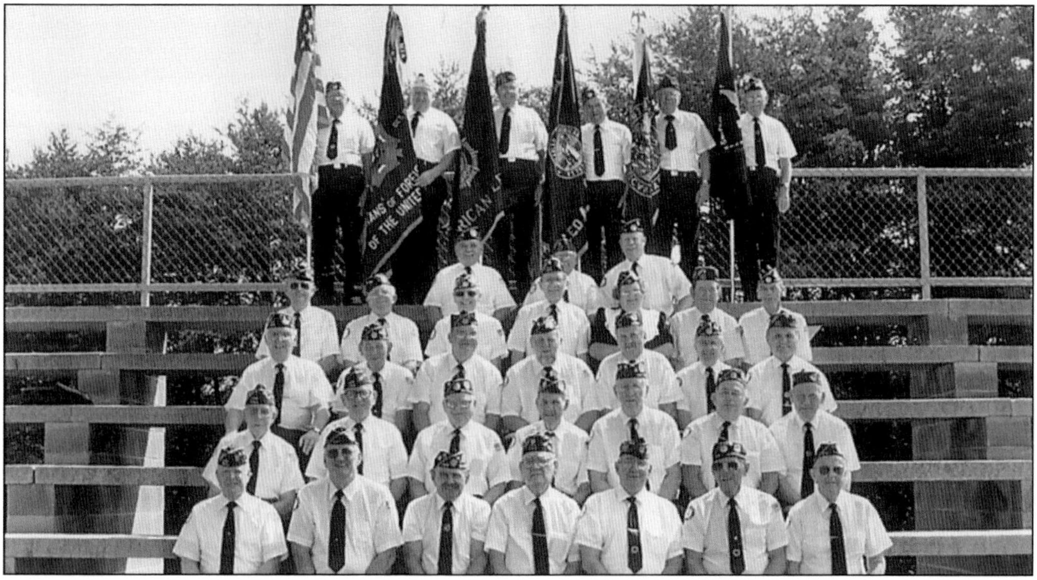

The North Georgia Honor Guard, in this August 3, 1996 photo, are, from left to right, (first row) Bill Curlee, Hubert Chappell, Johnnie Richards, Earley E. Turner, Charles Galloway, Weldon Pope, and James Gray; (second row) Fred Weaver, Hank Hall, Harry Hicks, Jack Nash, Floyd Collins, Bobby Flowers, and Elmer Couch; (third row) Al DeVita, Robert Butt, Marshall Kirkland, Otis Dillard, Joe Dyer, James Galloway, and Jack McCorkle; (fourth row) Gwen Williamson, Cecil Sisson, Earl Tierce, Kenneth Mountz, Myrtle Cook, Jimmy Cook, and Joe Hanson; (fifth row) Lewis Payne, William Fry, and Roy Hamby; (sixth row) Robert Martin, J.B. Brendle, Guy Spiva, Bill Bowers, Jack Reese, and Ira Van Orsdale. (Courtesy Georgia Department of Veterans Services.)

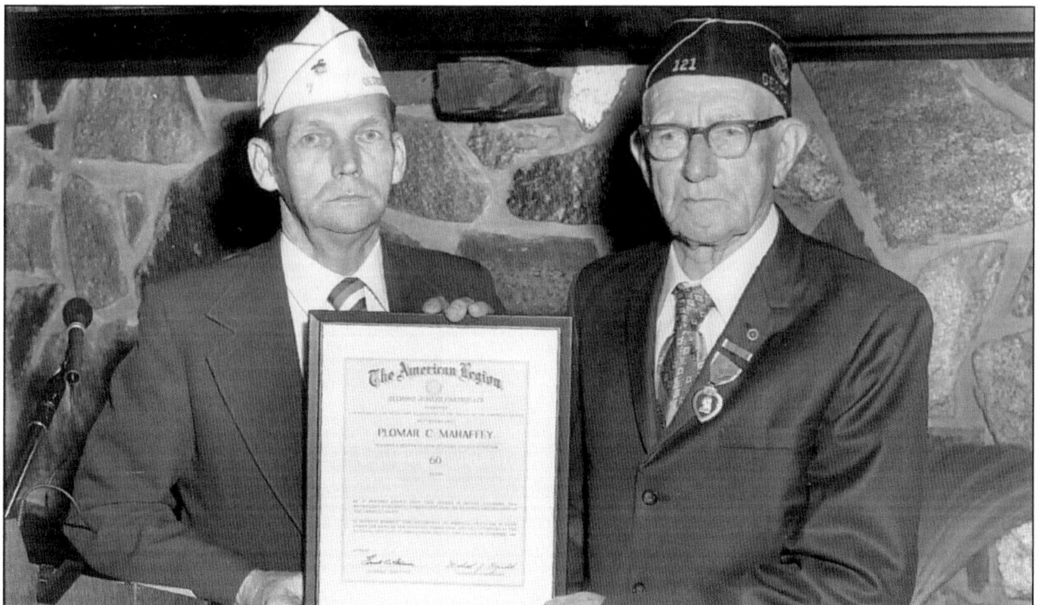

World War I veteran Polmar MaLaffey, wearing the Purple Heart, is presented a certificate from the American Legion. (Courtesy Martyne Jokela.)

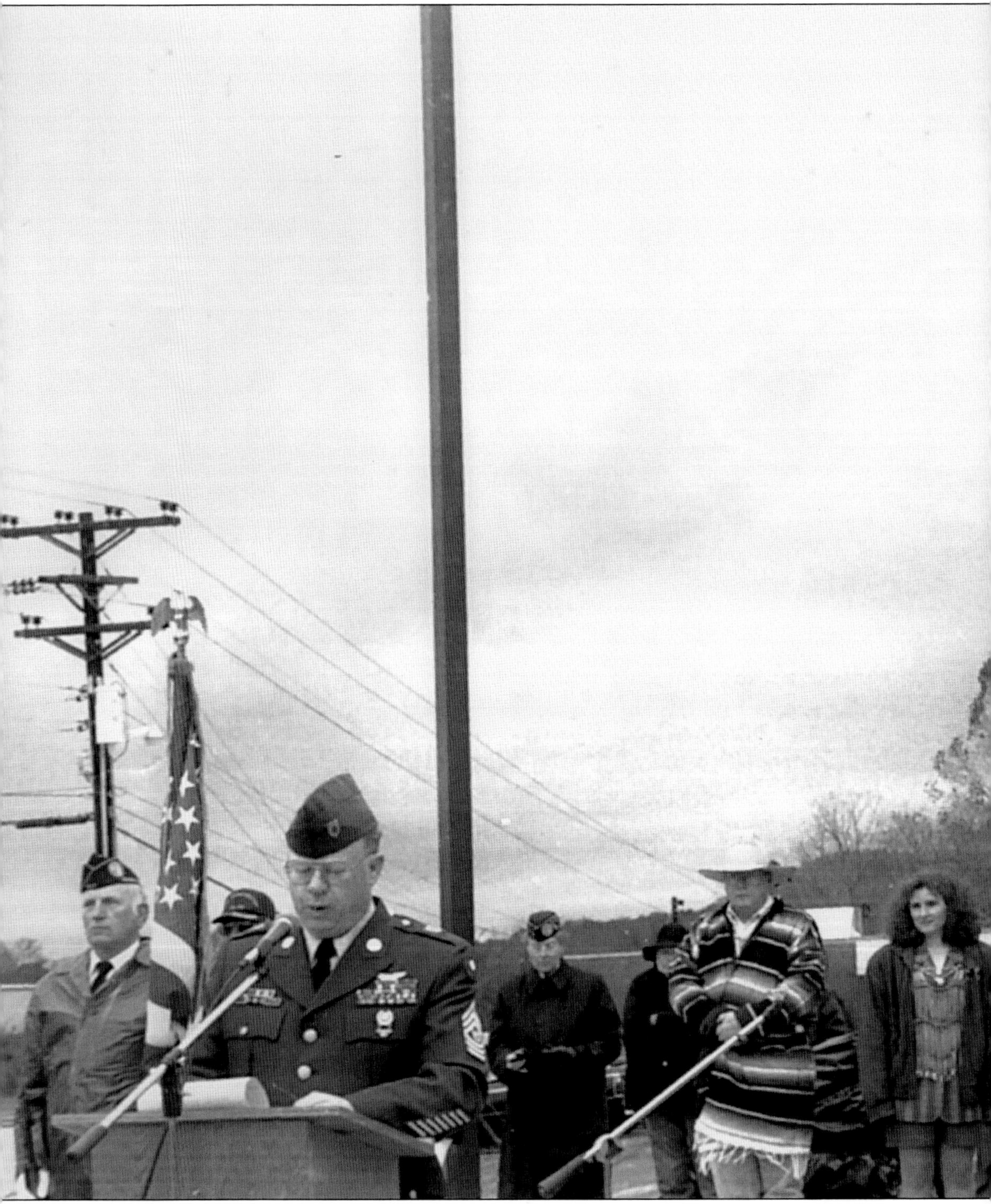

The Union County War Memorial was dedicated on November 11, 1995, the culmination of an 18-month project. Roy Hamby, master of ceremonies for the dedication, enlisted the help of citizens and civic organizations to help fund the project. The project got underway when

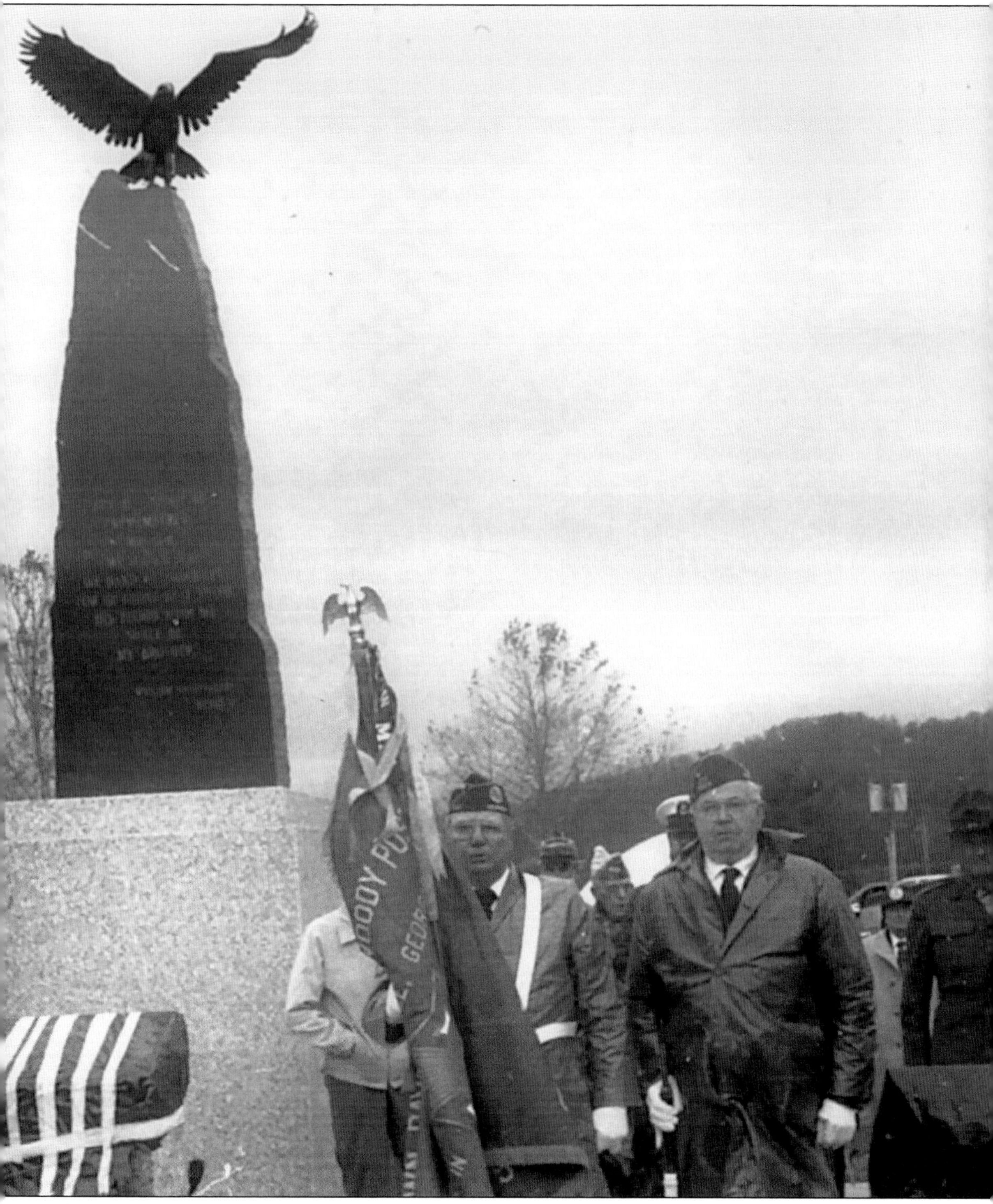

the Union County Board of Education donated a 1.13-acre site on school property. The board agreed to lease the land to the county for 99 years provided it be used as a memorial. The county maintains the land and the city pays the light and water bill. (Photo by Norman Cooper.)

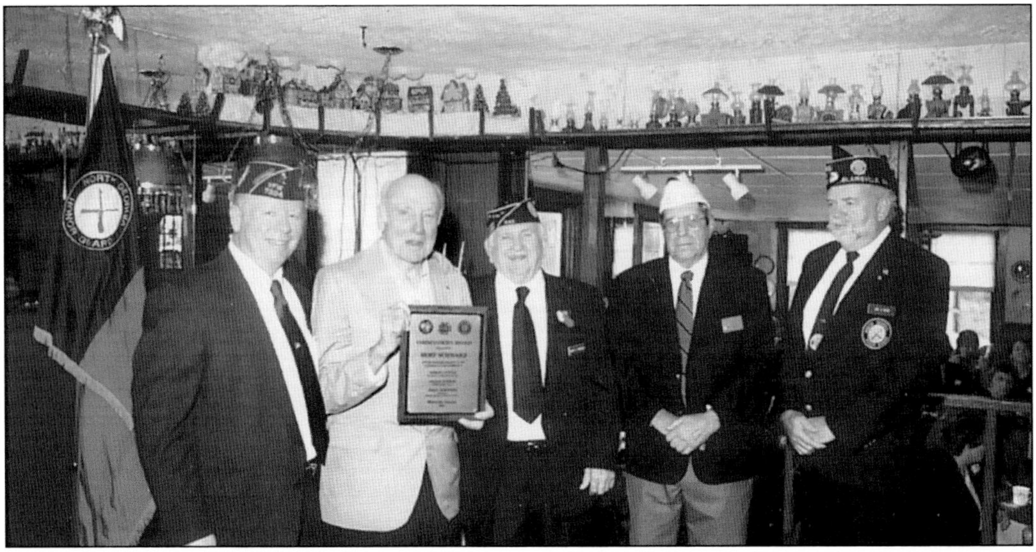

On November 11, Union County honors veterans during the annual Veterans Day ceremony. Guests of honor include former prisoners of war and their spouses and widows. Three veterans groups present a Commander's Award to the veteran who has done the most in the current year to assist veterans. Bert Schwarz, second from left, was presented the award in 2002. Roy Hamby, far left, assisted in the presentation with D.A.V. commander Jimmy Morrison, V.F.W. commander Robert Little, and American Legion past commander Joe Dyer. (Photo by Norman Cooper.)

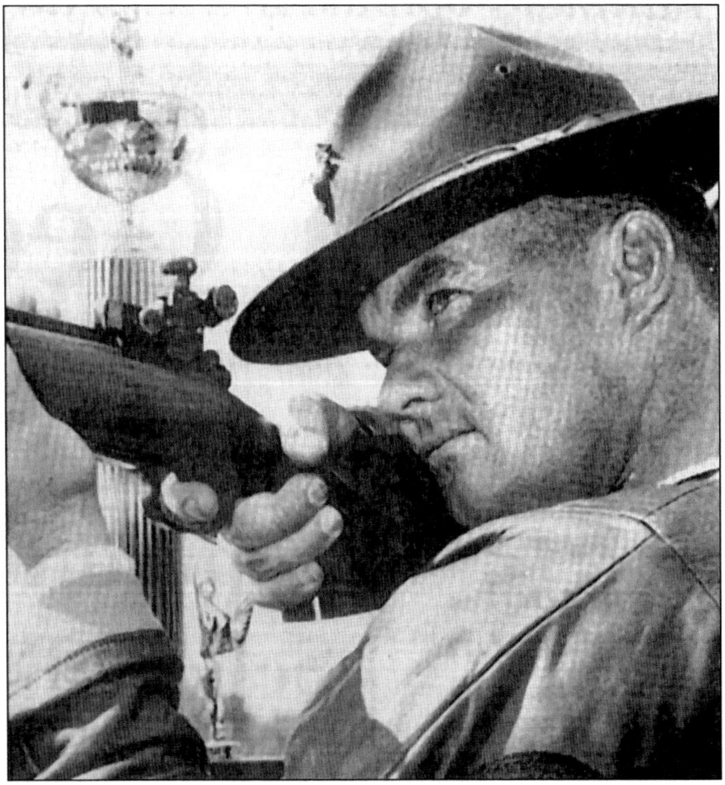

M.Sgt. Eric R. England entered the Marines in 1950 and distinguished himself as a sharp shooter during his 20-year career. He served in Vietnam as a sniper/scout and was an instructor for the USMC sniper school. He won competitions, set numerous records, participated on two Olympic teams, and won the Leach Cup. In recent years, England has worked with young shooters in the Union County 4-H. (Courtesy Georgia Department of Veteran Services.)

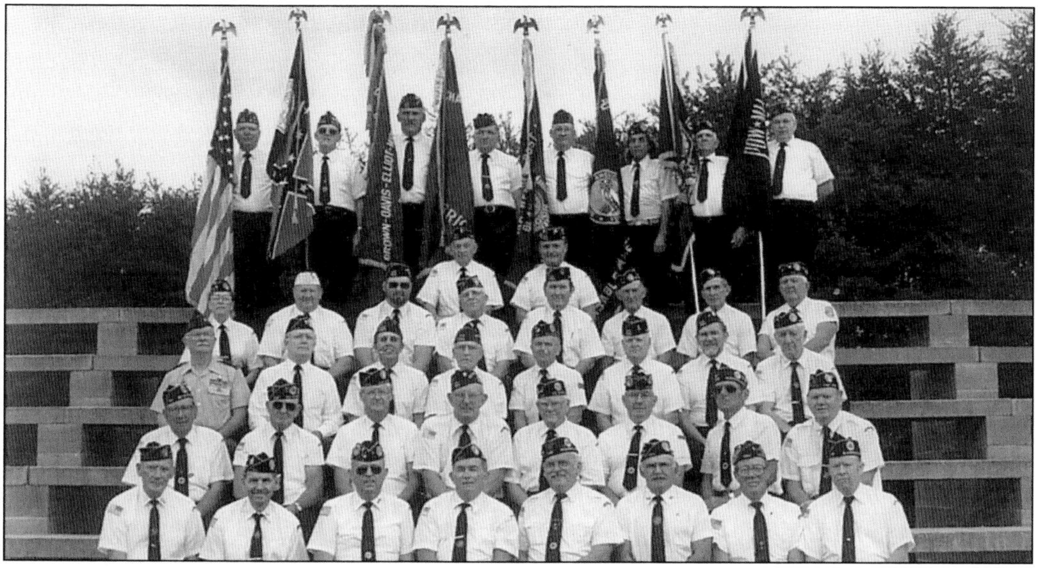

The North Georgia Honor Guard, in this October 3, 1992 photo, are, from left to right, (first row) Elmer Couch, Jack Nash, Gwen Williamson, Bobby Flowers, Grady Henson, Johnny Richards, David Kirkpatrick, and Roy Hamby; (second row) Robert Martin, Bill Weeks, Wayne Smith, Gordon Allison, Harry Hicks, Charles Galloway, Weldon Pope, and J.C. Wood; (third row) Arthur Estes, Bob Tackett, Lamar Ledford, Fred Weaver, James Galloway, Billy Curlee, Ken Mountz, and Floyd Collins; (fourth row) Florence Ford, J.B. Brendle, Gover Brendle, Cecil Sisson, James Cook, Bass Henderson, Robert Henderson, and Howard Johnson; (fifth row) Frank Ford and Jack McCorkle; (sixth row) Jack Reece, Earl Oliver, Rick Evans, Marvin Williamson, Marshall Kirkland, Jack Sigler, Jimmy Morrison, and Guy Spiva. (Courtesy Georgia Department of Veteran Services.)

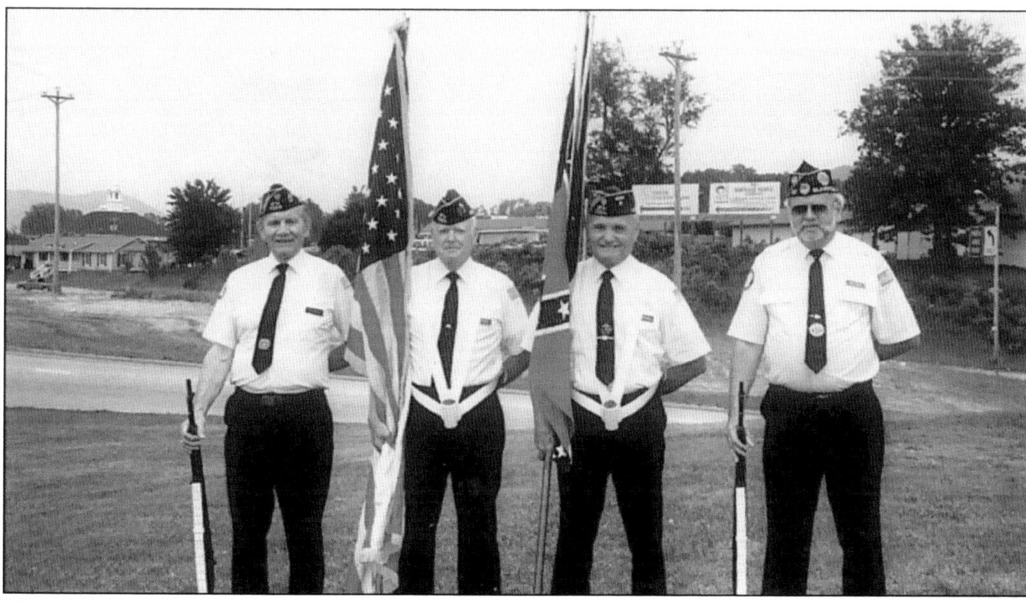

The North Georgia Honor Guard are, from left to right, World War II veteran Ken Mountz, North Georgia Honor Guard commander Bill Curlee, Korea 50th Anniversary coordinator Jack McCorkle, and American Legion commander Joe Dyer. (Courtesy Florence Ford.)

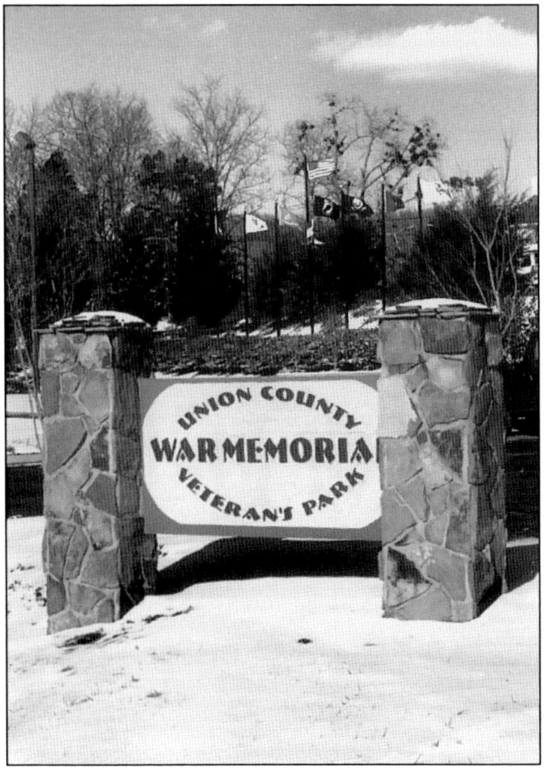

The Union County War Memorial is shown on a bright sunny day after snow covered the North Georgia Mountains. (Photo by Norman Cooper.)

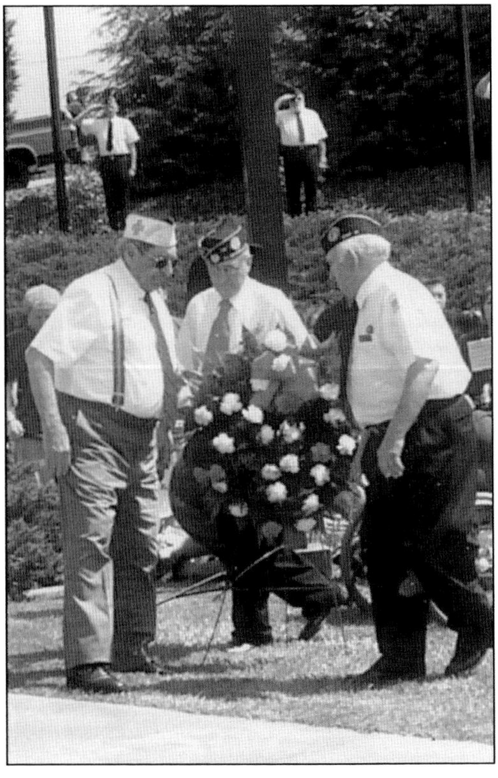

Commanders of the American Legion, V.F.W., and D.A.V. lay a wreath at the Union County War Memorial. (Photo by Norman Cooper.)

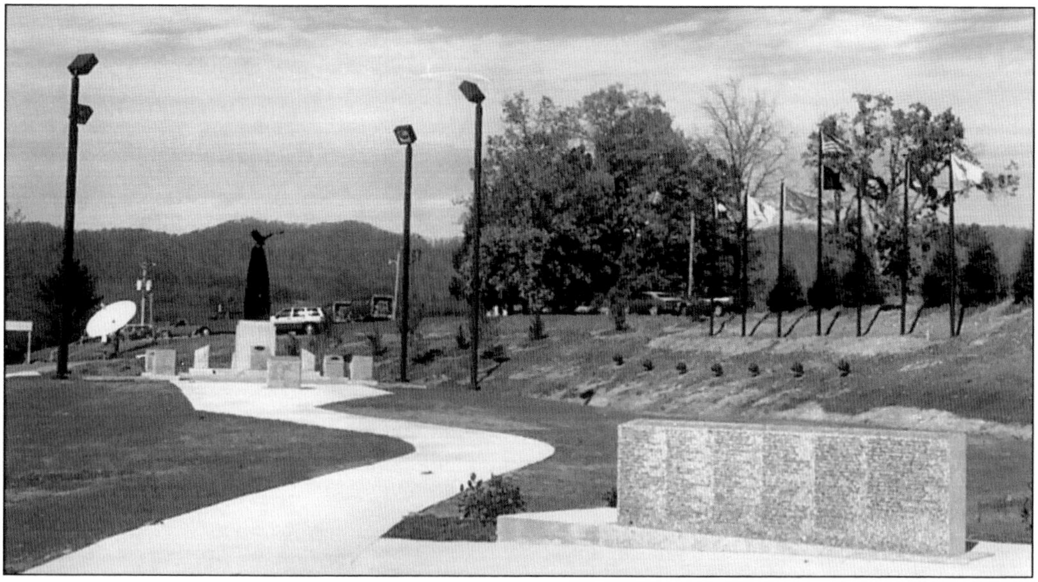

The Union County War Memorial, dedicated on November 11, 1995, depicts 11 major wars as they have impacted the county, state, and nation. Adjacent to the memorial are the American flag, P.O.W. flag, Georgia flag, and the flags of the U.S. Army, Marines, Navy, Air Force, and Coast Guard. The memorial honors the history of the Cherokees as they existed in Union County and the Trail of Tears, depicting their removal and the destruction of their nation. (Photo by Norman Cooper.)

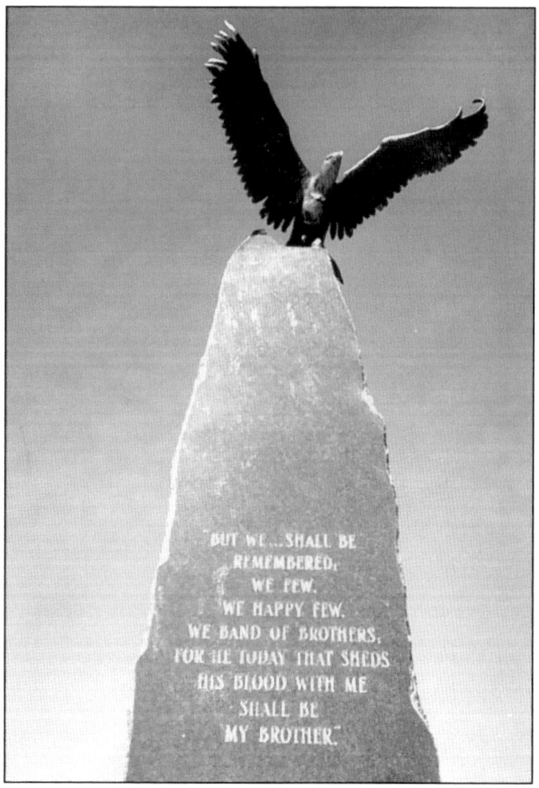

A bronze eagle, symbol of strength, unity, and courage, sits atop a 10-foot black granite with quotations from Shakespeare's *Henry V* and Douglas MacArthur. The eagle overlooks nine granite pedestals honoring 158 men from Union County who made the ultimate sacrifice in the service of our country during the Civil War, World War I, World War II, Korea, and Vietnam. Soldiers from Union County who fought and died for the Union and the Confederacy are honored. (Photo by Norman Cooper.)

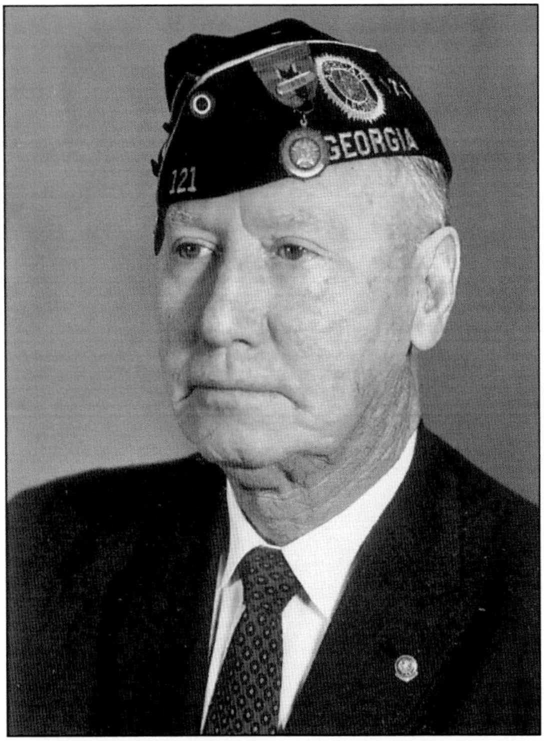

Obediah "Obe" Pruitt served in the army during World War I and was wounded in France. After the war, he served 23 years as U.S. deputy marshall for the Northern District of Georgia. Pruitt served 12 years as mayor of Blairsville. During his years as mayor, Blairsville built an airport, acquired a new water system, installed streetlights, acquired a fire truck, purchased its first police car, and paved many streets. (Courtesy Union County Historical Society.)

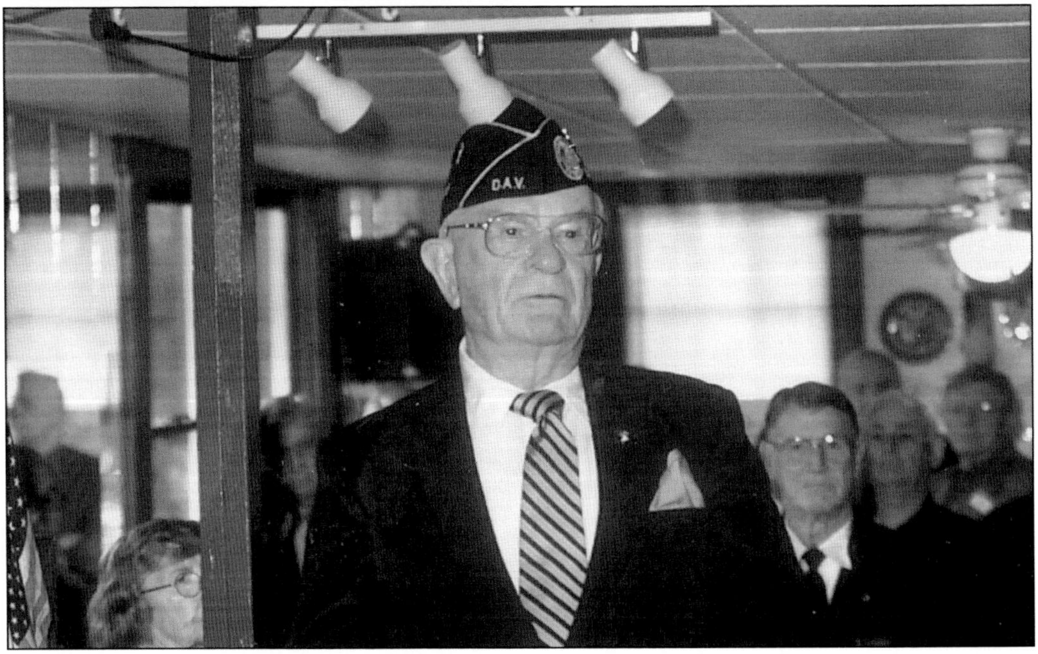

Chaplain Col. Arthur J. Estes, a Baptist clergyman for more than 50 years, was a master parachutist with over 100 jumps. He served during World War II, Korea, and Vietnam. Post chaplain at Fort Benning and Fort Lewis, Chaplain Estes served as staff chaplain of the army in Japan and chaplain staff advisor to the commanding general for U.S. Forces in Japan. He was promoted to colonel in October 1966. (Photo by Norman Cooper.)

Bert Schwarz, a pilot in World War II, arrived in the Philippines 18 days before the United States went to war. The planes never arrived and General MacArthur ordered the pilots to form infantry regiments. In February 1942, they surrendered and about 70,000 Americans and Filipinos became POWs. After horrible years as a POW, Schwarz was on a ship in September 1944 that was hit by two torpedoes. Only 82 people managed to swim almost three miles through intensive small arms fire to a friendly Philippine shore. Captain Schwarz was awarded a Bronze Star and a Purple Heart. Seen in the photo with Schwarz (standing) during Armed Forces Day are retired Col. Cheryl Bergeron and Jimmy Morrison. (Photo by Norman Cooper.)

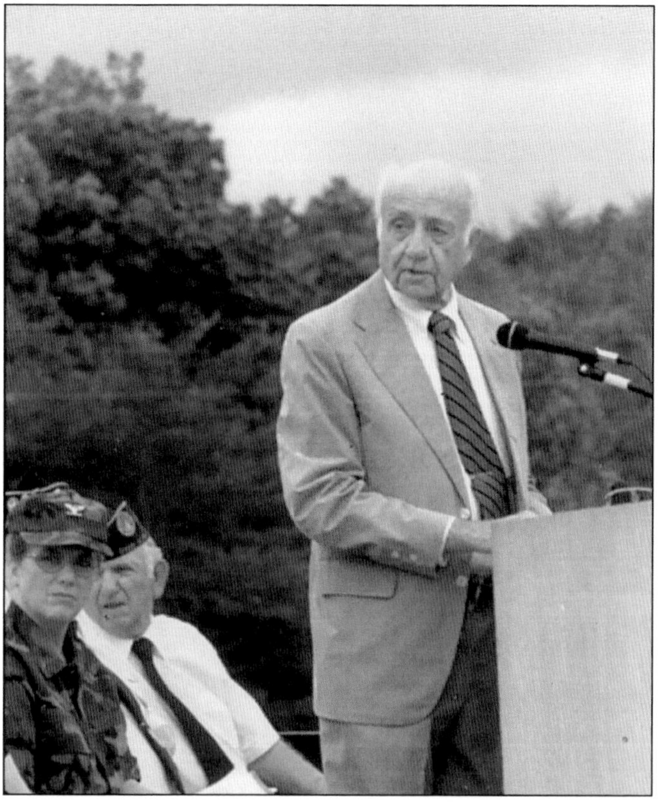

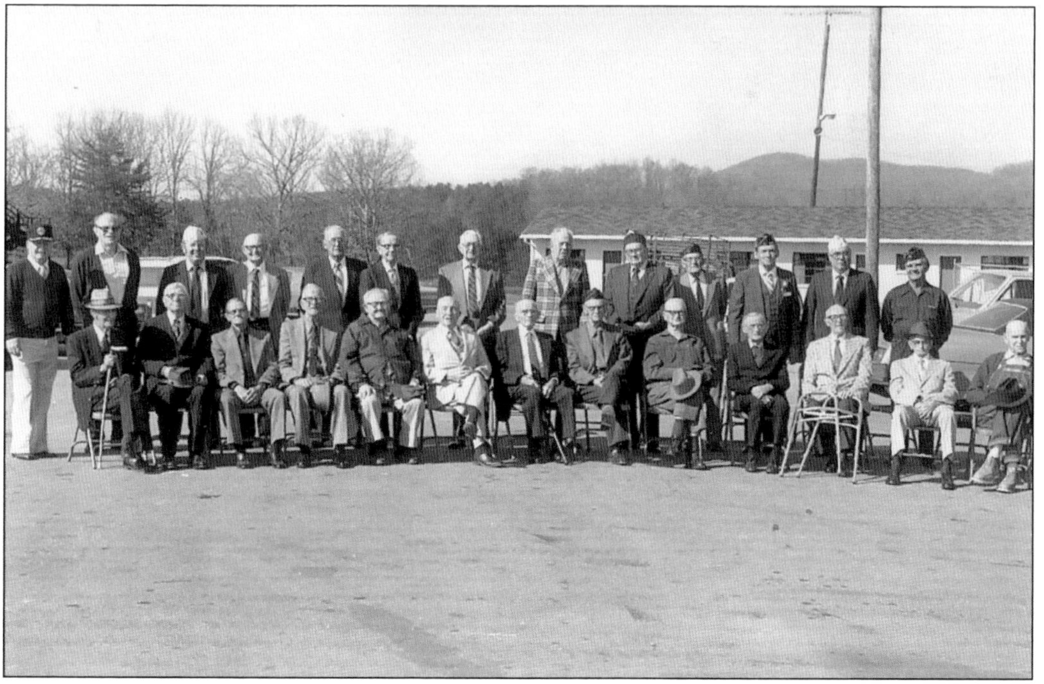

World War I veterans gather for a photo in Union County during the 1970s. (Courtesy Union County Historical Society.)

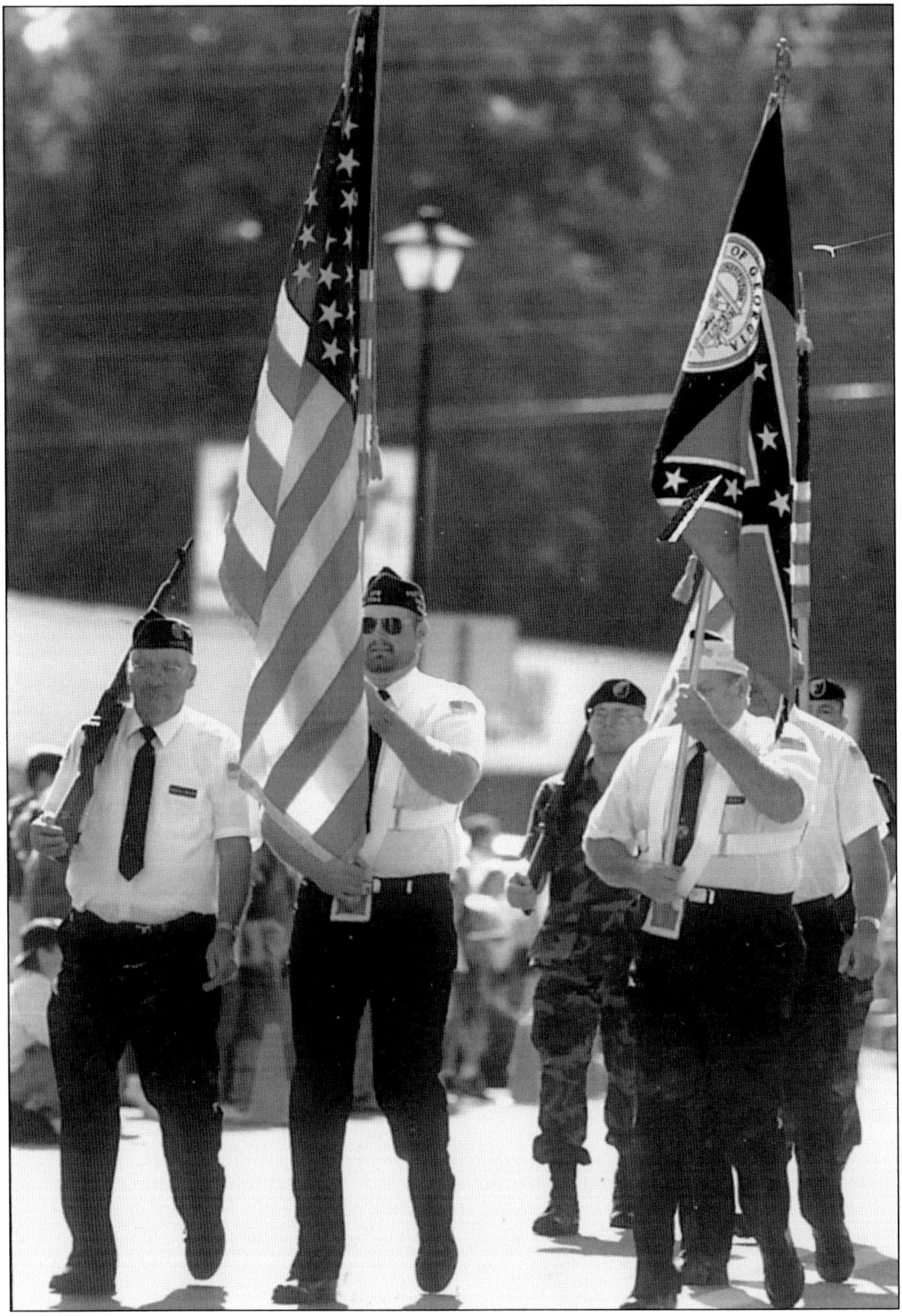

Union County features veterans at the front of each parade, including the Memorial Day Parade, Sorghum Festival Parade, and Christmas Parade, in the 1980s.

Three

ECONOMICS

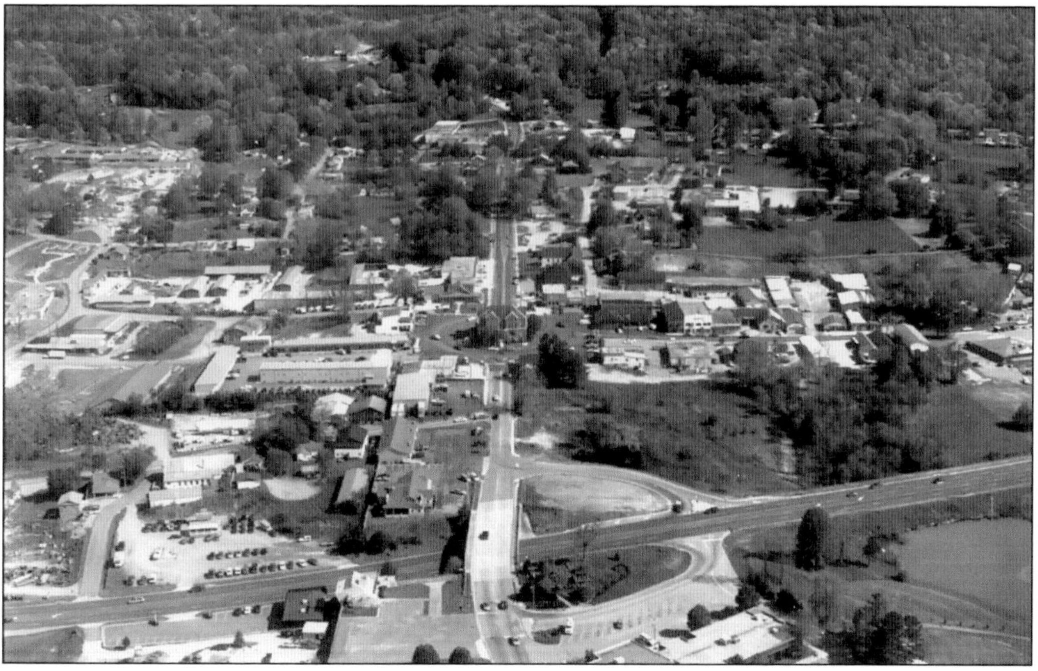

At the end of the 20th century, there were scores of entrepreneurs and small businesses and many who were self-employed. The work force exceeds 7,000 people, and unemployment is traditionally below the mountain region average and the state average. The photo shows the downtown business district of Blairsville during the 1980s. Even with the growth the county has seen, Union County has retained its unique small-town atmosphere. (Courtesy *North Georgia News*, photographed by Frank "Red" Carson.)

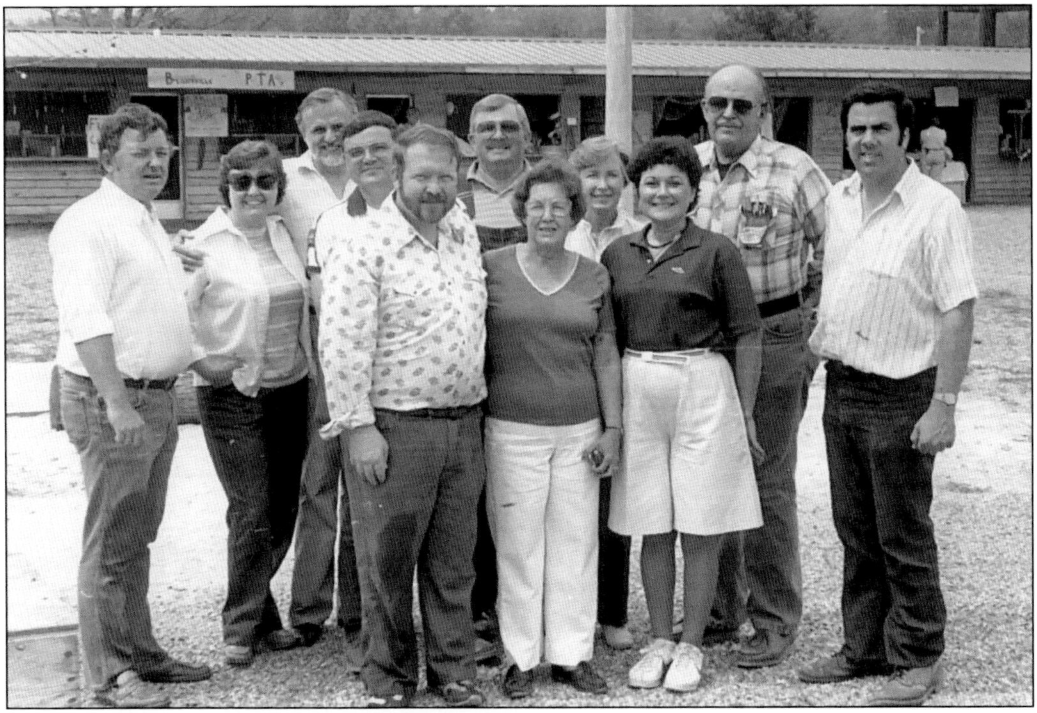

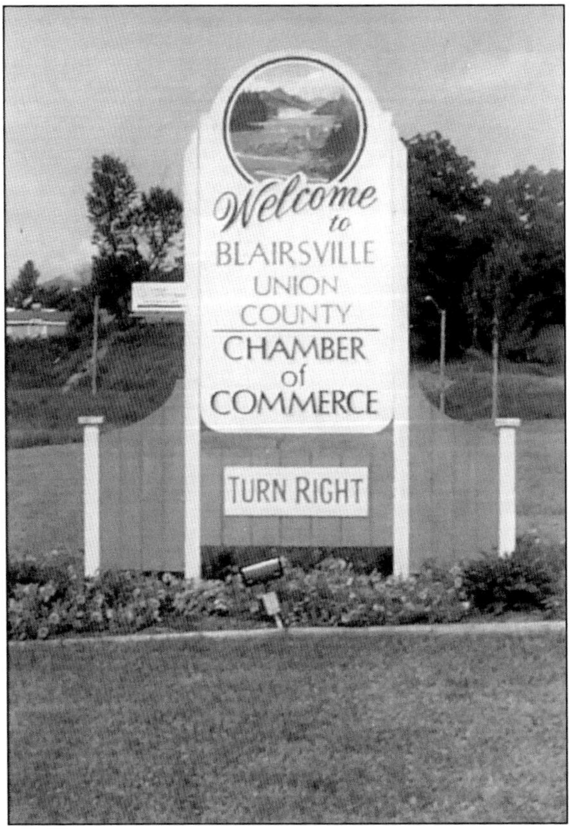

The Union County Chamber of Commerce has been in existence for over 50 years. In the early days, members met in a restaurant or business establishment until an office was provided in the old jail facility on Blue Ridge Street in the late 1980s. A Fourth of July extravaganza with fire-works and an annual Christmas parade were added to the community events through the efforts of its members. Donations and fund-raisers financed the chamber facility and tourist welcome station that exists today. Membership grew to more than 400 in the early 21st century. The group above at Fort Sorghum is, from left to right, (front row) Gene Sprayberry, president Faye Whitney, Louise Sprayberry, and Jim Arthur; (back row) Jacque Devereaux, unidentified, John Boemans, and unidentified. A beautiful sign in front of the Chamber of Commerce on Highway 515 welcomes visitors. (Photos courtesy Martyne Jokela.)

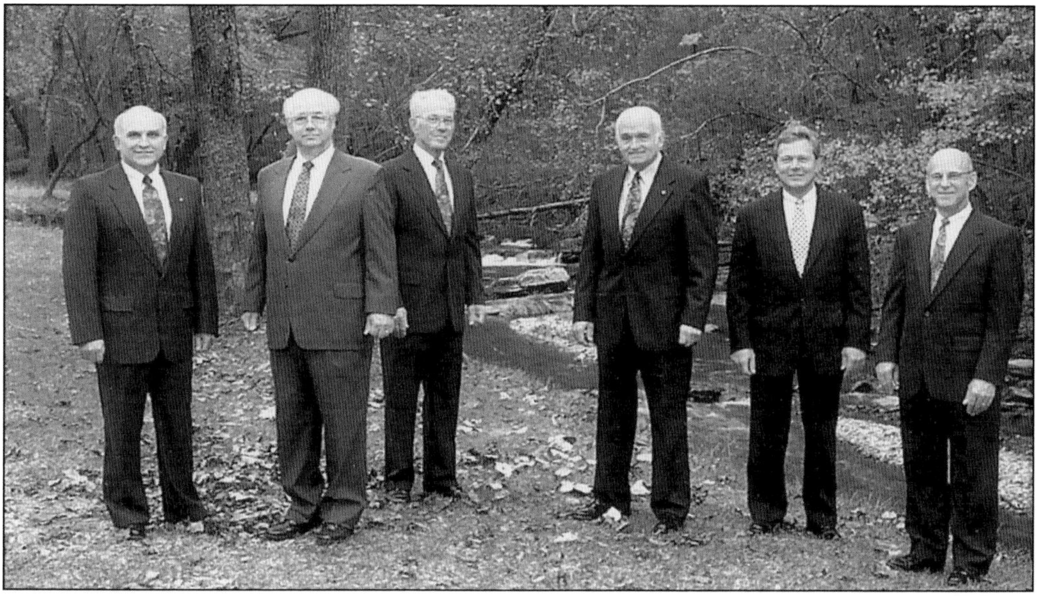

The positive impact United Community Bank, Union County (formerly Union County Bank) in Blairsville has had on the community cannot be measured. Established in 1950, the bank began to expand in 1990. The board of directors, above, in 1995 included vice chairman W.C. Nelson, Charles E. Hill, James A. Brackett Jr., chairman Robert L. Head Jr., president and C.E.O. Jimmy Tallent, and Billy M. Decker. United Community Bank offers the community dedication, growth, stability, expansion, and service, and it contributes to the development of the youth in the community. United Community Bank supplies financial support and its employees offer time, energy, and talent to schools, recreational programs, charity organizations, and other endeavors. The bank contributes human resources and leadership to the community. The Golden Club provides travel opportunities and entertainment to the elderly. The bank's services include the county's largest trust department and mortgage service. Throughout the years, United Community Bank has been the county's largest non-government employer. In 1995, United Community Bank saw its longest serving employee, Melva Lynn Drake, retire after 39 years of service.

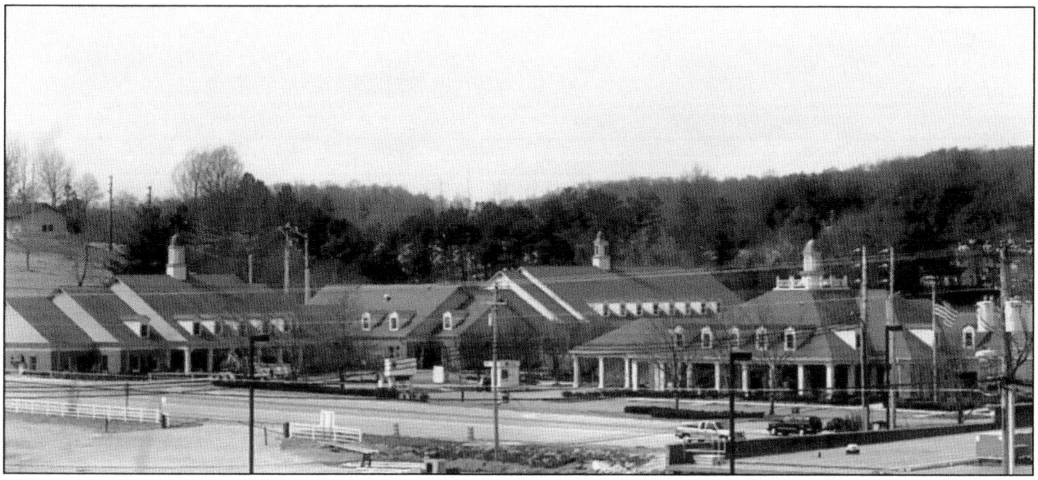

United Community Banks, Inc., is located in downtown Blairsville. (Photo by Norman Cooper.)

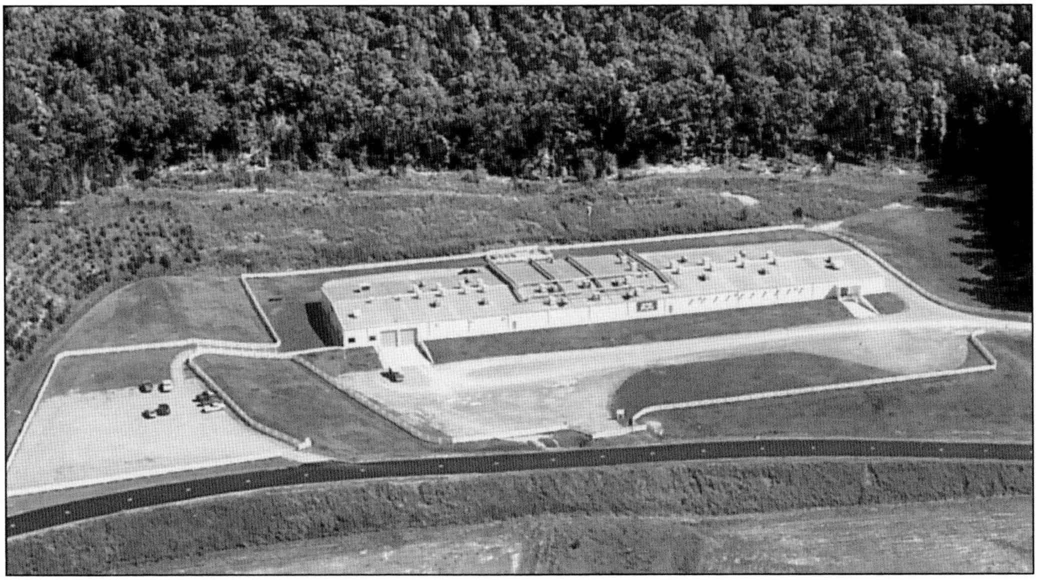

Arbor Acres, an international poultry company, established a Blairsville branch in 1957. The Blairsville farm started with six poultry houses, including a two-story poultry house and a six-incubator hatchery, seen below. It soon owned or leased 100 breeder houses in Union County and a neighboring county, seen above. Facilities housed 650,000 broiler grandparent chickens. A second hatchery facility in the Robert Jones Industrial Park became the largest production facility in entire system. Its two large hatcheries produce 18.5 million breeder chicks annually and employ 213 men and women in the Blairsville area. On a global scale, Arbor Acres stock comprise the parents for nearly one-third of the world's broiler meat supply, producing chickens in 28 countries and distributing to more than 70 nations on five continents. With a change to Aviagen Industries, the farm closed in 2003. The facilities at the hatchery in Robert Jones Industrial Park were still functioning in the early 2000s. (Courtesy Martyne Jokela.)

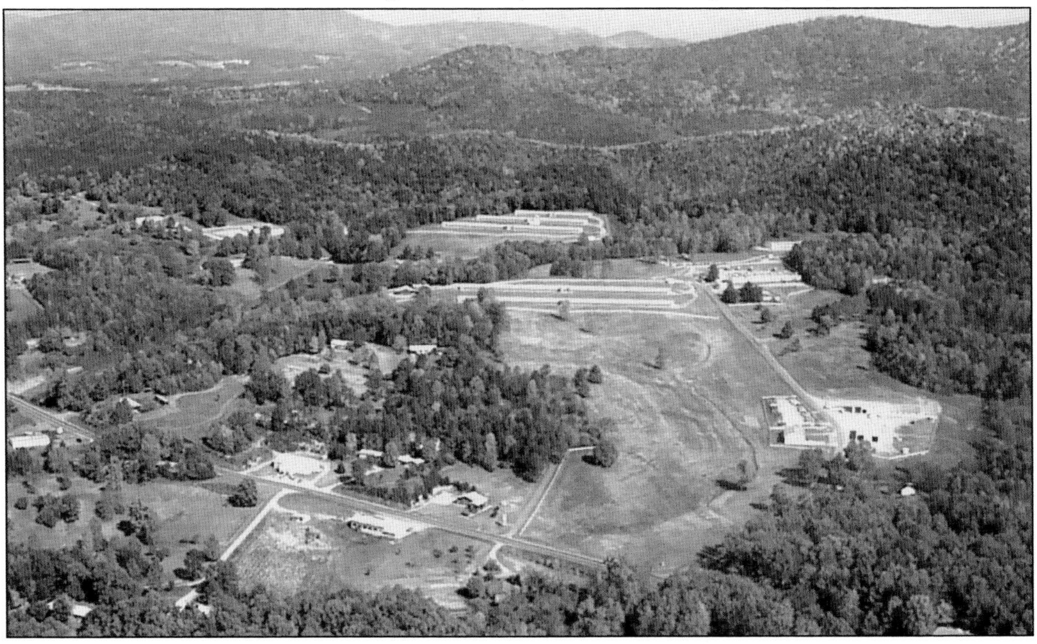

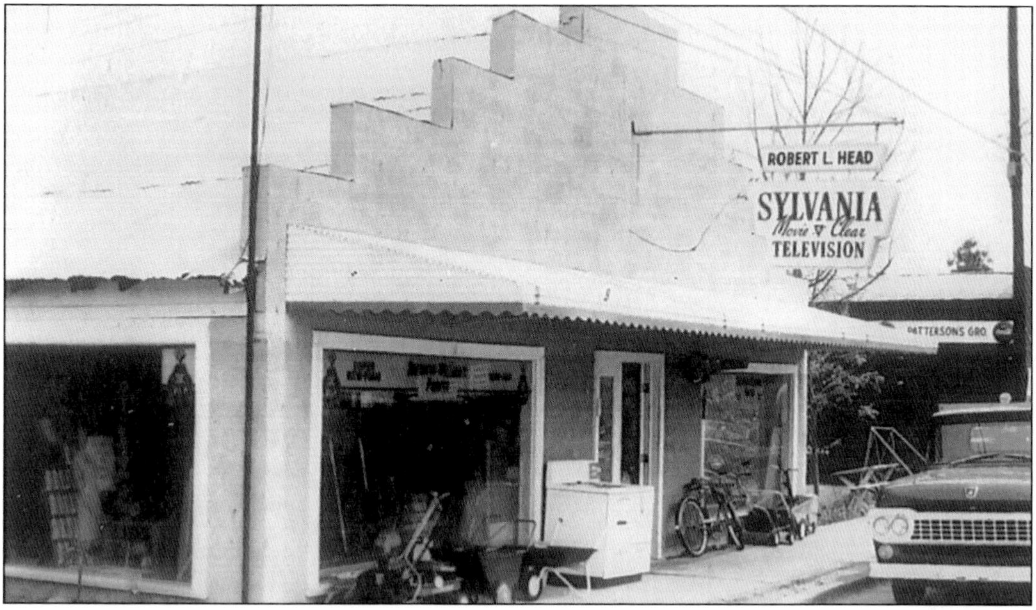

Robert L. Head Lumber Company began in 1949. Bob Head owned the company from 1963 to 1986. Head-Westgate began residential and commercial construction in 1976. Construction projects include the First United Methodist Church of Blairsville, the Union County Jail, United Community Bank, numerous buildings on the campus of Young Harris College, and the Media Center at Woody Gap School. Restoration projects include Woody Gap School's historic rock building and numerous projects for Young Harris College.

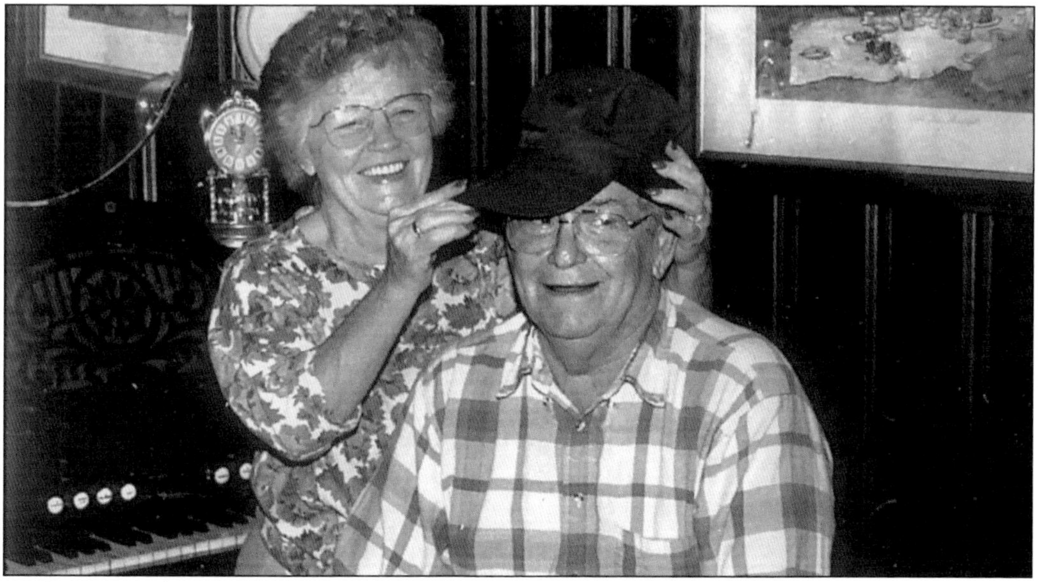

Tucker's Family Restaurant is remembered for exceptionally good food and the nostalgia-decorated dining facility. Numerous organizations used the restaurant for special occasions throughout the year, especially when it was decorated for Christmas. The train tracks above head level carried the engine, boxcars, and caboose with authentic train sounds to the delight of diners. The Tuckers are remembered for their cherished dessert, a chocolate-peanut butter pie. (Photo by Norman Cooper.)

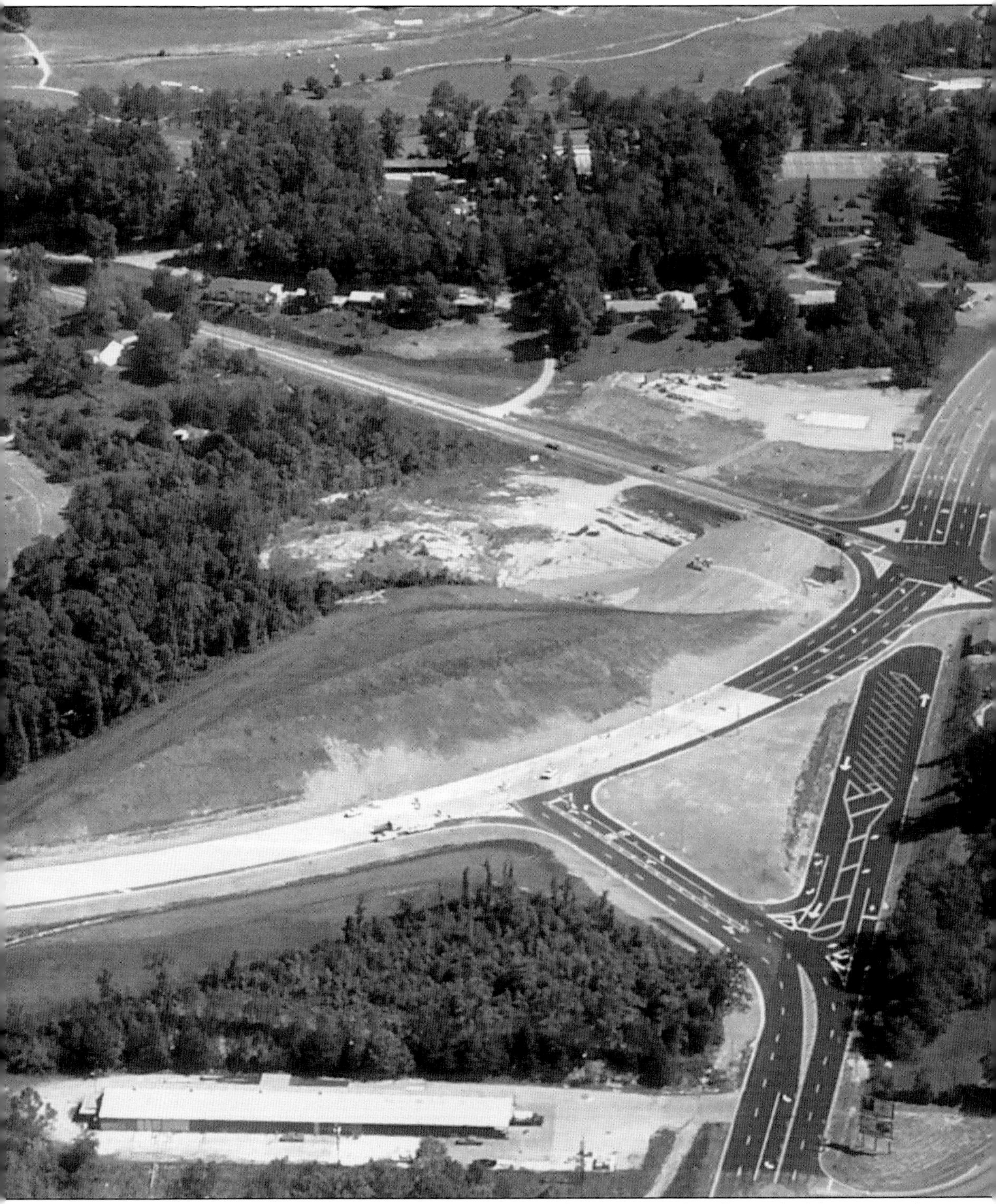

The economic landscape changed dramatically with the opening of Highway 515, known as the Zell Miller Parkway. The impact of the divided four-lane from Union County to the interstate highways was similar to replacing the horse and buggy with a car. With the four-lane came more

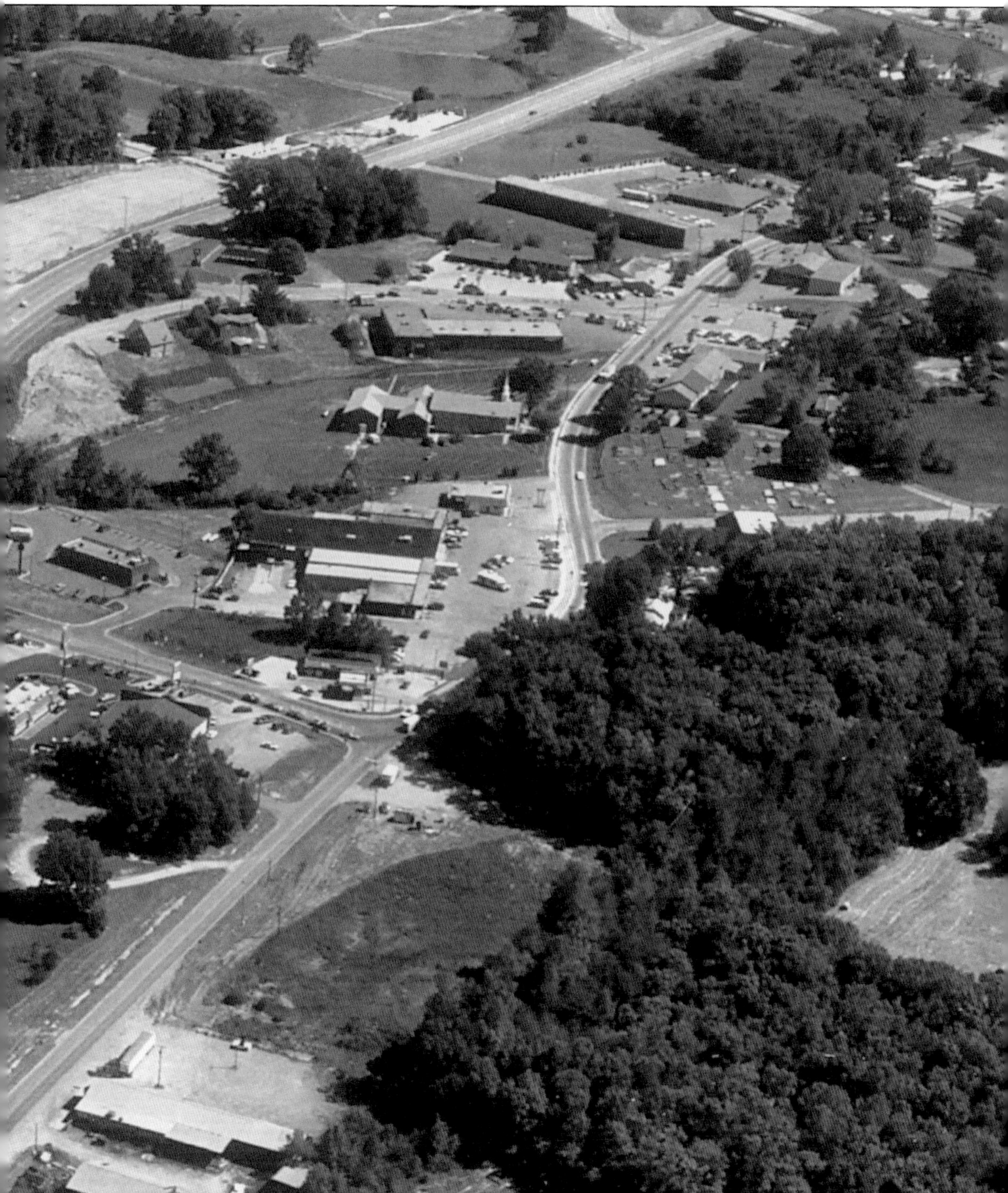

tourists and more people moving to the mountain community. As more people moved in, more businesses opened up. (Courtesy *North Georgia News*, photographed by Frank "Red" Carson.)

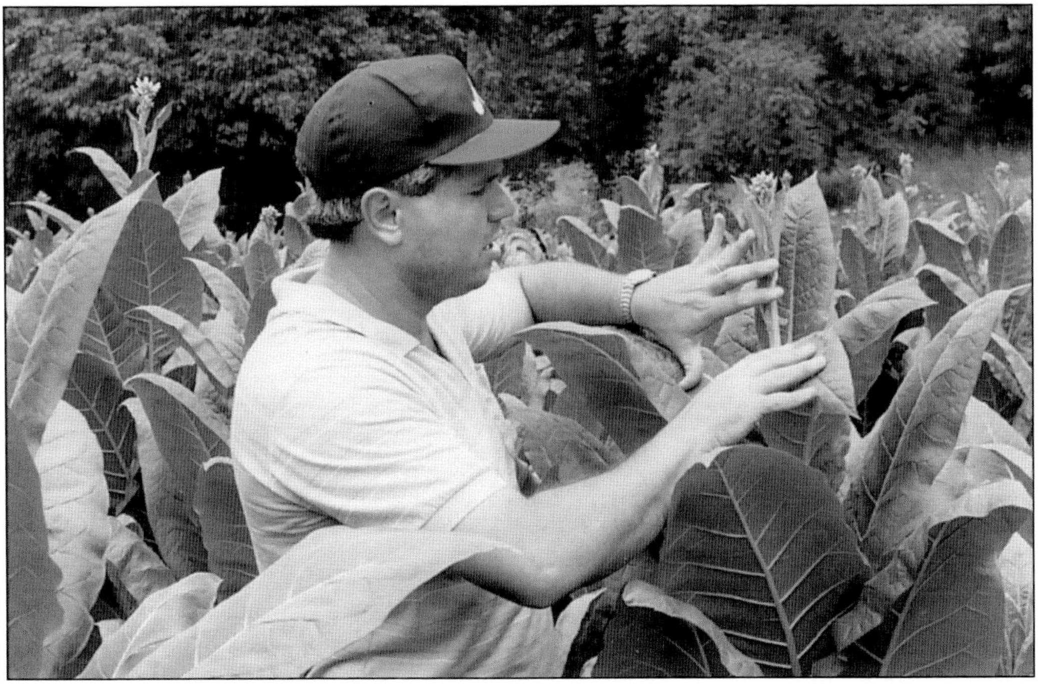

A resurgence of burley tobacco in the 1990s led to research work on area farms. County extension agent Mickey Cummings is scouting for tobacco budworms in a tobacco field in Union County.

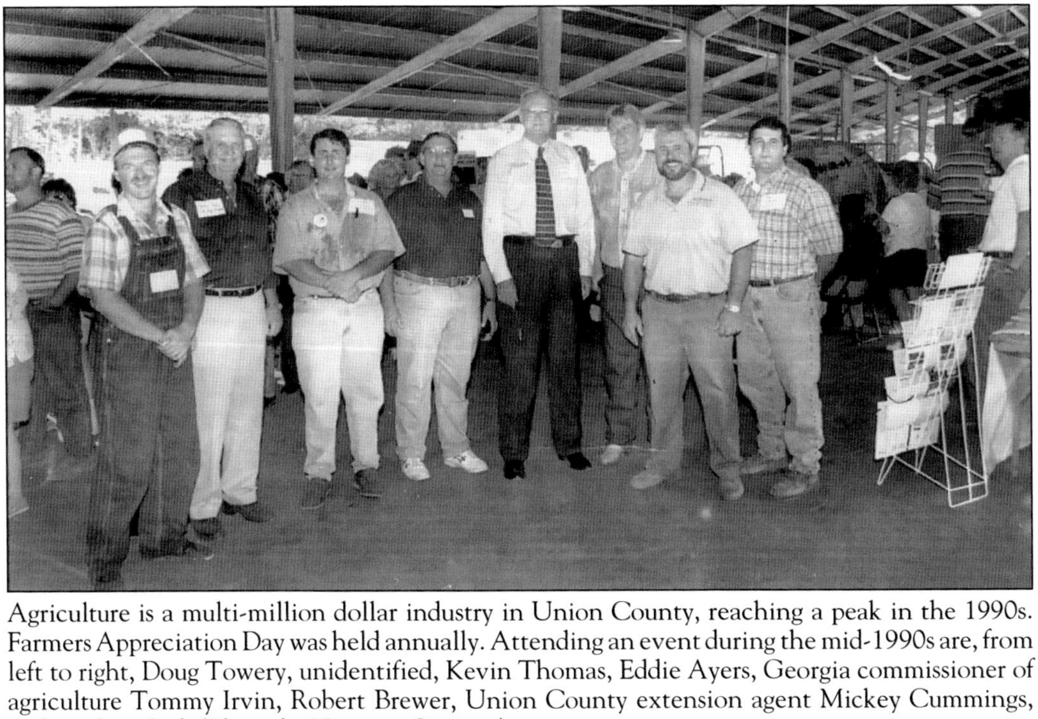

Agriculture is a multi-million dollar industry in Union County, reaching a peak in the 1990s. Farmers Appreciation Day was held annually. Attending an event during the mid-1990s are, from left to right, Doug Towery, unidentified, Kevin Thomas, Eddie Ayers, Georgia commissioner of agriculture Tommy Irvin, Robert Brewer, Union County extension agent Mickey Cummings, and unidentified. (Photo by Norman Cooper.)

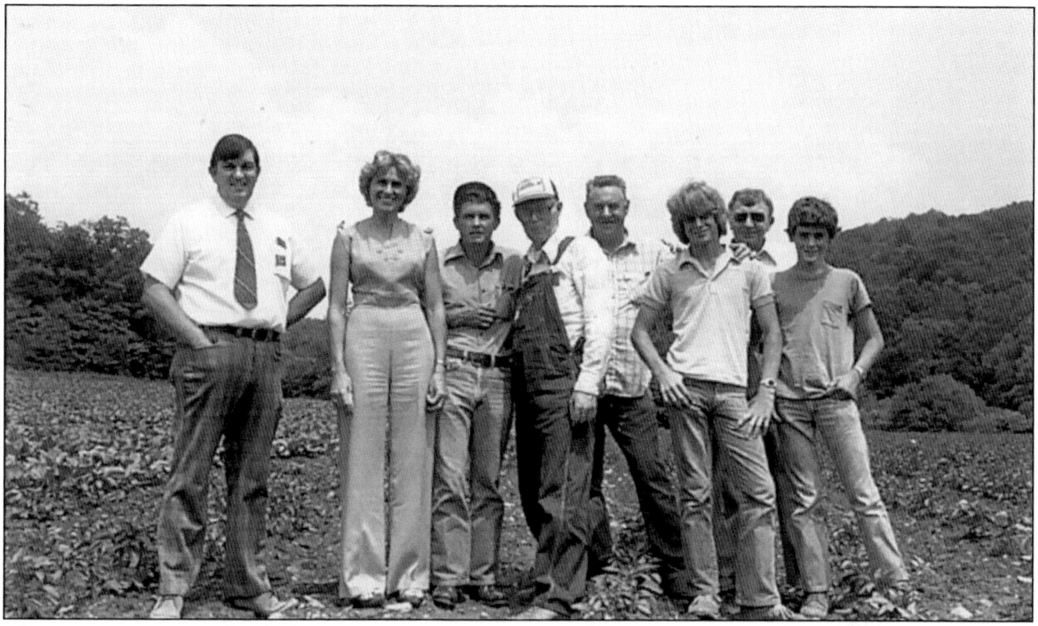

This group received funds from the Tennessee Valley Authority to do research on an individual farm during the 1970s, when this photo was taken. Pictured from left to right are Neal Moon, Pat Parker, Franklin Hunter, and five unidentified people.

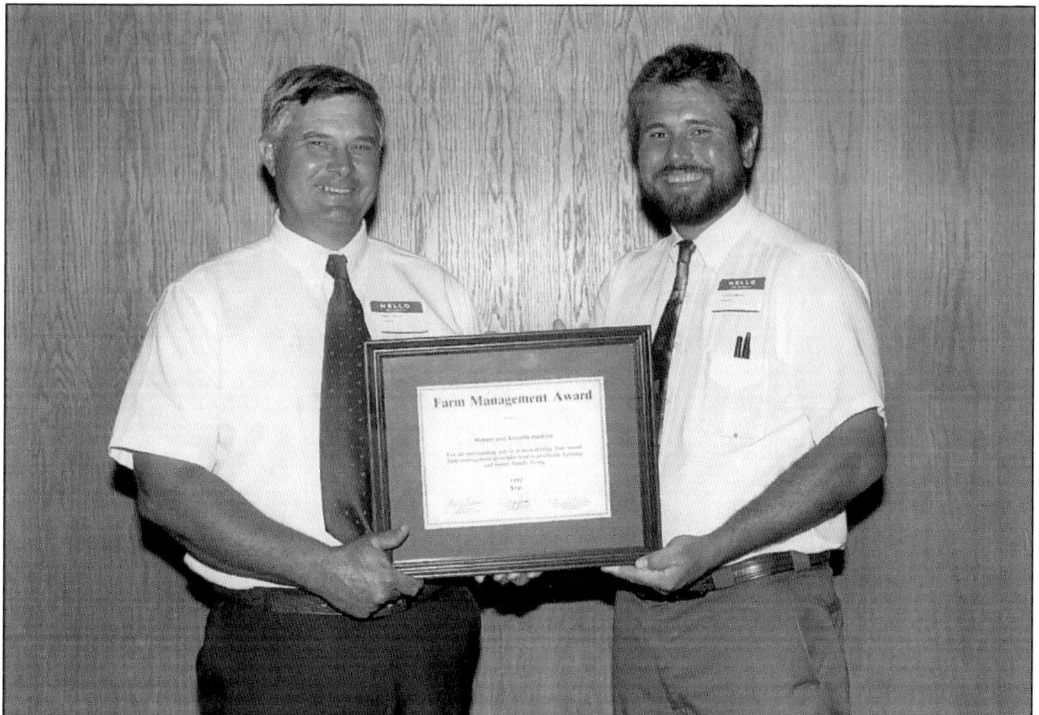

Robert Harkins is presented a Farmer of the Year Award by Union County extension agent Mickey Cummings on behalf of the Tennessee Valley Authority in the early 1990s. The award recognized the Suches resident for conservation efforts on his farm.

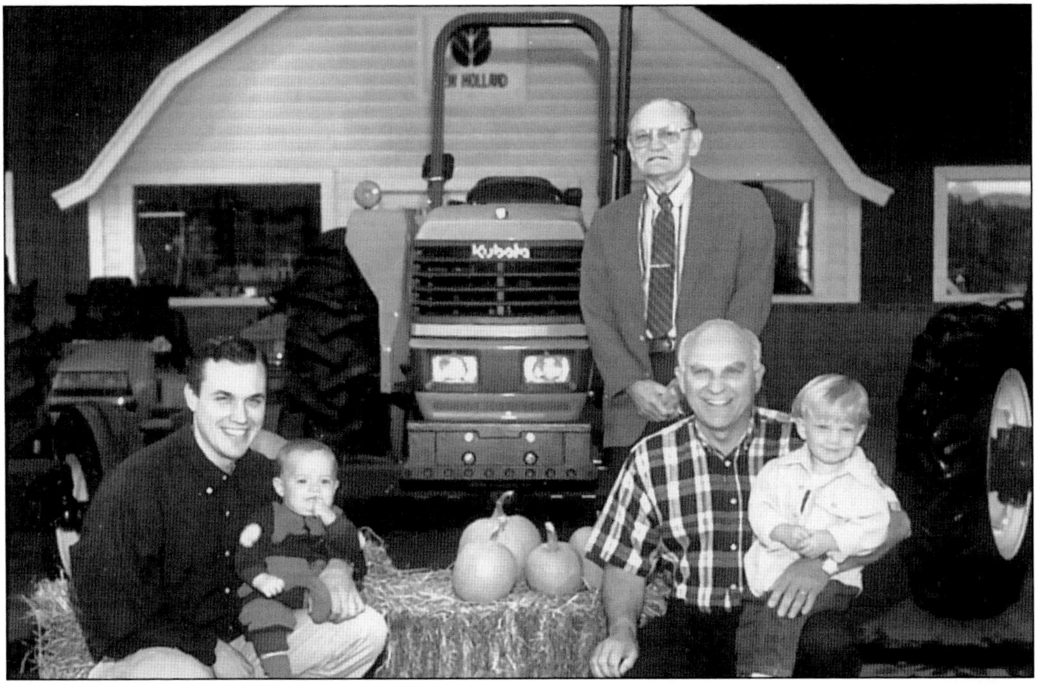

Nelson Tractor Company dominated the landscape in downtown Blairsville for more than half a century, the business being run by the same family through three generations: Cecil Nelson, standing; W.C. Nelson Jr., kneeling on right; and Will Nelson, kneeling on left. Established in 1949, the company moved to Highway 515 in 1982. The company had a huge jump in volume in the early 1990s. During 2003, Will Nelson, grandson of the founder, announced plans to relocate the company outside of the downtown district.

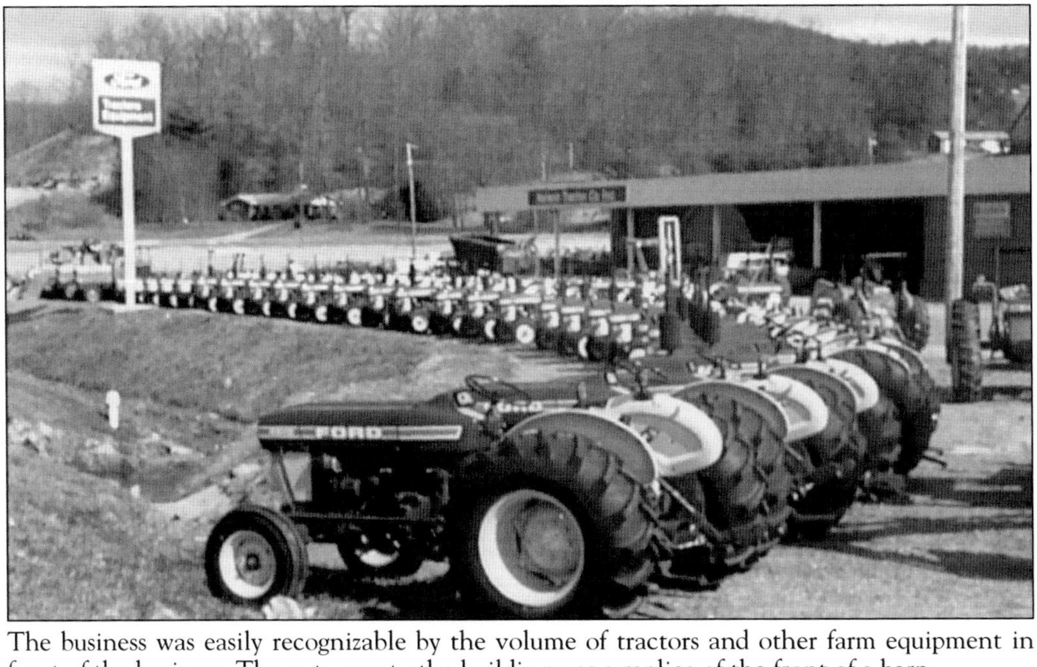

The business was easily recognizable by the volume of tractors and other farm equipment in front of the business. The entrance to the building was a replica of the front of a barn.

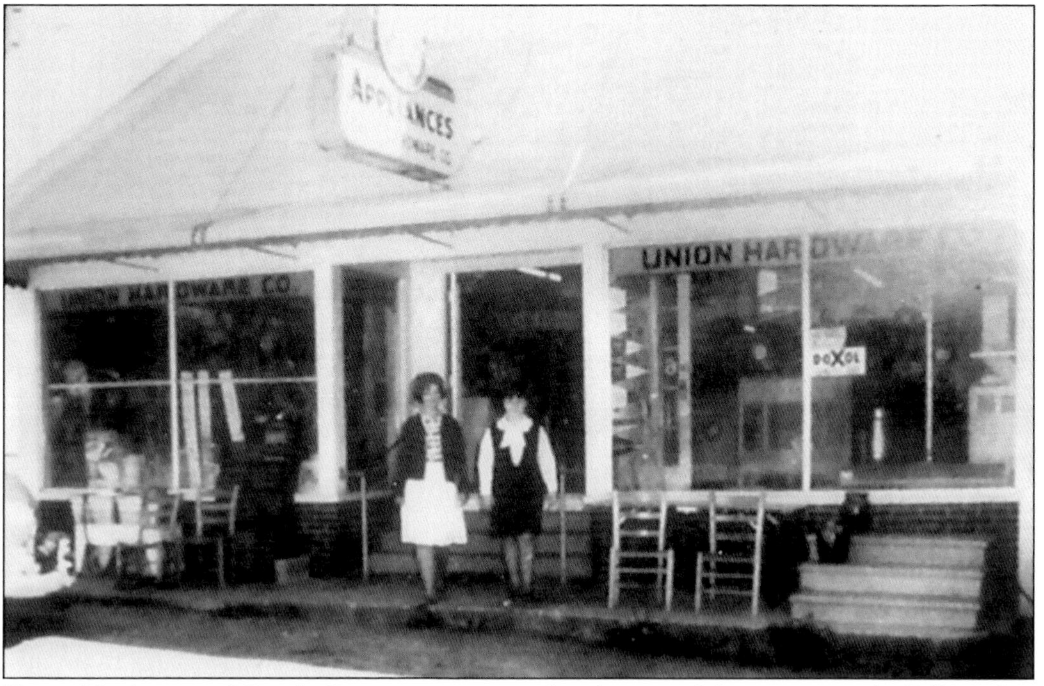

Union Hardware and Supply Company was owned and operated for many years by Bill Meeks.

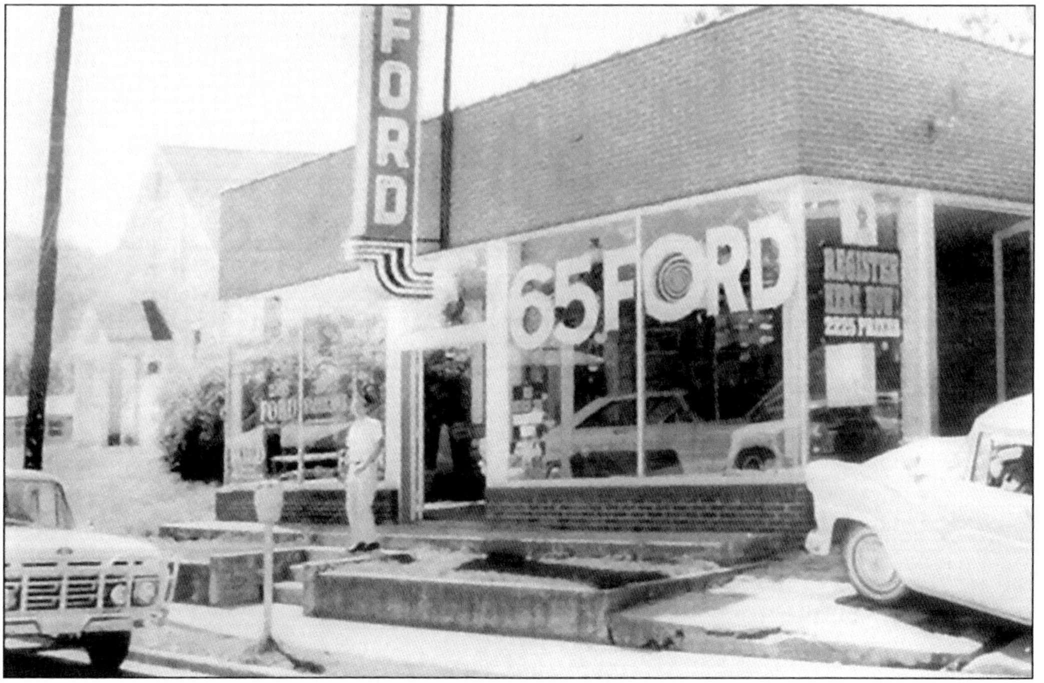

Blairsville Ford Company was located on Cleveland Street just south of the square in Blairsville in the 1970s.

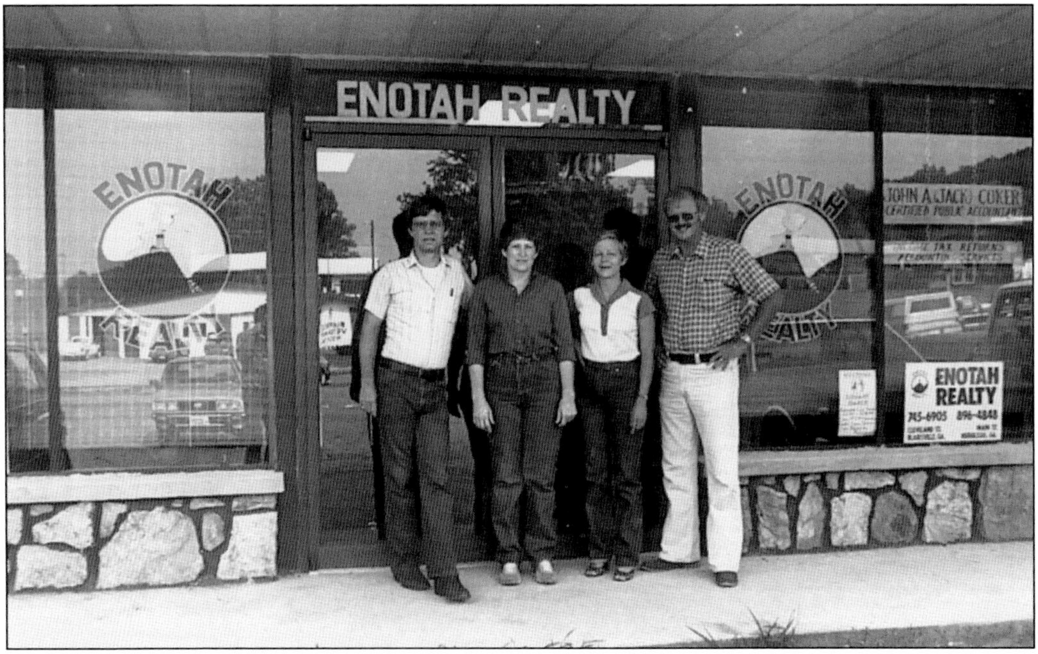

Real estate companies in the 1980s opened as independent agencies. As market conditions changed, many joined national networks. Among the earliest real estate companies in the county were Enotah Realty, Union Realty, Blairsville Realty, Griffin Realty, Jenkins Realty Group, and Howard O. Thomas Realty Company. Seen above are Cecil Teboe, Ann Barnes, Cindy Sparks, and Jim McAfee at the Enotah Realty office.

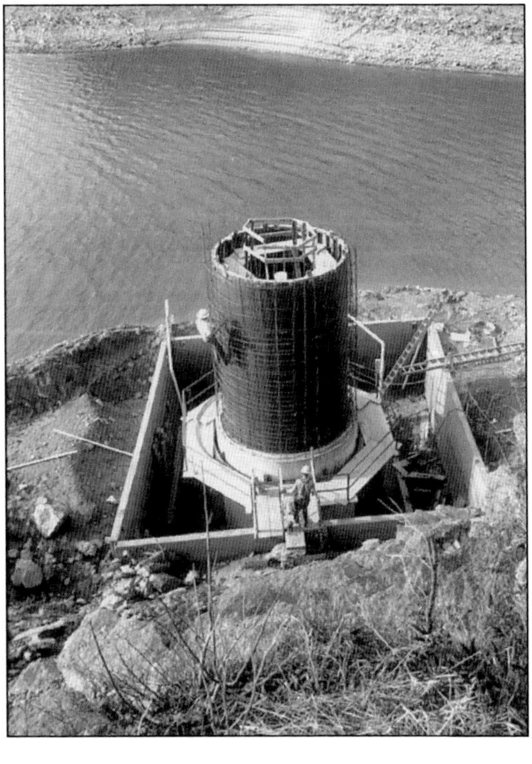

At the end of the 20th century, many homes and farms in Union County still used wells, but three major water suppliers were established and expanding. Those suppliers included Notla Water Authority, Coosa Water Authority, and the City of Blairsville. Only the City of Blairsville offered sewer service as the 21st century began. Notla Water Authority dramatically increased its service capacity by drawing water from Lake Nottely. The equipment, seen here on the edge of the lake, pumps water to another location, where it is prepared for distribution through new water lines. (Photo by Norman Cooper.)

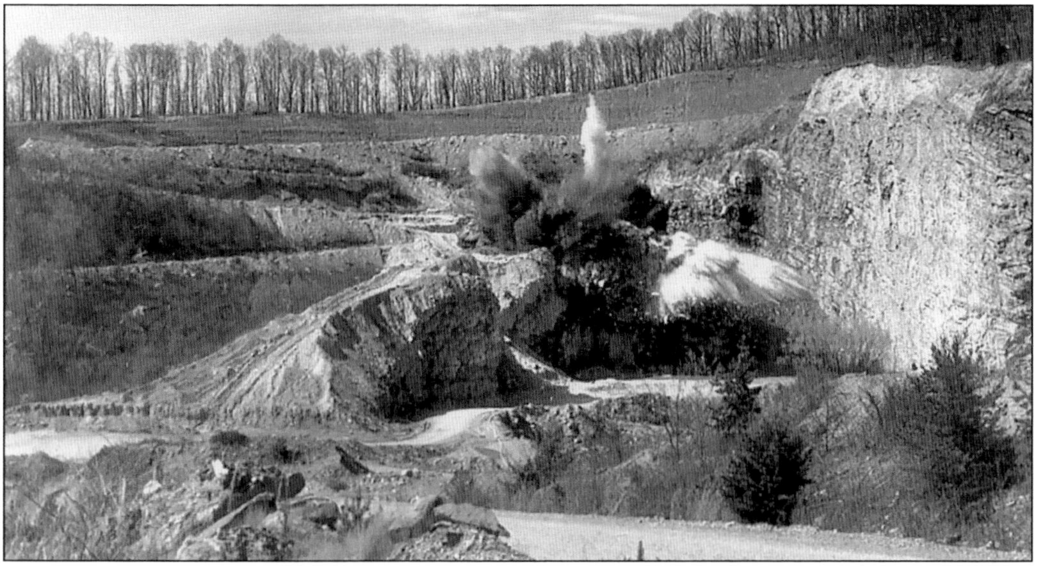

Colwell Construction traces its origins to the late 1960s when Carlton Colwell, Bob Colwell, and Pat Colwell Jr. opened the rock quarry. Since then, Colwell Construction has processed millions of tons of rock in Blairsville. The company cleared land, built fishponds, and constructed dams. The company began paving in the late 1980s. Colwell Construction has been a major employer in Union County for decades, providing jobs for hundreds. Carlton's children—Curtis, Steve, Doug, Tom, and Carla—have worked for the company. Colwell Construction has always been active in the community, generously donating needed resources to recreation, school, and charities. (Courtesy Carlton Colwell.)

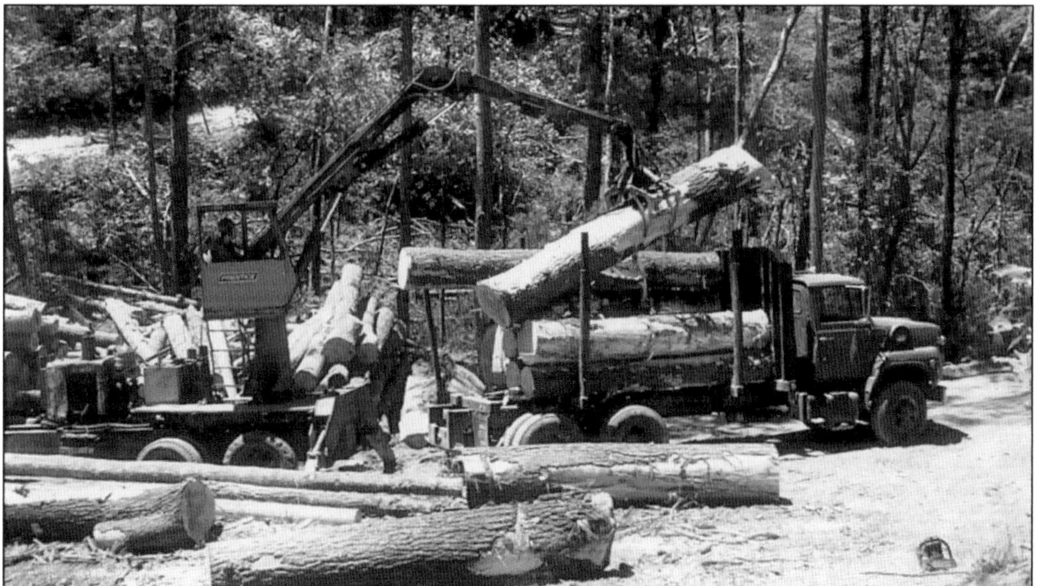

Logging provided economic opportunities for generations in Union County. Sean Dwyer started logging in 1984 and established Timberline Logging Company. Many trees are over 100–150 feet tall and have a circumference of 3–4 feet, requiring the fine art of felling trees within a predetermined space, causing minimal damage around the site.

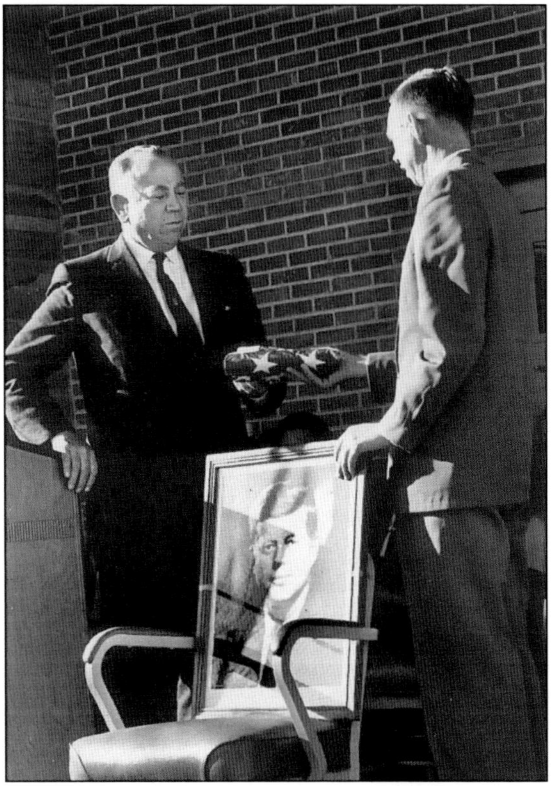

The U.S. Post Office has played a major role in economics. The volume of mail includes bills, payments, packages, and receiving supplies from points around the globe. In addition, the post office is an employer to local residents. The photo at right shows Charles Conley and Phil Landrum during the dedication of the old post office. (Courtesy Union County Historical Society.)

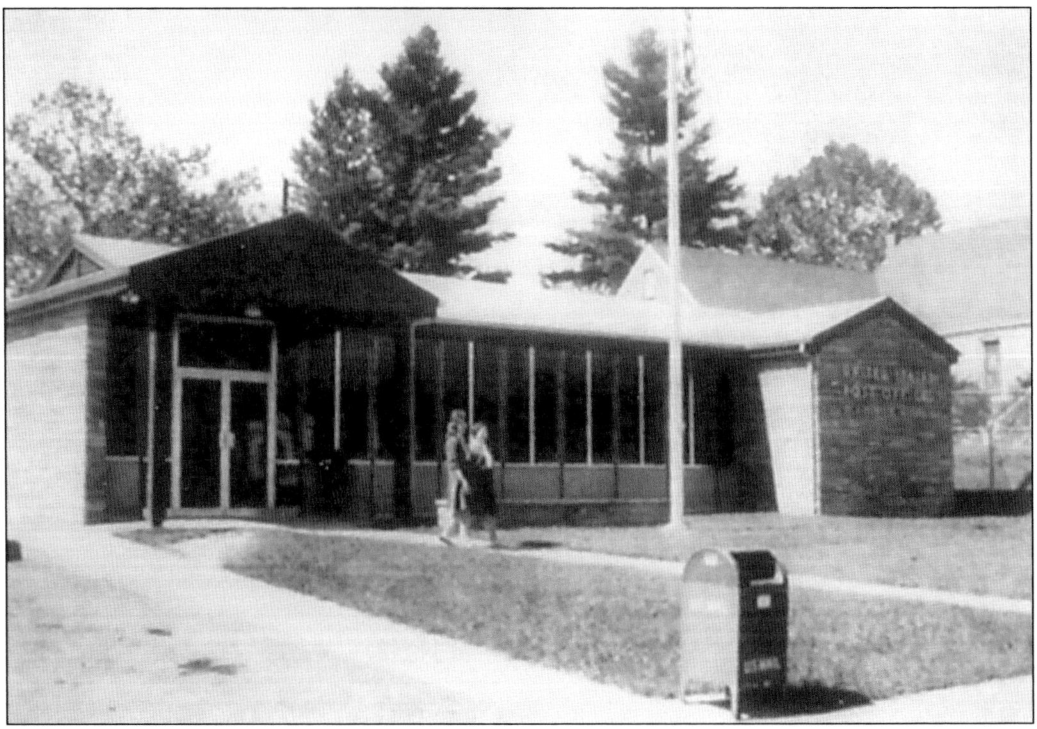

Pictured here is the Blairsville Post Office in 1970.

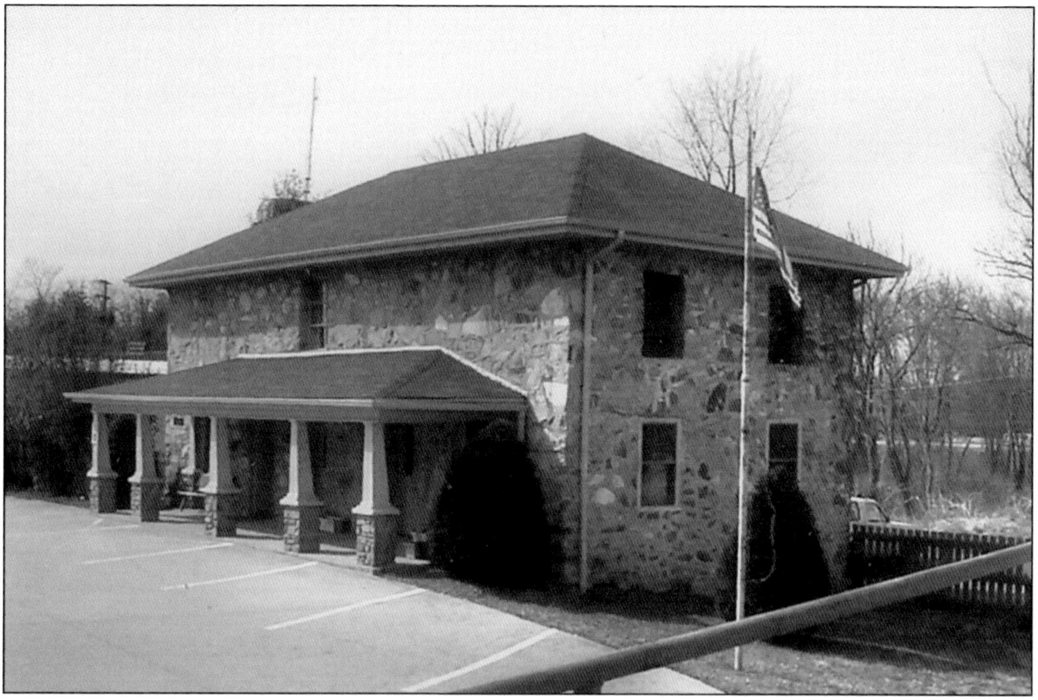

Blairsville's city hall is listed on the register of historic places. Sheriff Virge Kelley lived downstairs and the prisoners were kept in the jail upstairs. Virge's daughter Betty later became a Blairsville City Council member in the very room she slept in as a child. The building underwent renovation and today houses the mayor's office and city hall office. (Photo by Norman Cooper.)

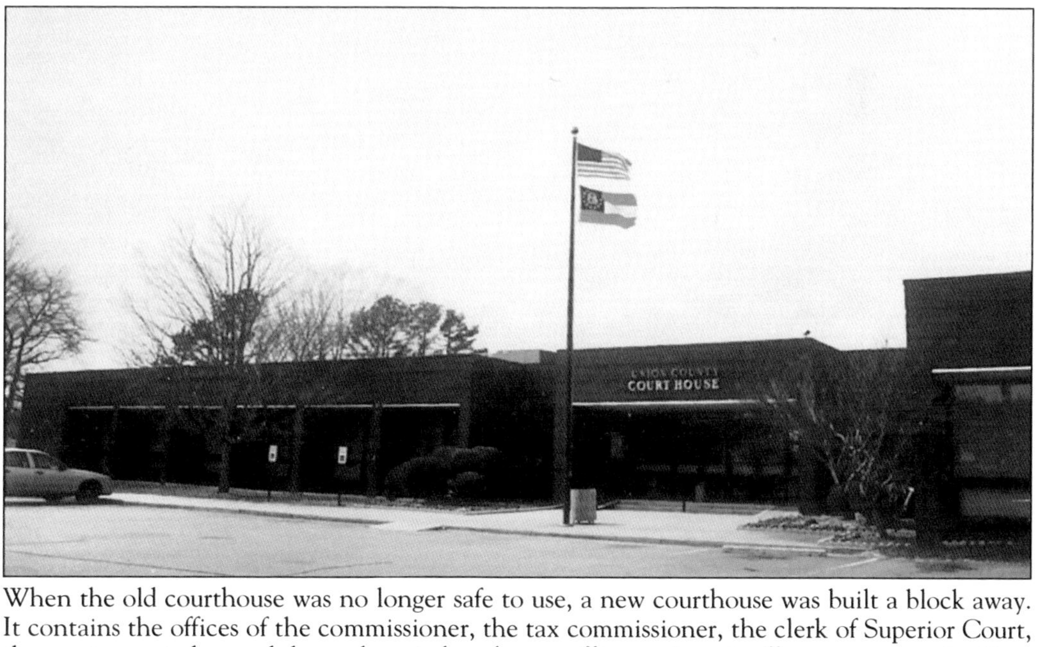

When the old courthouse was no longer safe to use, a new courthouse was built a block away. It contains the offices of the commissioner, the tax commissioner, the clerk of Superior Court, the magistrate judge, and the probate judge, the tag office, registrar's office, tax assessor's office, mapping office, and one courtroom. (Photo by Norman Cooper.)

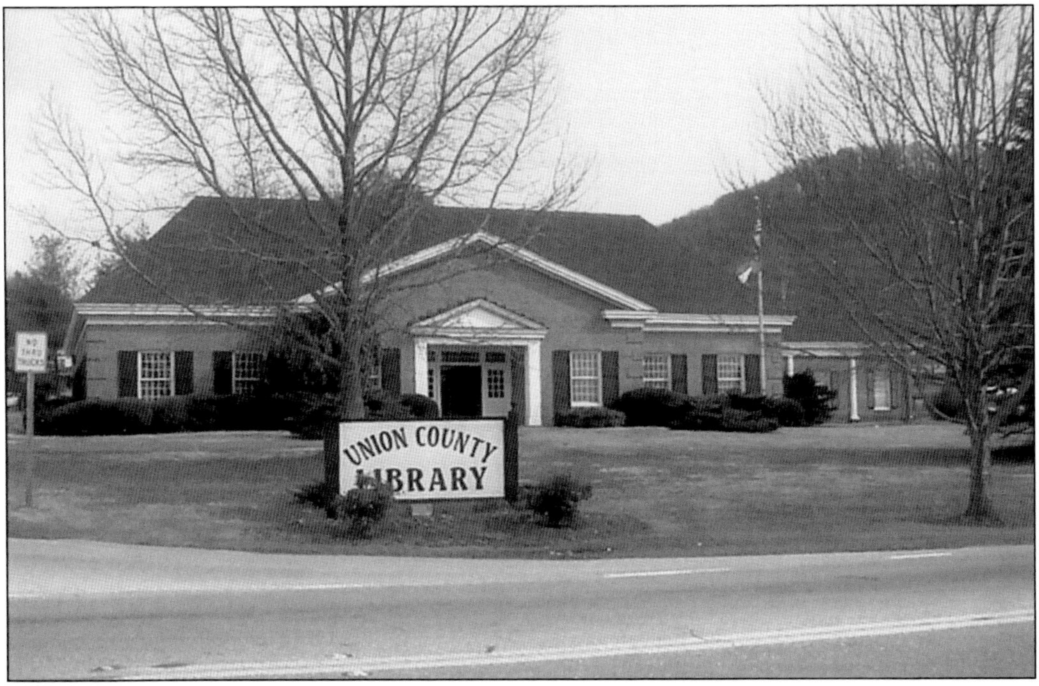

The Union County library has served the needs of the community for many years. Wilma Ash, the librarian who worked in the system for more than 40 years, has seen the use of the facility grow through the years. (Photo by Norman Cooper.)

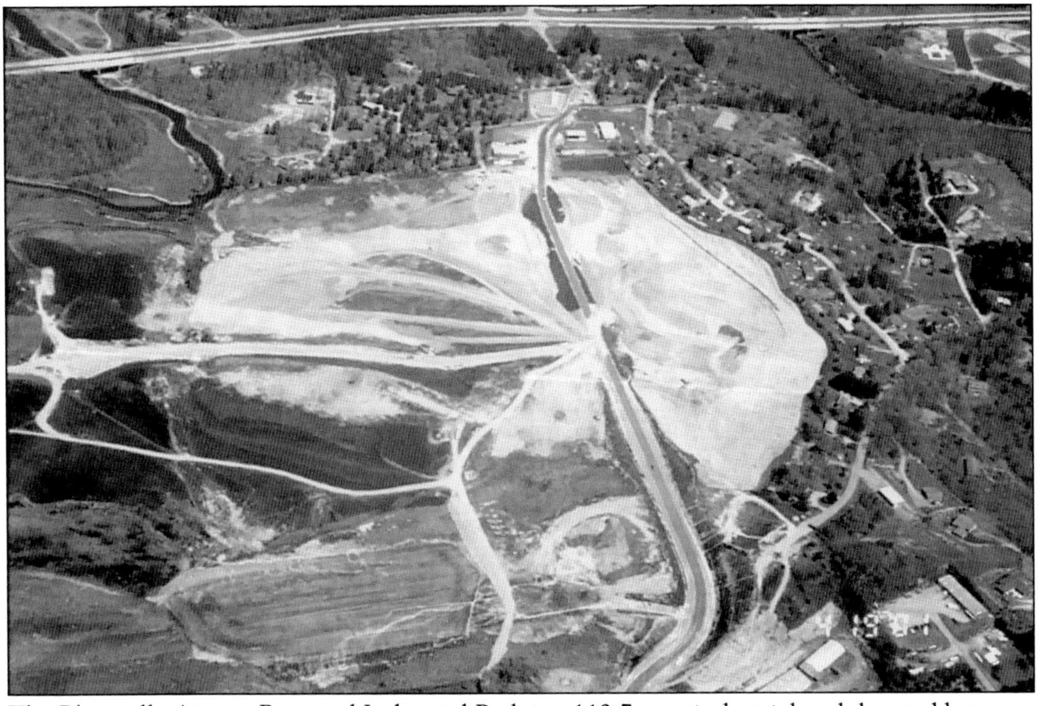

The Blairsville Airport Regional Industrial Park is a 112.7-acre industrial park located between the Blairsville Municipal Airport and the Zell Miller Parkway. (Courtesy Tom Murphy.)

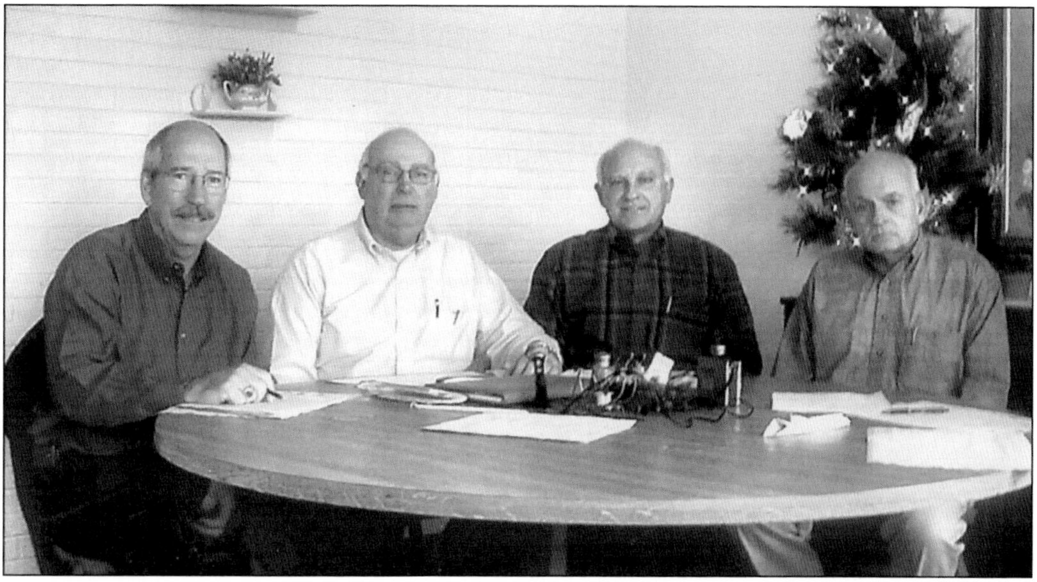

The charm of a small town grocery store still exists in Union County. The store was originally Bill Hunter Superette; Wayne Abercrombie and Tony Dyer bought the store in 1971, when it was known as A and D Supermarket. A year later the name was changed to Foodland. The vertical sign with the white squares and red letters at the edge of the parking lot still remained as the 2000s began. (Photo by Norman Cooper.)

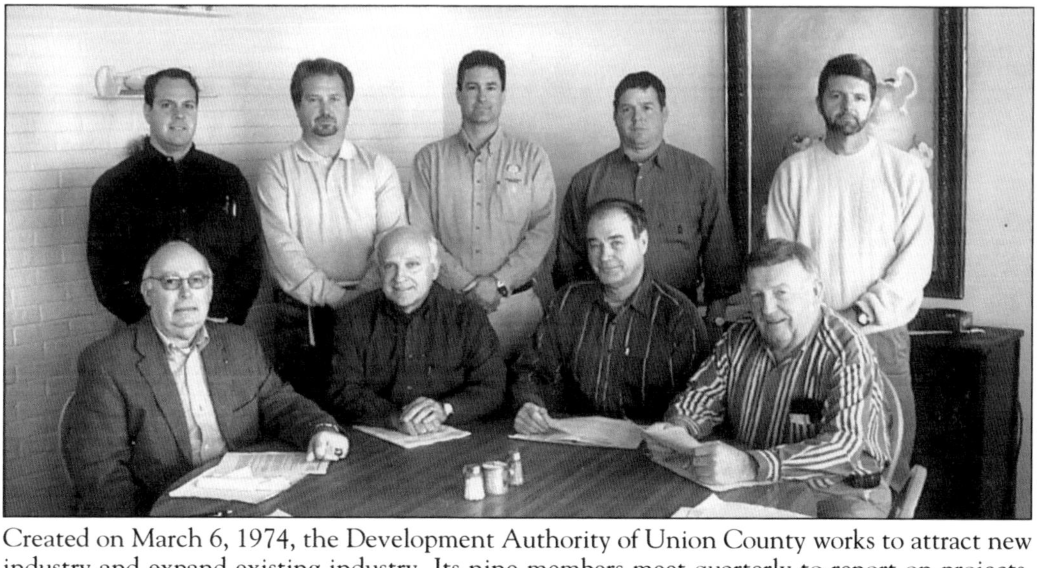

Created on March 6, 1974, the Development Authority of Union County works to attract new industry and expand existing industry. Its nine members meet quarterly to report on projects, plan strategy, consider inducement resolutions for new industries, and to acquire and develop industrial buildings, sites, and parks. Development Authority members in 2003 include, from left to right, (seated) Tom Murphy, executive director/secretary; chairman W.C. Nelson; treasurer Gene Windham; and vice chairman Eddie Graham; (standing) Mike Kiernan; Gary Davenport; Scott Carter; Jeff Kelley; and Earl Sullivan. Among those serving in previous years were Robert Head, Brenda Conley, Earl Odom, Mike Jones, R.B. Brown, Bill Parker, Bob Jones (chairman for several years), Mickey Cone, D.L. Martin, Jack Lance, Charles Hill, and Eldon Collins. (Photo by Norman Cooper.)

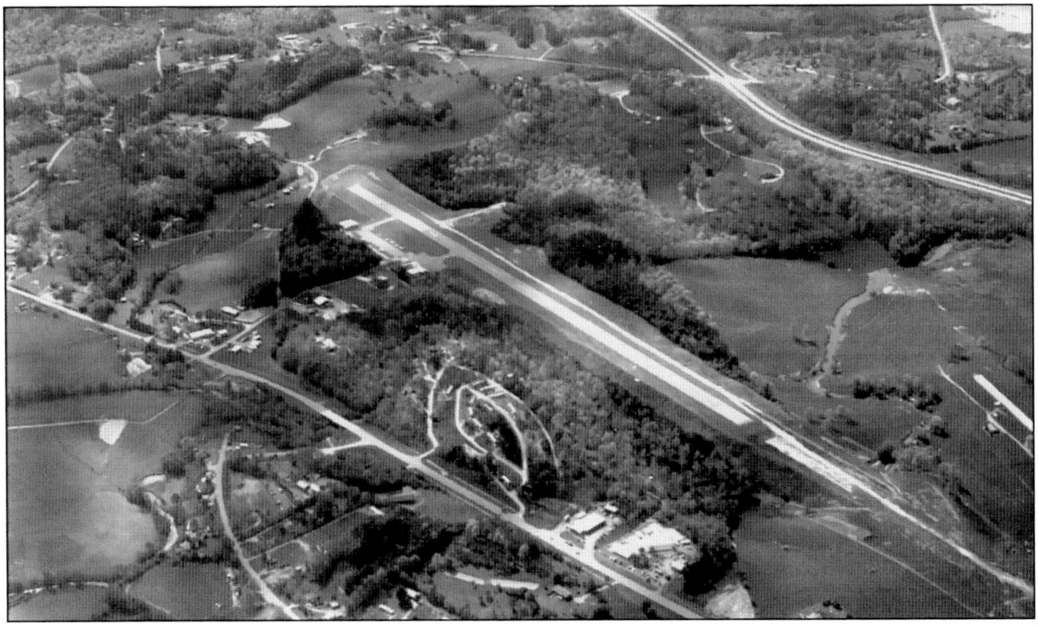

The Blairsville Airport opened with a 3,800 by 75-foot runway three miles southwest of Blairsville. Gov. Zell Miller provided $3 million for expansion to 5,500 feet in length and 100 feet in width. The Union County Development Authority developed the Blairsville Airport Regional Industrial Park (BARIP), a 112.7-acre industrial park located between the Blairsville Municipal Airport and Highway 515. Because of the mountainous terrain, no rail service is available to industries and industrial sites in Blairsville. The nearest rail is 32 miles west of Blairsville. (Courtesy of *North Georgia News*, photograph taken by Frank "Red" Carson.)

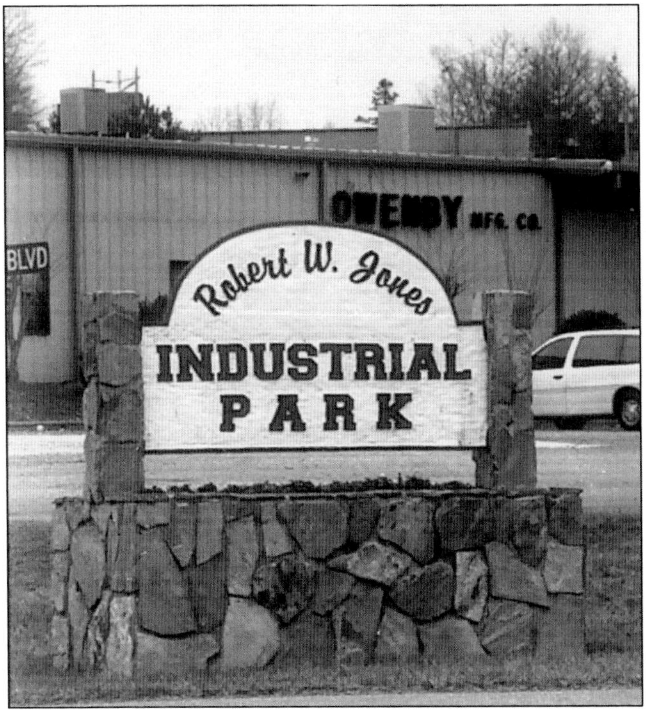

The Robert Jones Industrial Park is a 100-acre site near downtown Blairsville named in honor of the former chairman of the Development Authority of Union County. In the background is the Owenby Manufacturing Company, one of Union County's oldest businesses and a major employer in Union County. (Photo by Norman Cooper.)

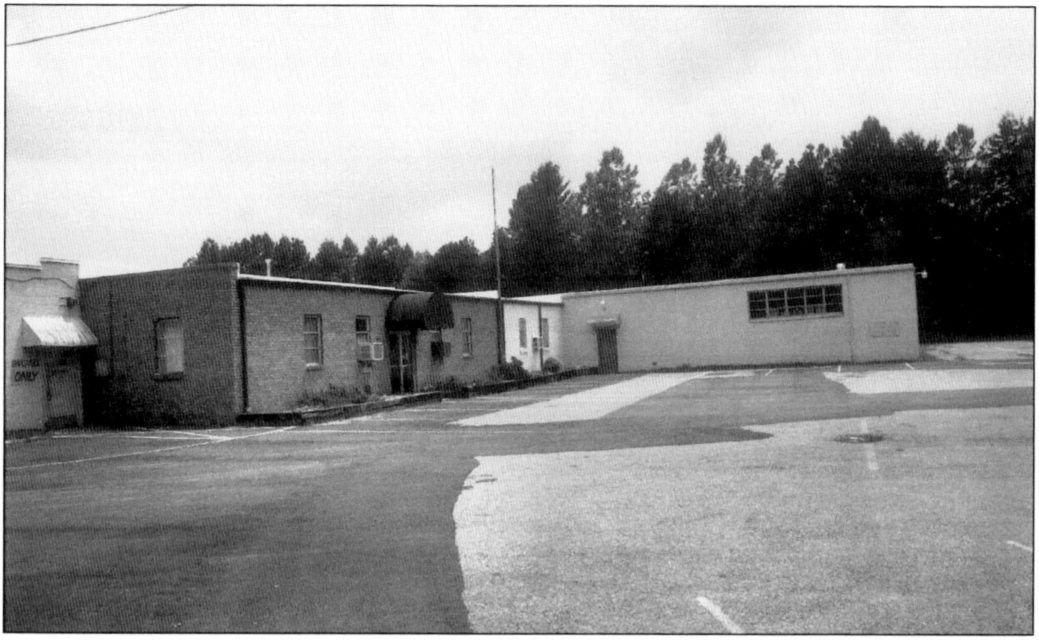

Georgia Boot has been a major employer in Union County for decades. During its peak, the company employed several hundred workers. It was not uncommon for three generations of people in one family to have jobs at Georgia Boot. The plant was eventually acquired by E.J. Footwear. Like many manufacturers in the United States in the 1990s, the North America Free Trade Agreement forced the shoe factory to close. (Photo by Norman Cooper.)

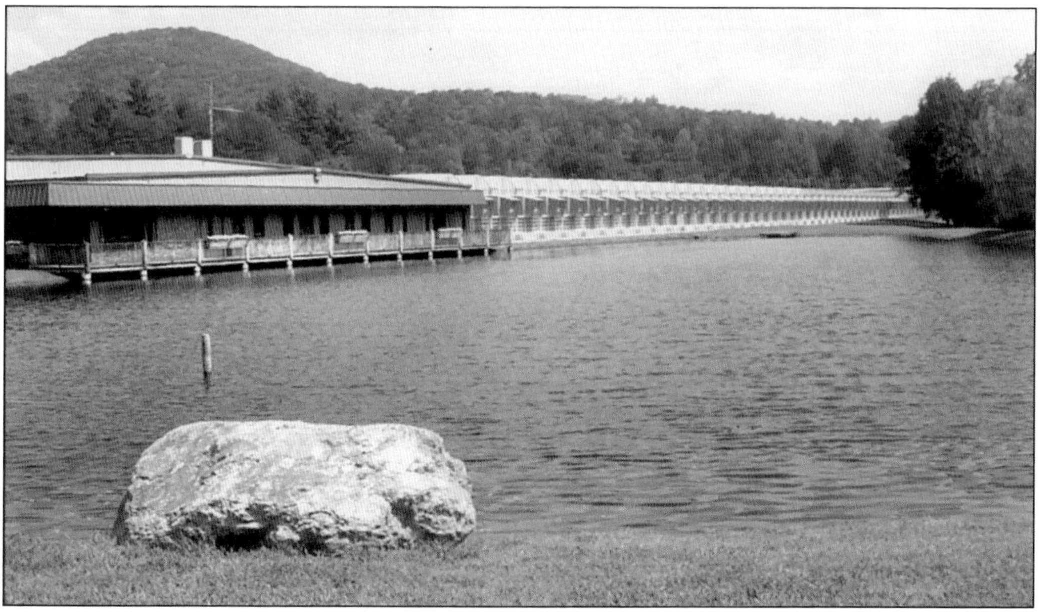

This facility, first known as Greiling Farms, was acquired by Speedling in the 1990s. The nursery provides exceptional quality ornamental plugs. Greenhouse capacity can accommodate 150,000 plug trays and approximately 50,000 hanging baskets grown under glass cover. Within the 720 by 430 foot growing area is a totally climate-controlled environment. (Photo by Norman Cooper.)

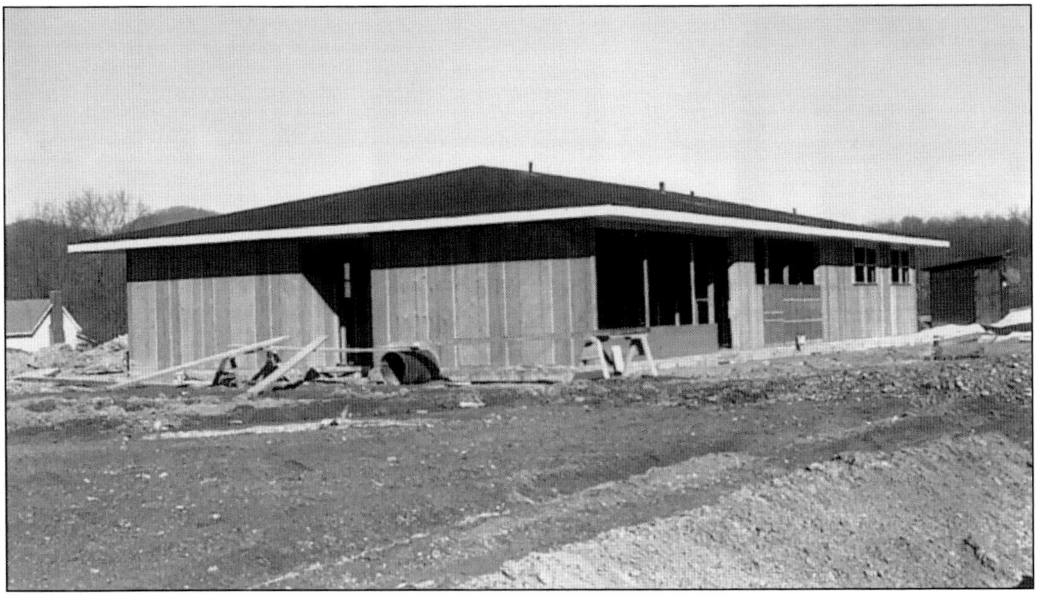

Blairsville's first clinic was made possible with a $20,000 bond referendum. The clinic opened January 1959 with a staff of Dr. George D. Gowder, Dr. Charles H. Little, and nurses Jane Mahaffey Truelove and Bessie Fields. In the fall of 1959, plans were drawn to change it to a 16-bed general hospital, including an emergency room, delivery suite, operating suite, and kitchen. By 1964 need for a larger facility called for a $48,000 referendum overwhelmingly voted in by the citizens. (Courtesy Union County Historical Society.)

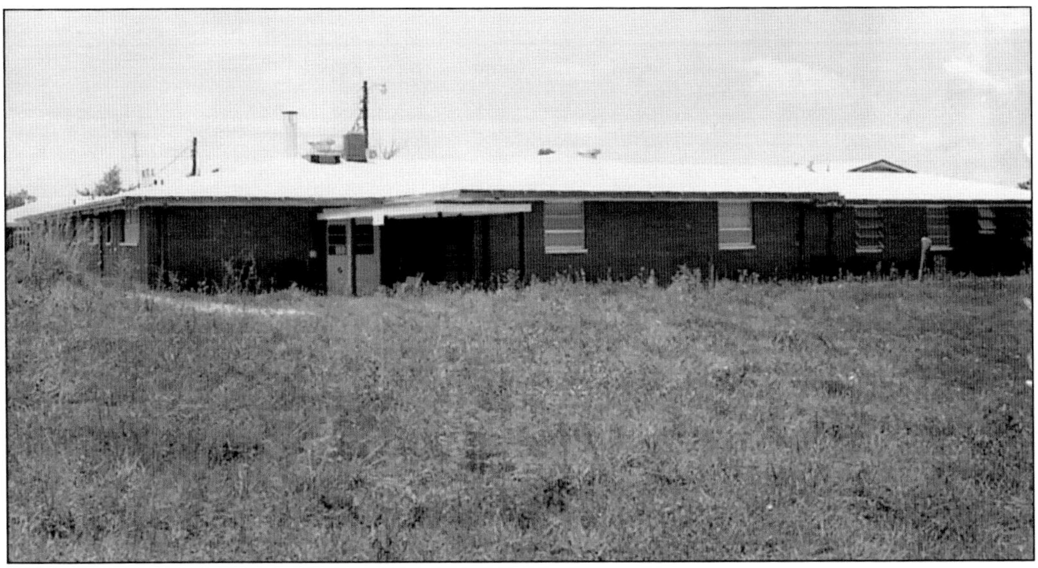

Completion of the new additions in 1968 made 33 beds available, along with other improvements. In 1979, after concerned efforts of Hospital Authority members Warren Souther, Tom Burnett, Edith Paris, Larry Daniels, Charles Hill, and administrator Leon Davenport, a loan was acquired to purchase a private hospital that closed in 1976. It was renamed the Union General Hospital. In 1980 the old hospital was converted to additional nursing home beds. The facility is now used as offices for diversified organizations. (Courtesy Henley Hamby Collection.)

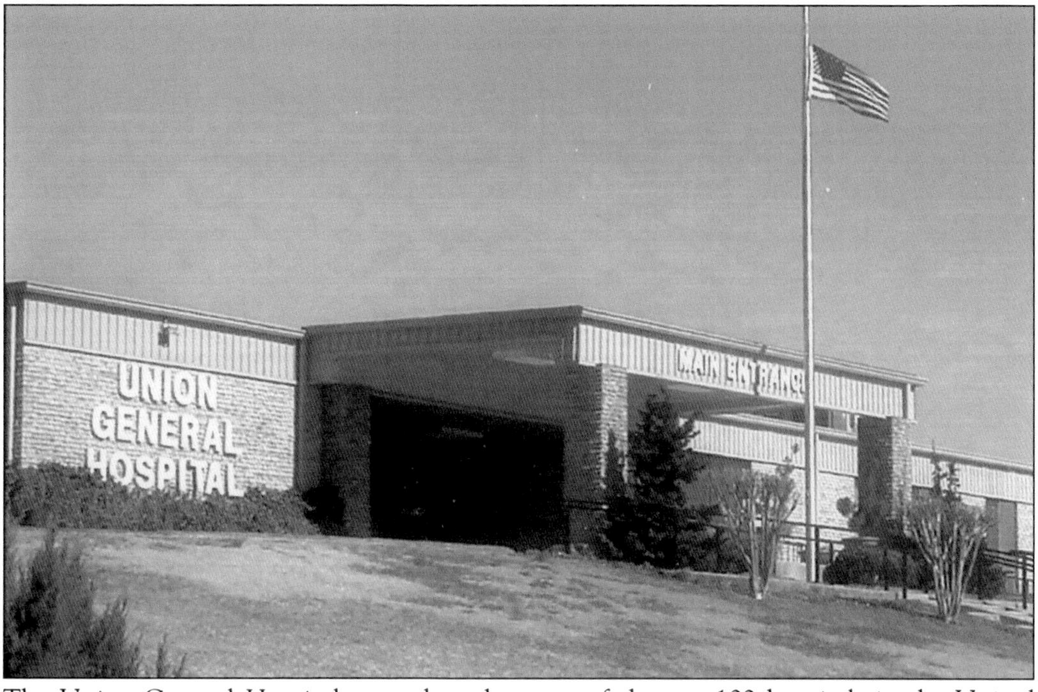

The Union General Hospital was selected as one of the top 100 hospitals in the United States in 1994. The study evaluated hospitals based on several characteristics. (Photo by Norman Cooper)

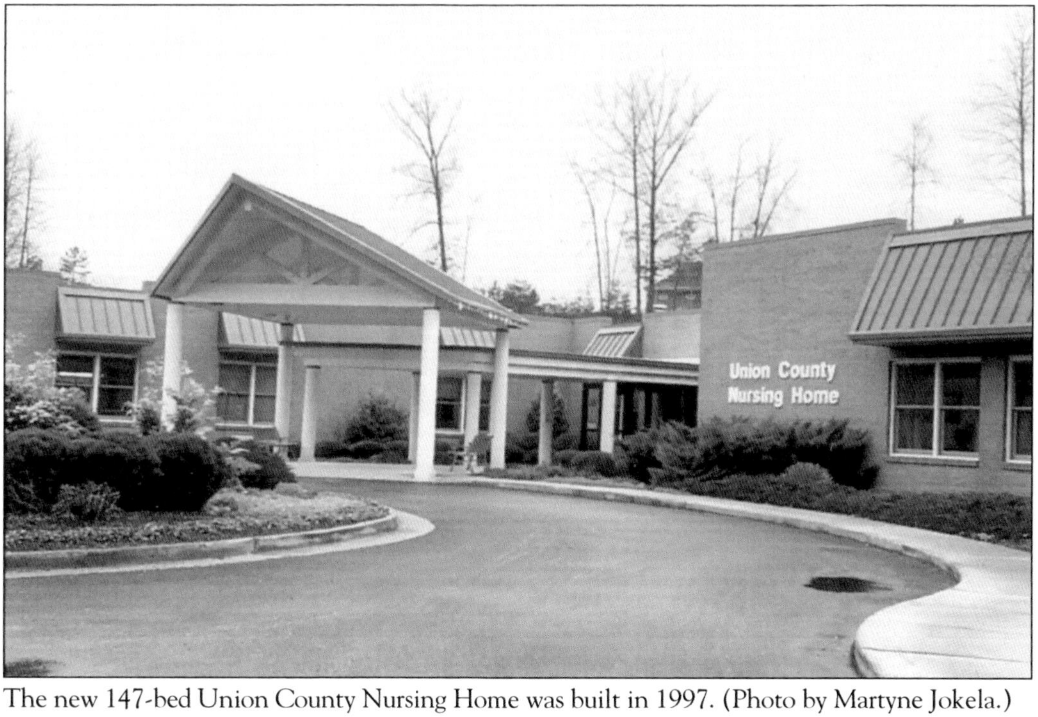

The new 147-bed Union County Nursing Home was built in 1997. (Photo by Martyne Jokela.)

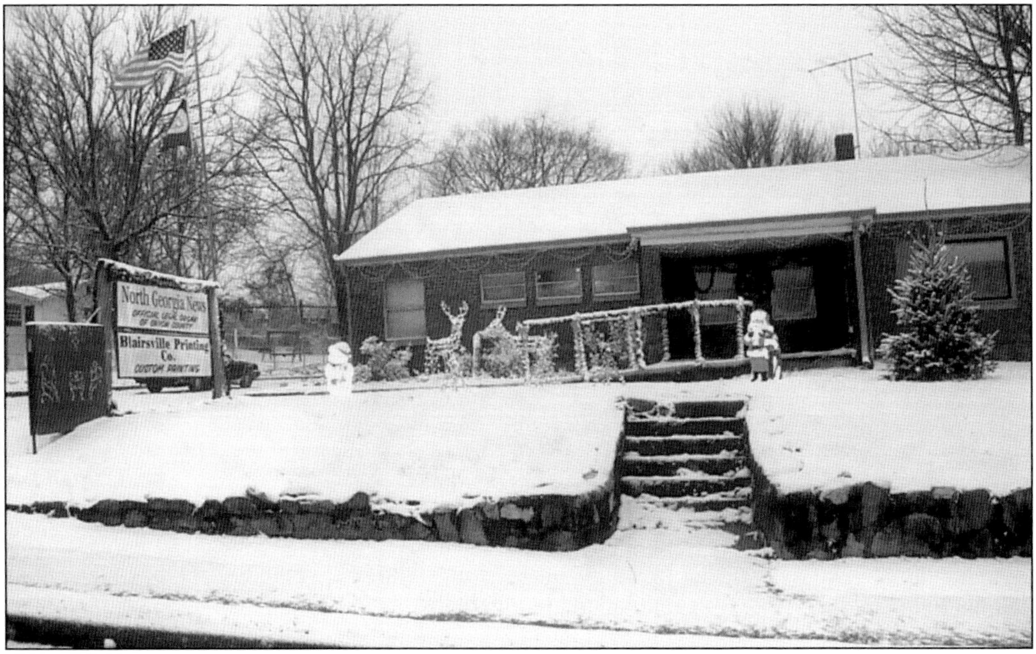

The oldest business in Union County is the *North Georgia News*, established in 1909. "Land of Lakes, Scenic Beauty, and Friendly People" has been part of the banner of the newspaper for decades. The publication has served as the legal organ of Union County for decades. (Photo by Norman Cooper.)

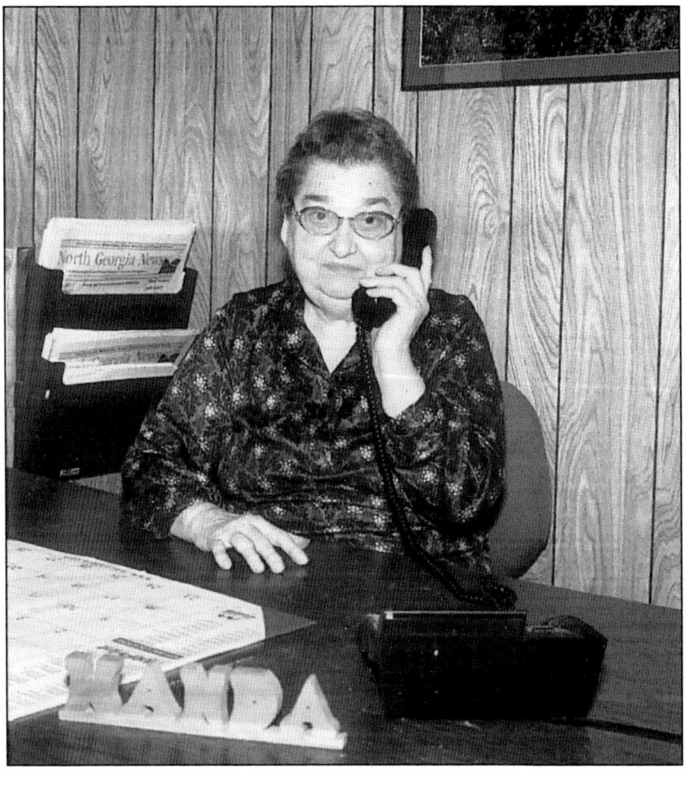

Harold and Wanda West purchased the newspaper in the early 1950s. Harold West passed away in 1976. Wanda West, seen here, is the publisher of the *North Georgia News*. Kenneth, son of Harold and Wanda West, is the general manager of the *North Georgia News*. Harold and Wanda's daughter, Donna, was involved with the newspaper for many years. (Photo by Norman Cooper.)

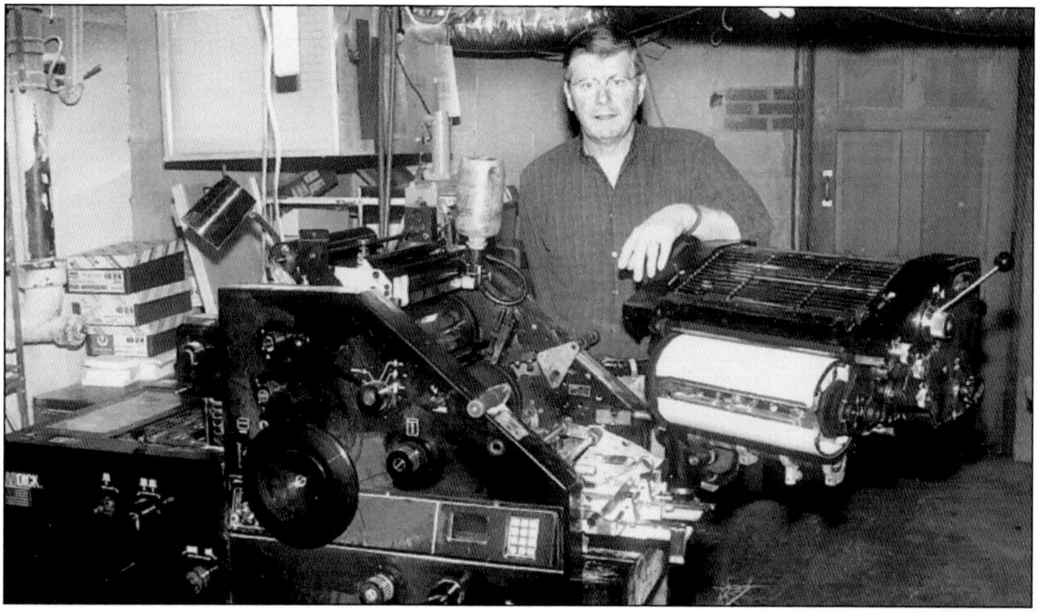

The *North Georgia News* included a commercial print shop since the early 1950s. During the mid-1970s, Blairsville Printing Company was formed independent of the newspaper, although it was located in the same building. One of the original presses is on display in the museum inside the Old Courthouse in Blairsville. Kenneth West is shown in this photo with a two-color offset press at Blairsville Printing Company. (Photo by Norman Cooper.)

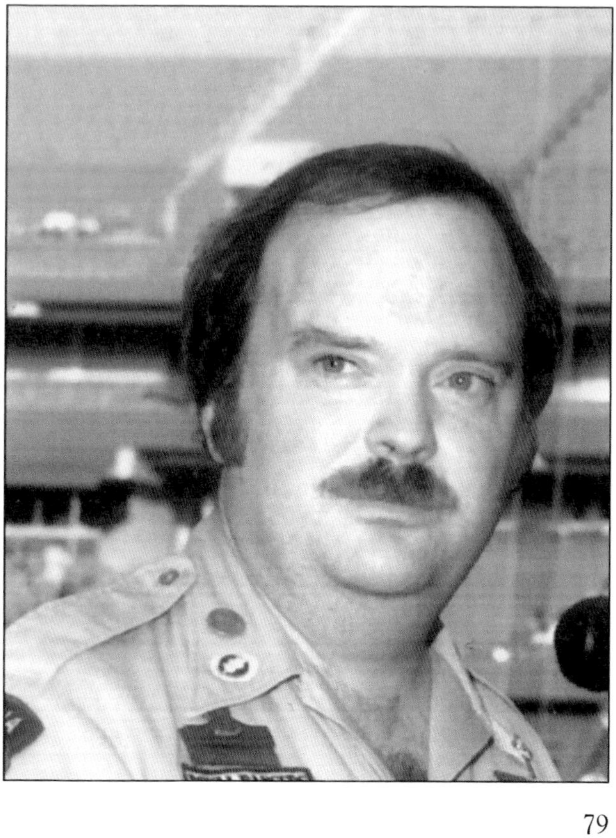

Norman Cooper joined the staff of the *North Georgia News* in October 1994 and became editor, sports editor, and photographer in 1995. He has won two awards from the National Newspaper Association, eight awards from the Georgia Press Association, and 26 awards from the Georgia Sports Writers Association. He was presented the Beacon Award by the Georgia School Boards Association. He has served as vice president of the Georgia Sports Writers Association and serves on the Education Committee of the Georgia Press Association. As chairman of the Union County Red Cross Committee, he pioneered the program of giving 25 percent of the proceeds from fund-raisers to local groups in Union County. He also serves as chairman of the Lifelong Learning Center Advisory Committee. (Photo from *Georgia Trend* magazine.)

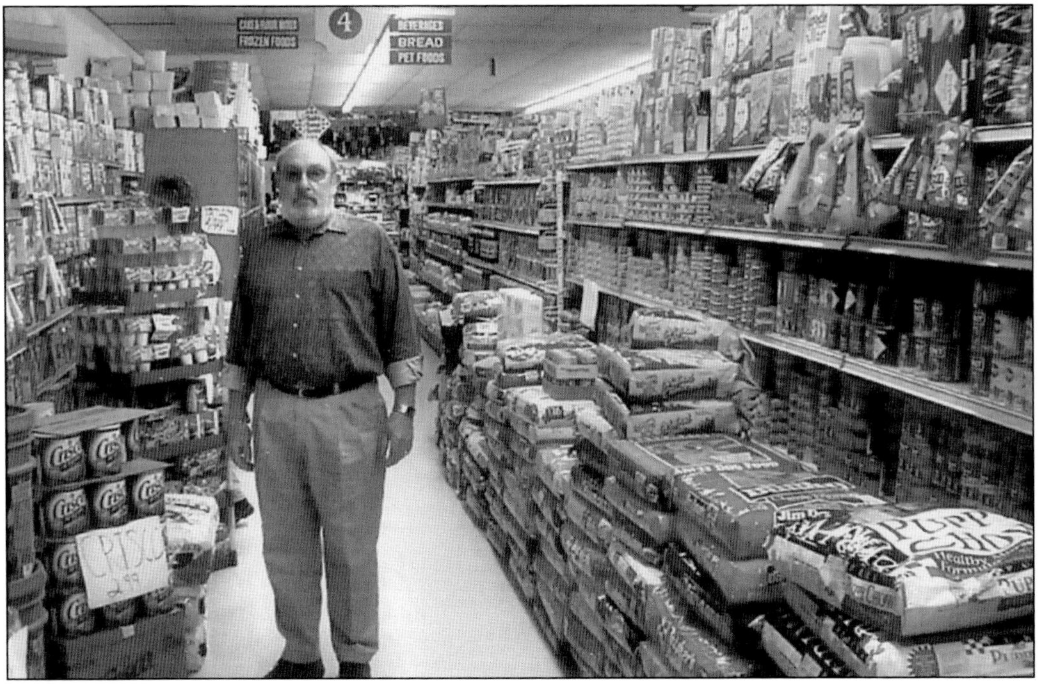

Anchoring the square for decades is one the last of the hometown grocery stores, Foodland, owned by Wayne Abercrombie. (Photo by Norman Cooper.)

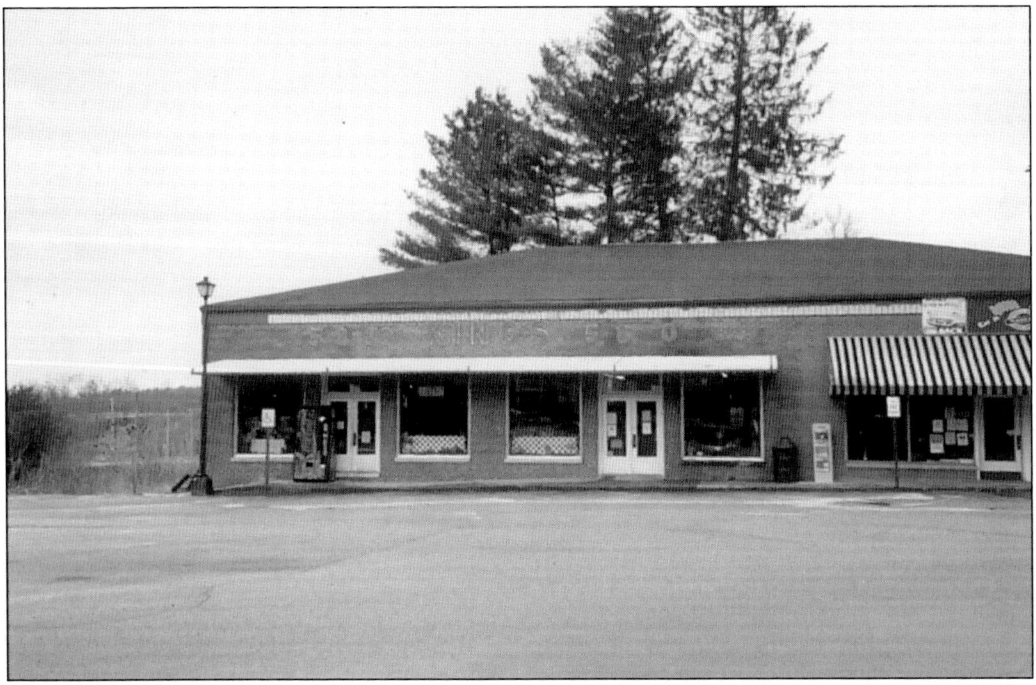

While businesses build, companies expand, and strip malls are created, one of the stores in the county that maintains its rural charm is Kings 5 & 10 on the Square in Blairsville. (Photo by Martyne Jokela.)

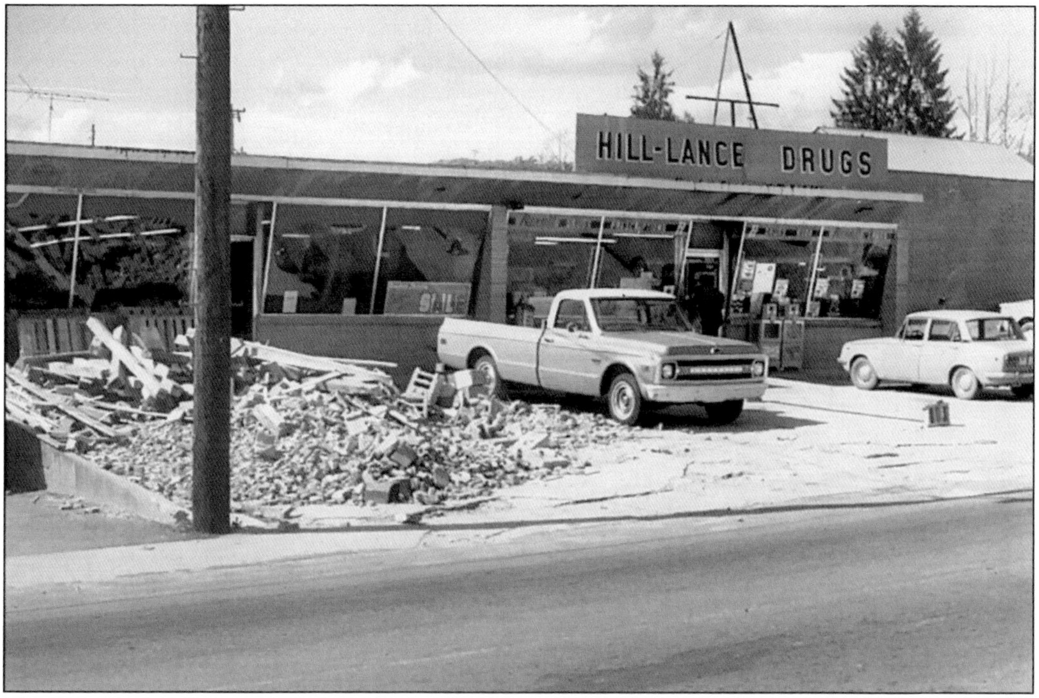

Hill-Lance Drugs just off the square in Blairsville served the area from the early 1960s until it was sold in 1985. During the late 1950s it was known as Akins Drugs. Charles Hill bought it in 1960 and Jack Lance joined him in business in 1962. Renovation work was underway when this photo was taken. (Courtesy Jack Lance.)

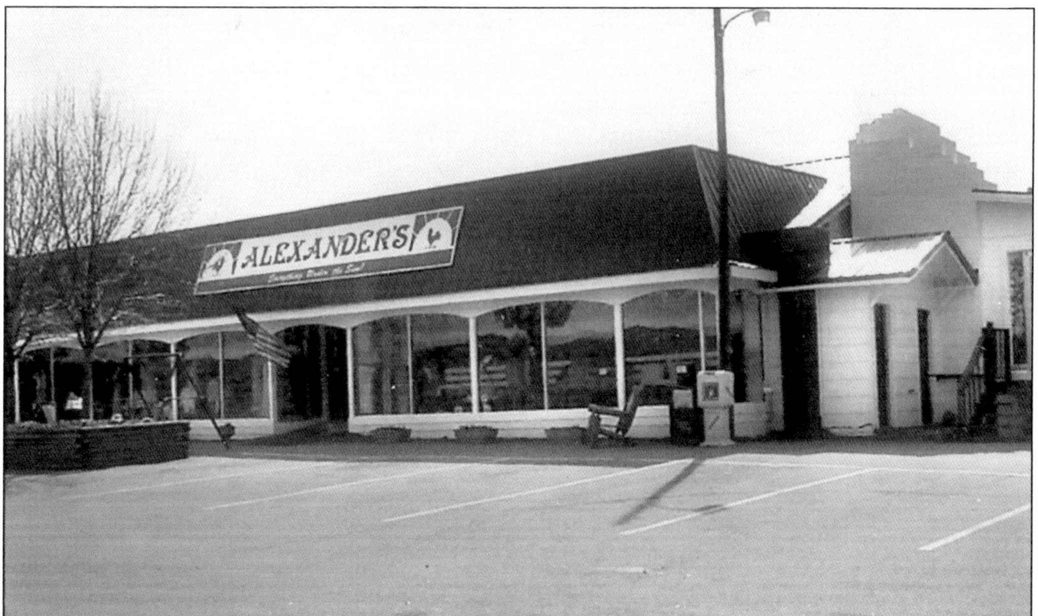

Alexander's Store has always been known as the store with "everything under the sun" and has been in the same family for generations. Hoyt Alexander bought the store in the middle of the 20th century. It is still a family business owned and operated by Eddie and Sandy Alexander.

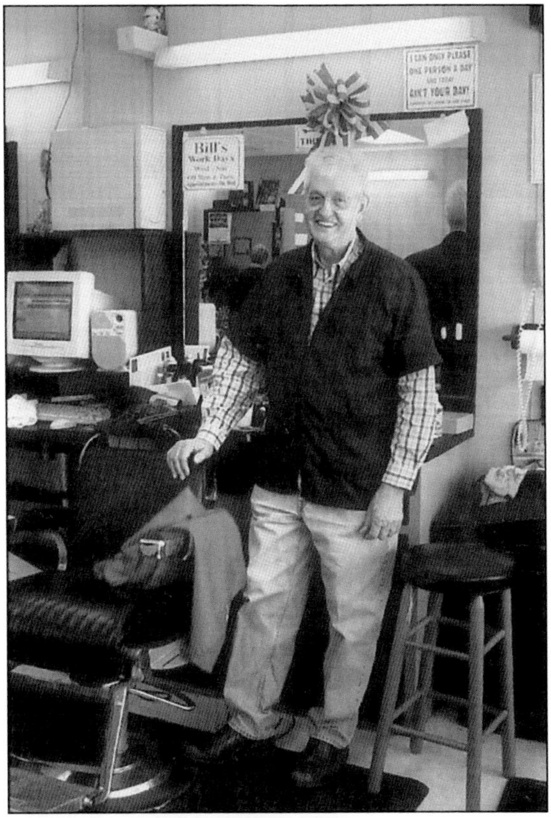

Bill Kuykendall opened a hair shop in Union County in the 1970s and has been at his present location with The Hair Shoppe for more than two decades.

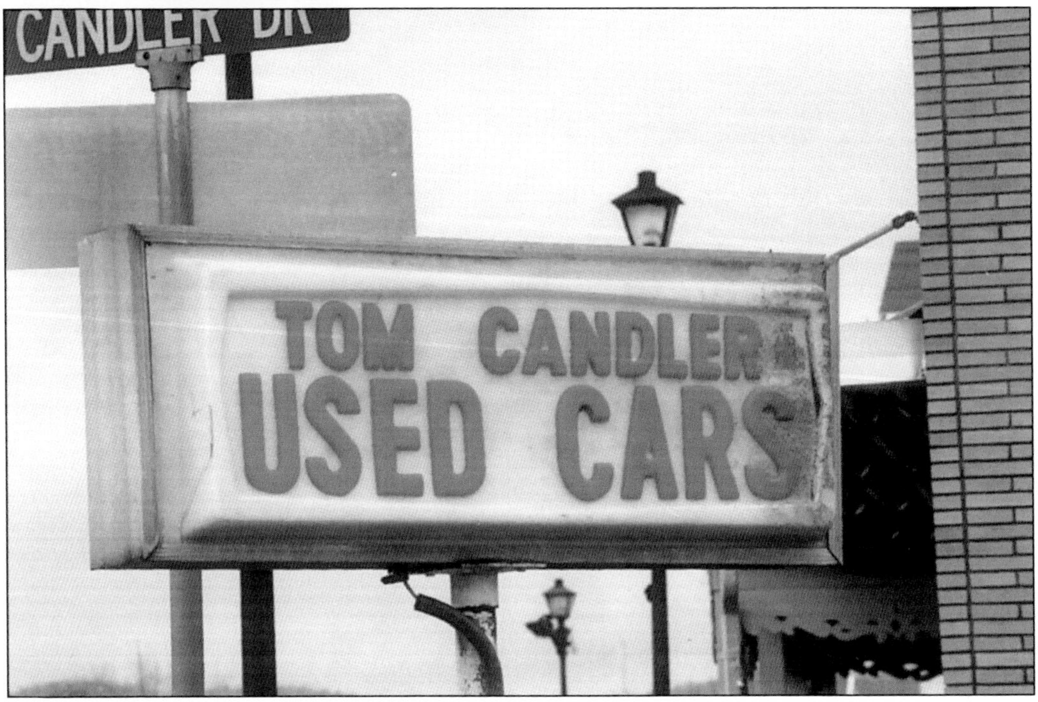

Tom Candler owned and operated a car lot on the Square for many years.

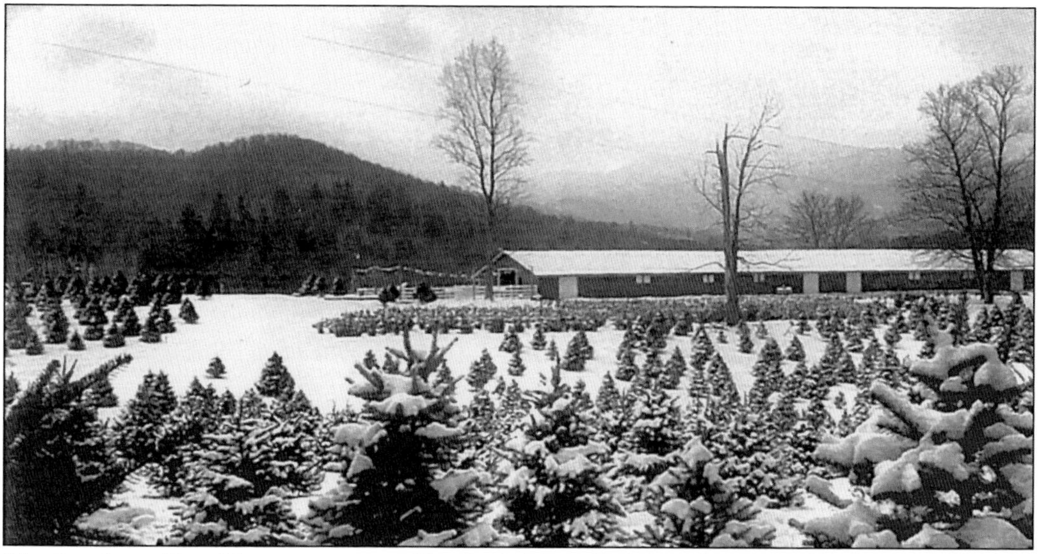

The Southern Tree Plantation, owned by the McCombs family, began in the 1980s. Thousands visit the farm annually. Georgia Forestry provided 1,500 white pine seedlings and the first sales were in 1987. Howard McCombs transformed the part-time venture into a full-time business in 1992. The plantation grew to 25,000 trees of eight species. The plantation features a holiday barn, petting farm, and hayrides, which attract hundreds of students annually on field trips. (Courtesy of McCombs family.)

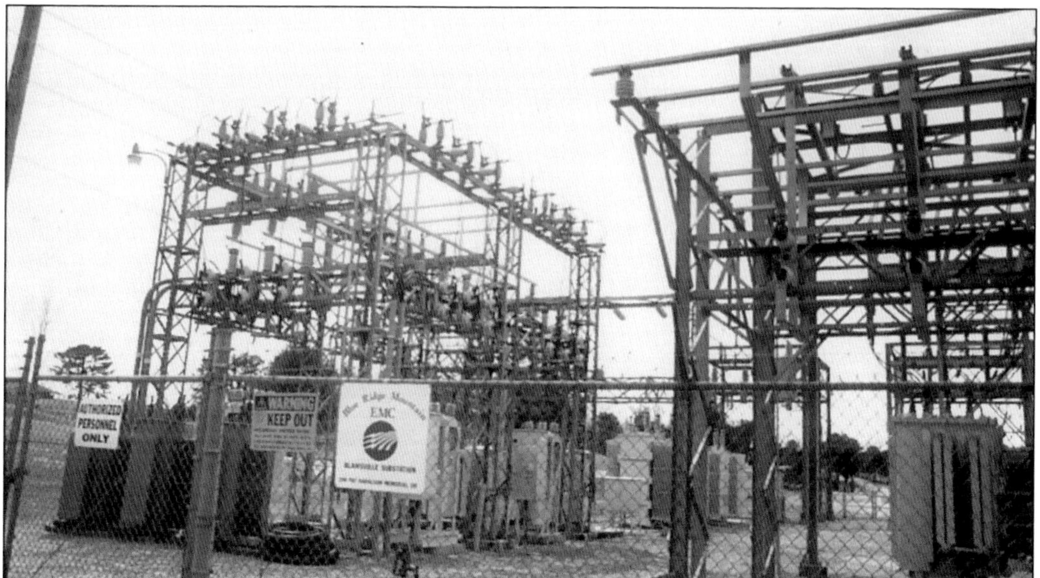

In 1936 the Rural Electrification Act, part of the New Deal, was passed. Rural electric cooperatives were formed to provide service to rural areas across the United States. Blue Ridge Mountain Electric Membership Corporation (EMC) was organized in 1937 when a group of businessmen met and decided that this rural area needed power, too. An agreement was made with the Tennessee Valley Authority to supply electricity and with the Rural Electrification Administration to borrow money for construction. Three employees were hired and volunteers were recruited. EMC has grown to serve over 40,000 customers. (Photo by Norman Cooper.)

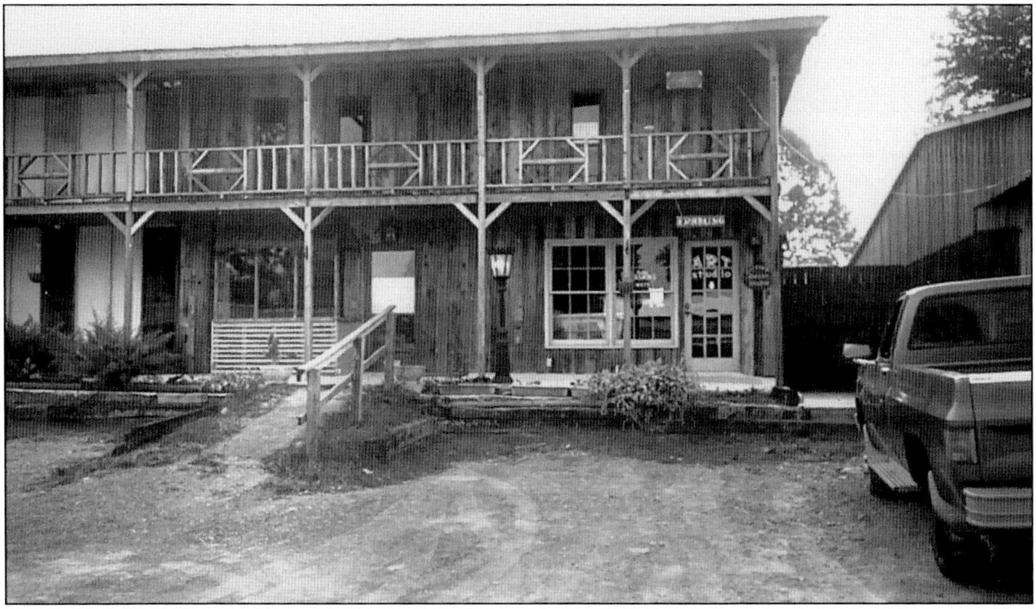

Merchant's Walk in downtown Blairsville has housed numerous businesses over the years. This photo, *c.* 1986, shows the appearance of one of the buildings after Carriage House opened its picture framing addition in 1985.

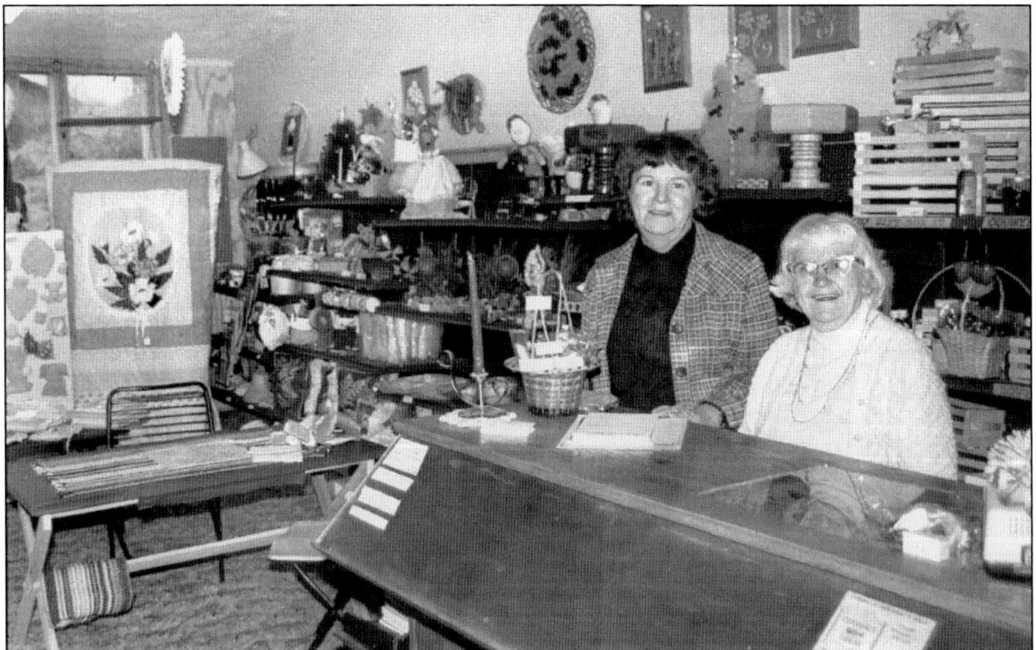

Martyne Jokela and her mother Mrs. McMonigle are pictured inside the Carriage House in December 1984. Martyne began coming to Blairsville in 1954 and taught leather craft and other arts and promoted mountain artisans and their work to the general public. Moving to Union County permanently in 1970, Martyne became Blairsville's artist-in-residence. She played a role in getting artists' works exposed through the Sorghum Festival, which she helped get off the ground.

Four

EDUCATION

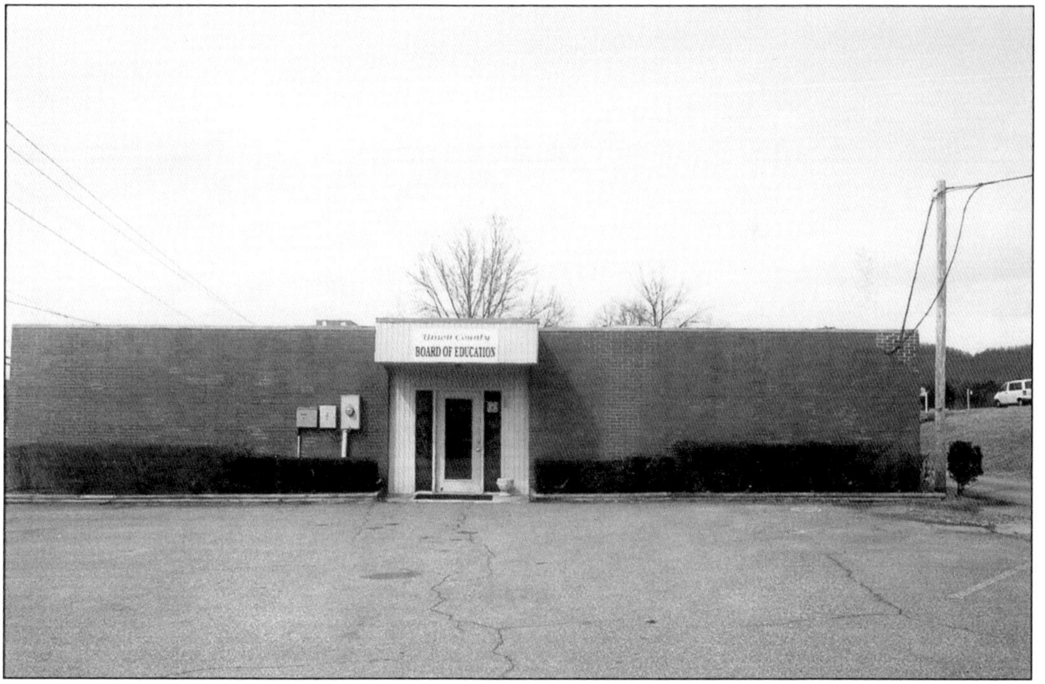

Union County's educational opportunities have grown since one-room schoolhouses were scattered through the community in the early 1900s. In 2003, more than 2,600 students were enrolled at Blairsville's Union County Primary School, Union County Elementary School, Union County Middle School, Union County High School, and Suches's Woody Gap School, which includes all grades. Union County collaborates with other counties through the Mountain Education Center, North Georgia Technical College, and the Lifelong Learning Center. (Photo by Norman Cooper.)

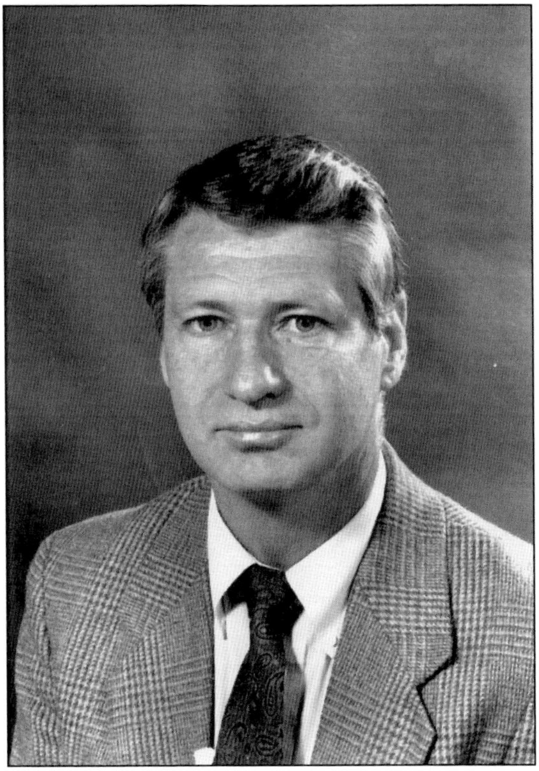

Tommy Stephens grew up in Union County and graduated from Union County High in 1966. He attended Truett McConnell College for two years before enlisting in the air force, serving four years with a tour of duty in Southeast Asia. He graduated from North Georgia College with a bachelor's degree in psychology and returned to North Georgia College for his master's in physical education. He taught and served as an assistant principal and principal at Union County Middle School. He was elected superintendent of Union County Schools in 1992 and continues to serve in that position.

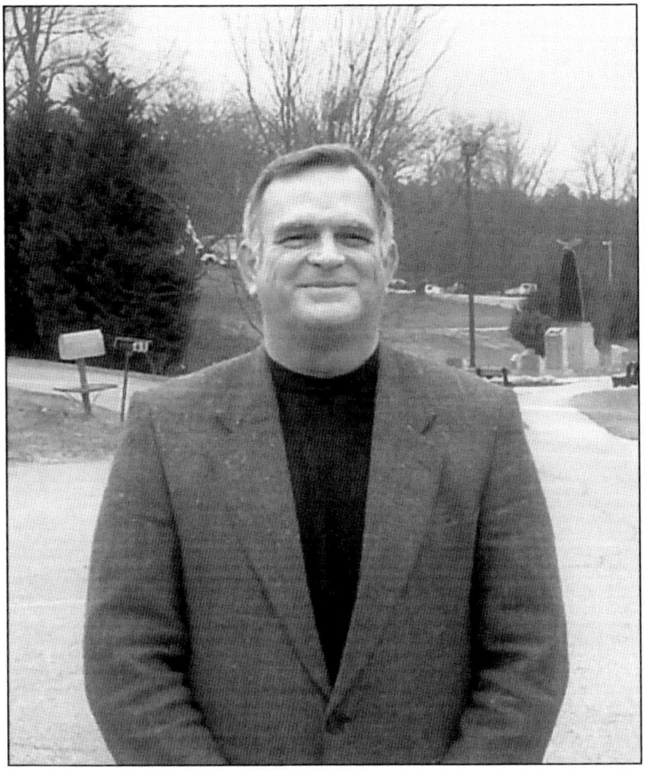

Ron Byers graduated from Union County High School in 1968 and went to Appalachian State University on a football scholarship. He graduated from Piedmont College and earned his graduate degree from the University of Georgia. In 1977, he began work at the Union County Middle School helping with seventh- and eighth-grade football and physical education. He was director of student services for Union County Schools and coached football, girls' basketball, and girls' and boys' tennis until 1992, when he became assistant superintendent of operations.

Dr. Lewis McAfee graduated from Union County High in 1967. In 1970, he joined the U.S. Army Reserve and served two years active duty. He graduated from North Georgia College in 1977 and taught at Union County High School. In 1983, he became principal of Union County Middle School. After four years he became the principal of Union County High School, and one year later he became curriculum director. Currently, he is the assistant superintendent for Curriculum and Instruction.

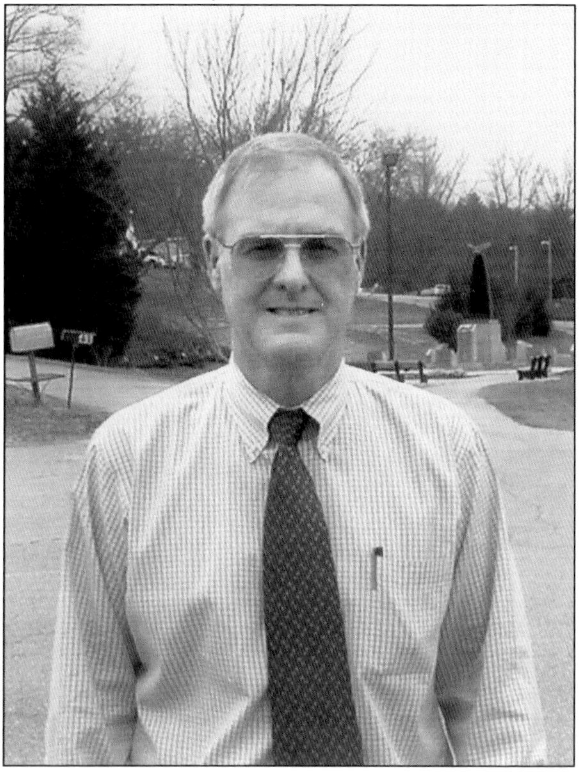

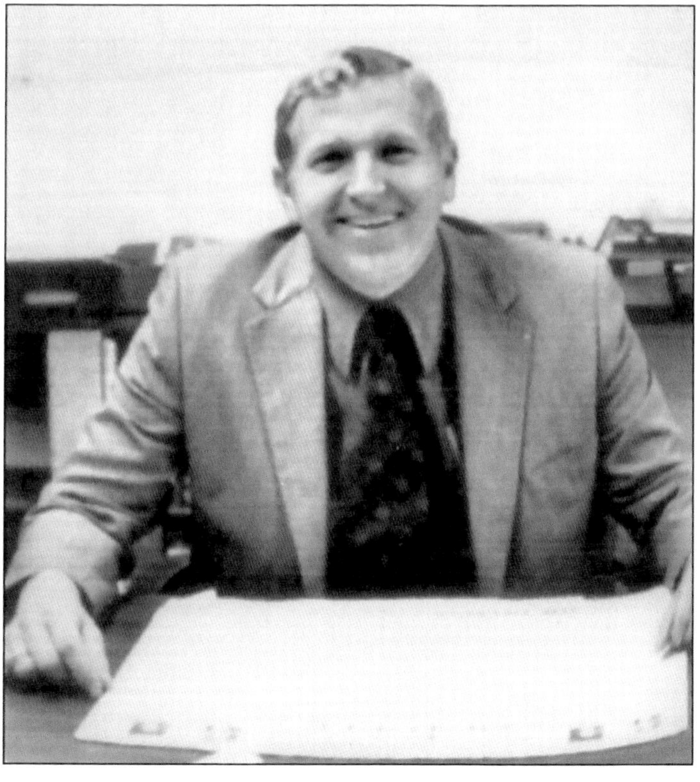

Jim Allison taught at Union County High School in 1965. After a few years he left to go into business and returned to Union County High School again as a vocational teacher in 1971. Six years later he took the position as director over the entire vocational department. In 1992 Allison was asked to take the job as technology director. He retired 10 years later. Jim helped take the Union County School System from a non-technological system to a school system with over 600 computers on one network.

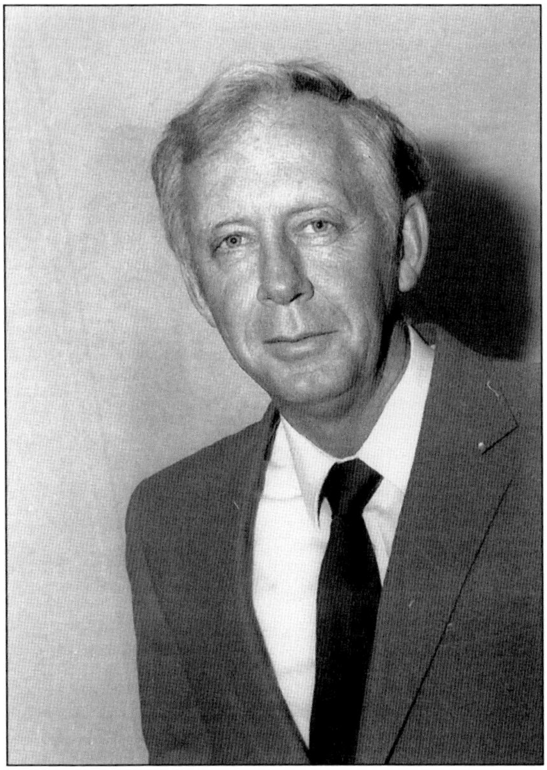

Earl Odom served twice as Union County school superintendent, once in the early 1970s and again for 15 years until his retirement in March 1993. He began his career at Union County High School in 1963. He started the track team at the school and coached basketball. He was named Coach of the Year many times. He served as assistant principal for several years and returned to the classroom and coaching after his first term as superintendent.

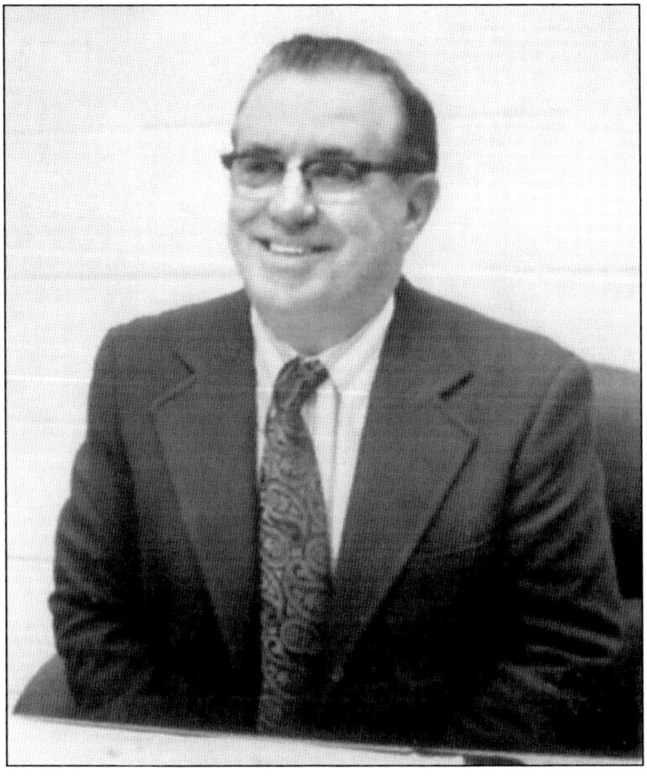

Clyde Collins was principal of Town Creek Elementary School in 1957, serving until 1962, when he returned to Union County High School as a teacher of American history and government. While principal of Ivy Long Elementary School from 1966 to 1968, he received a master's degree in school administration. He returned to Union County High School as principal in 1968 and served until 1976, when he was elected as Union County superintendent. This picture is *c.* 1974. Collins retired in 1981.

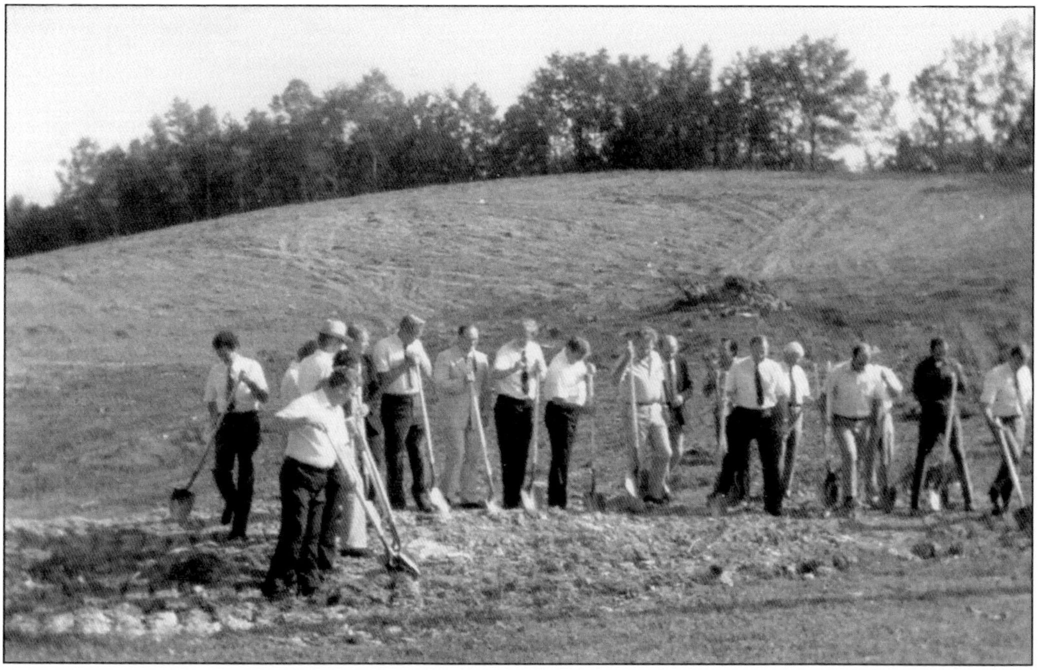

An innovative financing plan allowed Union County to open a new elementary school in 1984. The new building was designed to hold 850 students, replacing a 50-year-old wooden structure. Union County Elementary School is believed to be the first school built in Georgia using a limited tax; the referendum was supported by 83 percent of the voters in 1982. Union County School Superintendent Earl Odom noted at the time that Union County was 155th out of 159 Georgia counties in per capita income. Odom began working for a new school in the early 1970s. (Courtesy of Gwen Odom.)

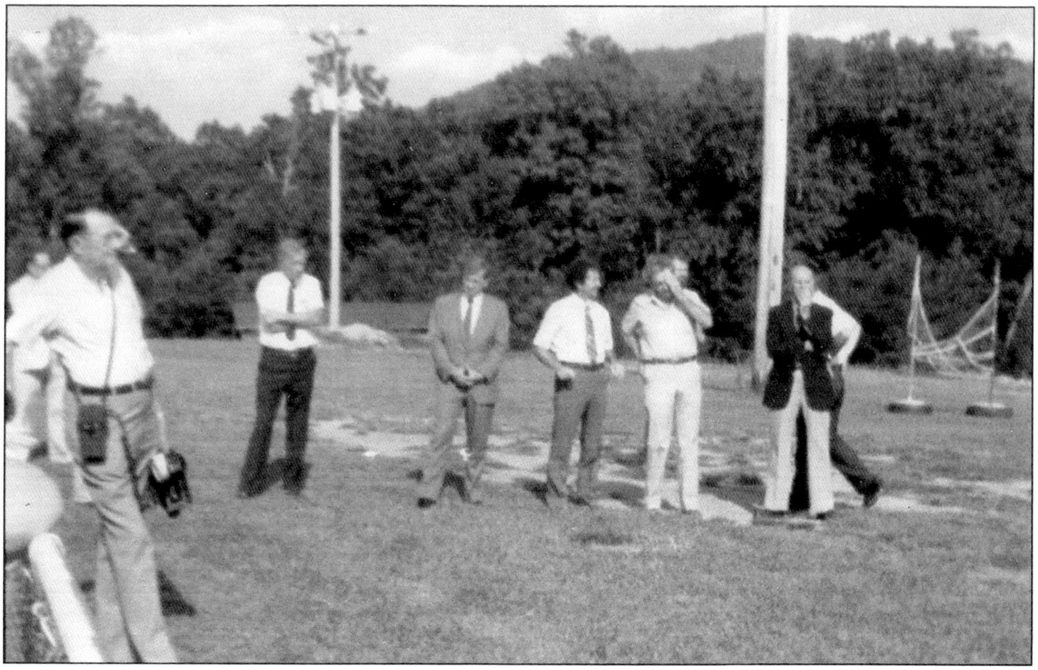

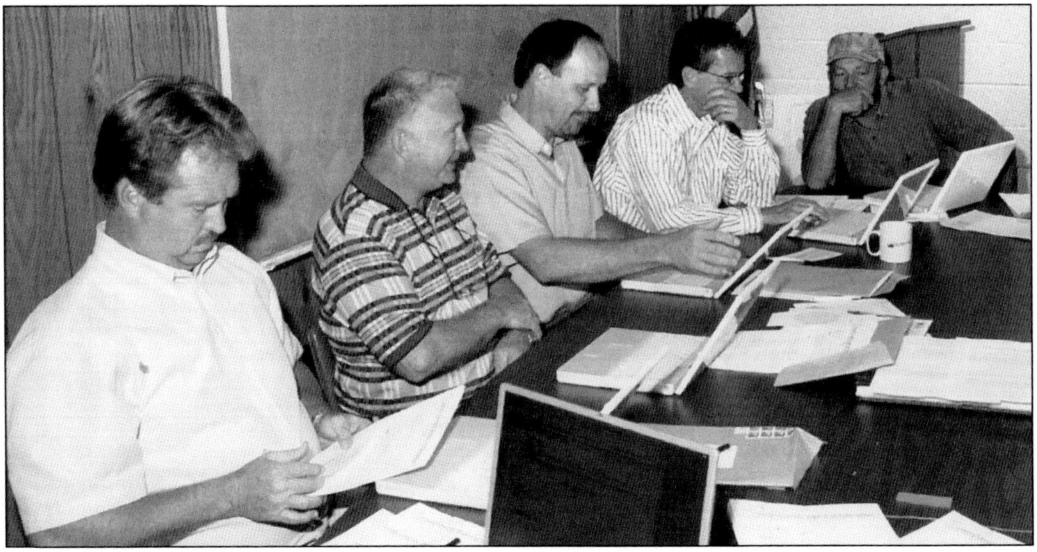

Union County School Boards have a legacy of professionalism, cooperation, integrity, and a reputation for making decisions in the best interest of the education of students. School board members in 2003 were Gary Davenport, Larry Akins, Jerry Dyer, Rick Davenport, and Jerry Gilreath. Past school board members included Ernie Pruitt, Larry Duff Conley, Myron Turner, Gene Dyer, Mickey Cone, Hobert Lunsford, Barry Collins, and Johnny Jones. (Photo by Norman Cooper.)

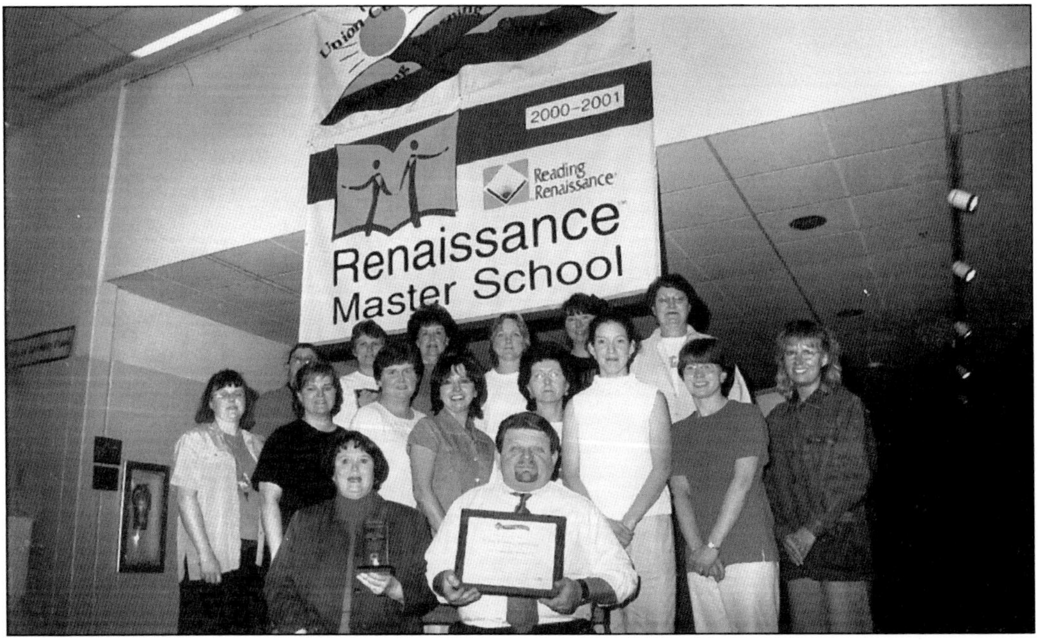

Union County Elementary School adopted the Renaissance Reading program to improve the reading skills of students. Under the guidance of principal Jim Colwell, holding the certificate, assistant principal David Ueltzen, and coordinator Lynn Harbin, front left, the students' skills increased dramatically, so much so that they were awarded the distinction of Renaissance Master School. Many of the faculty attended a convention in Las Vegas where they were recognized as one of the leading schools in the nation. (Photo by Norman Cooper.)

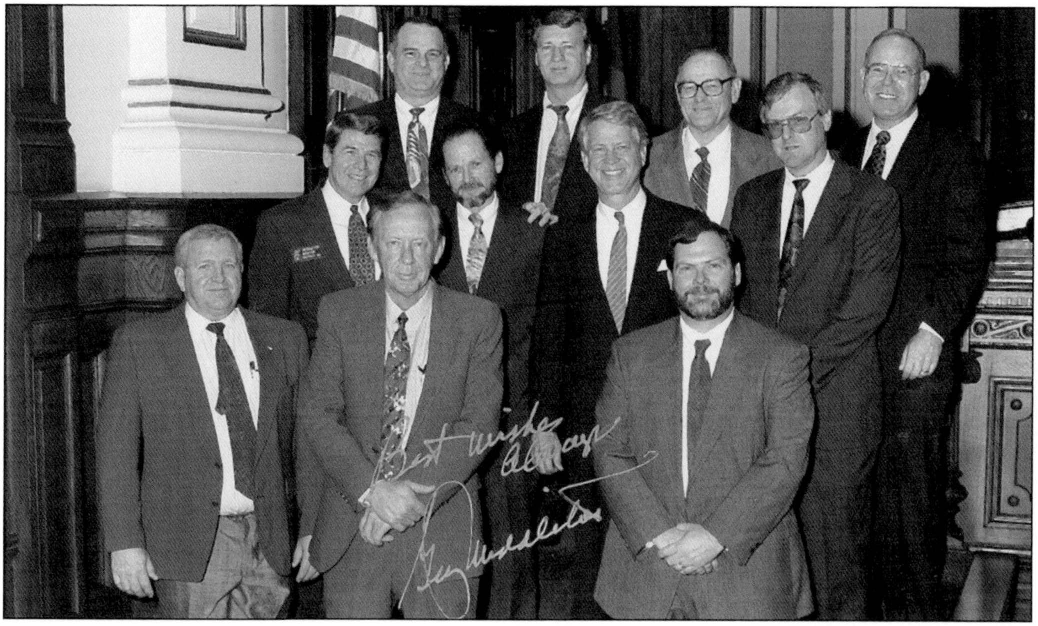

Bill Parker was honored at the State Capitol for his 30-plus years as teacher, principal, and curriculum director. Pictured in this c. 1990 photo are, from left to right, (front row) Union County vocational director Jim Allison, Union County past superintendent Earl Odom, and Michael Plott; (middle row) Georgia state senator Guy Middleton, Parker; Georgia Lt. Gov. Pierre Howard, and Union County assistant superintendent Lewis McAfee; (back row) Union County assistant superintendent Ron Byers, Union County superintendent Tommy Stephens, and two unidentified people.

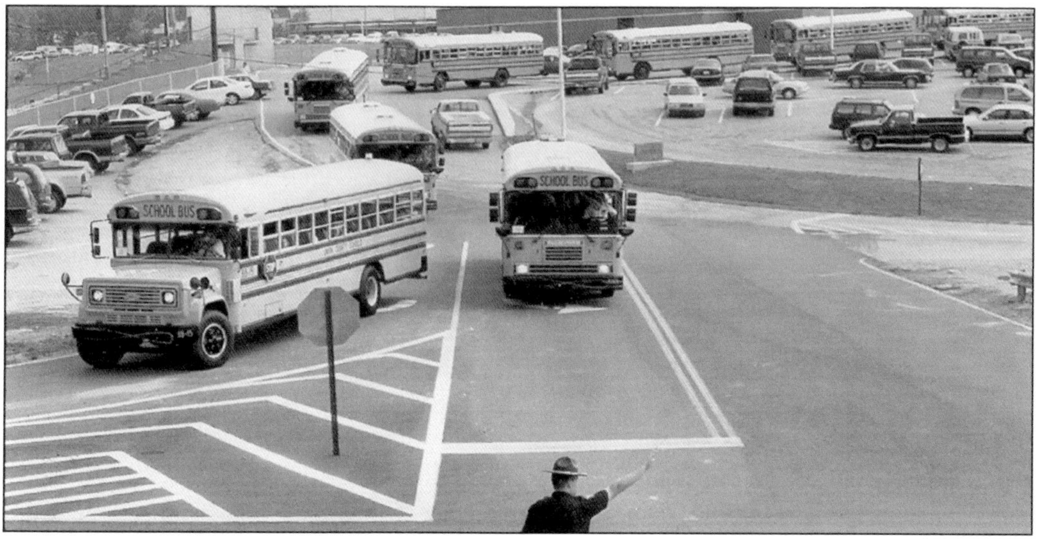

Safe transportation is a priority of the Union County School System. In the past, many roads were unpaved; the school board contracted a wrecker company to pull school buses out of ruts and mud holes. School officials credit Stanley Garrett, transportation director for nearly three decades, for keeping the buses in top running order. Annual inspections by the Georgia State Patrol testify to the exceptionally good job Garrett and his staff does. (Photo by Norman Cooper.)

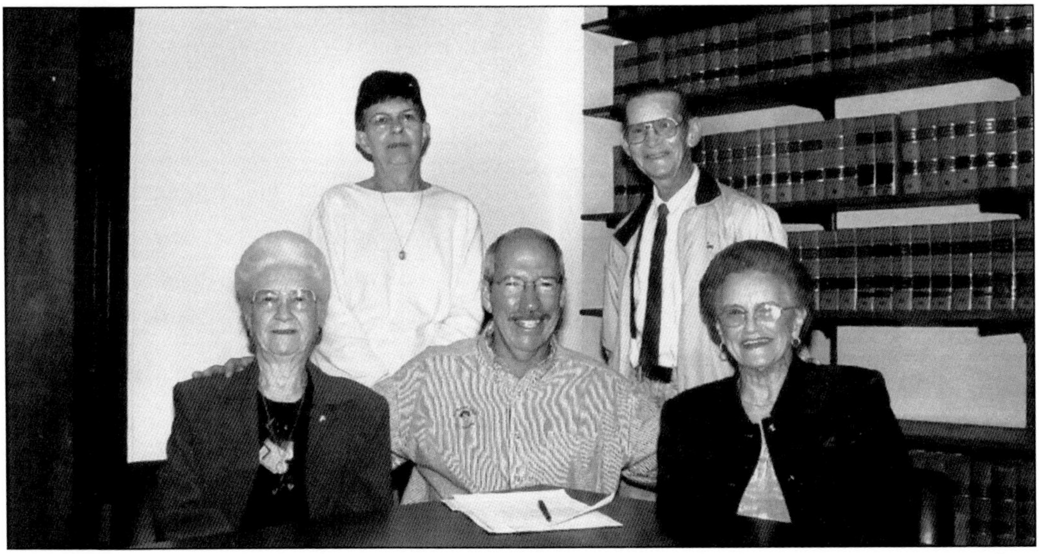

Retired educators are honored annually with a Georgia Retired Educators Day in November. In the late 1990s, Jack Parker spearheaded a proclamation recognizing the exceptional service provided by the retired educators to Union County, and he encourages citizens to recognize the lasting contributions of retired educators to the lives of citizens and the welfare of the city and county. Blairsville mayor Ray Potts, not pictured, and Union County commissioner Lamar Paris, seated center, issued the proclamation in 2003. Paris's mother, Edith Paris, was a retired educator. Attending the 2003 signing were retired educators Dora Spiva, seated left, Doris Souther, seated right, Mary Barksdale, standing, and Jack Parker. (Photo by Norman Cooper.)

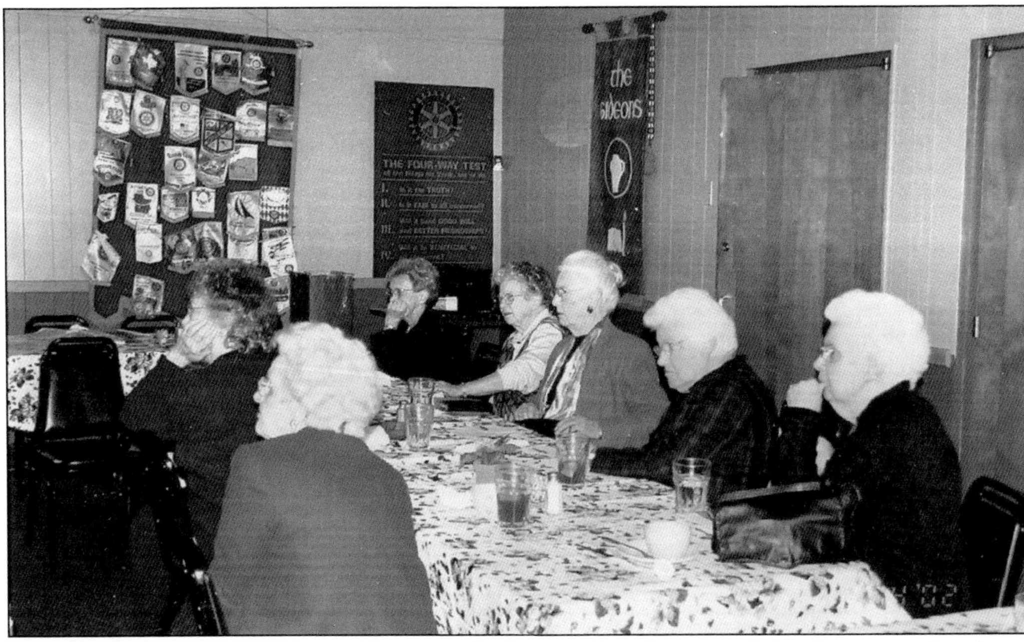

Retired educators devoted time, energy, and talent to the educational development of students. Retired educators are a major source of insight and direction for the county. They possess valuable knowledge and use their experiences and skills to enrich the educational process in a variety of settings. (Courtesy Jack Parker.)

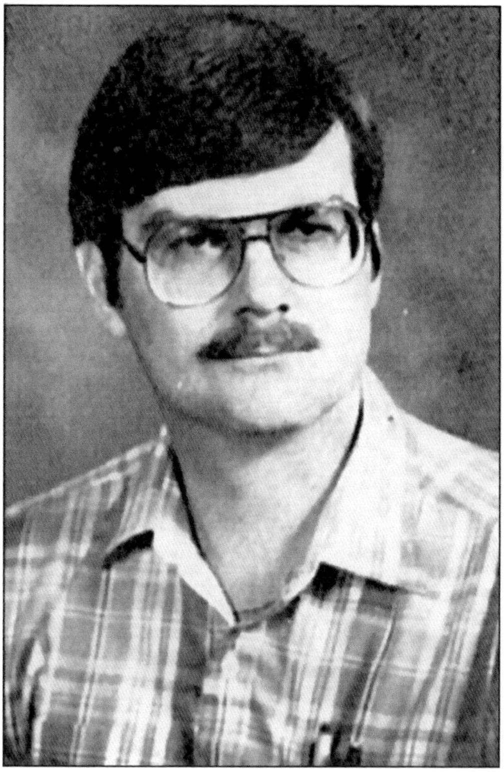

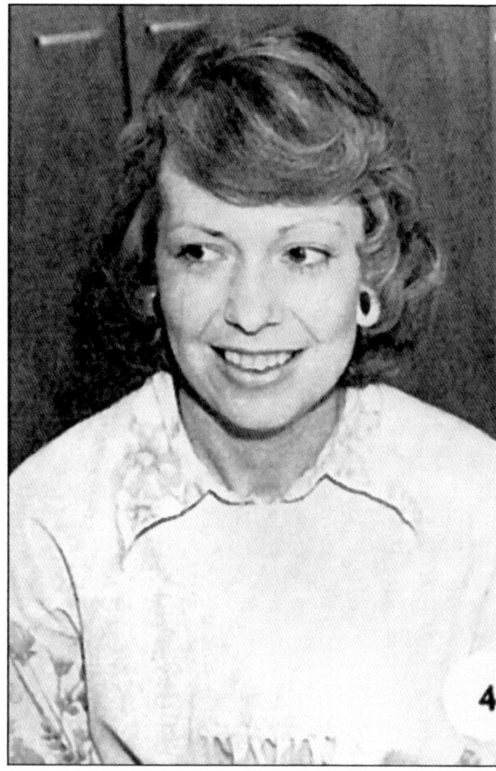

(Above, left) Pictured here *c.* 1984 is Jim Clark, who taught mathematics for many years. He has served the school system as an assistant principal and principal.

(Above, right) This is Sandra Akins *c.* 1978. She taught home economics and sponsored the F.H.A.

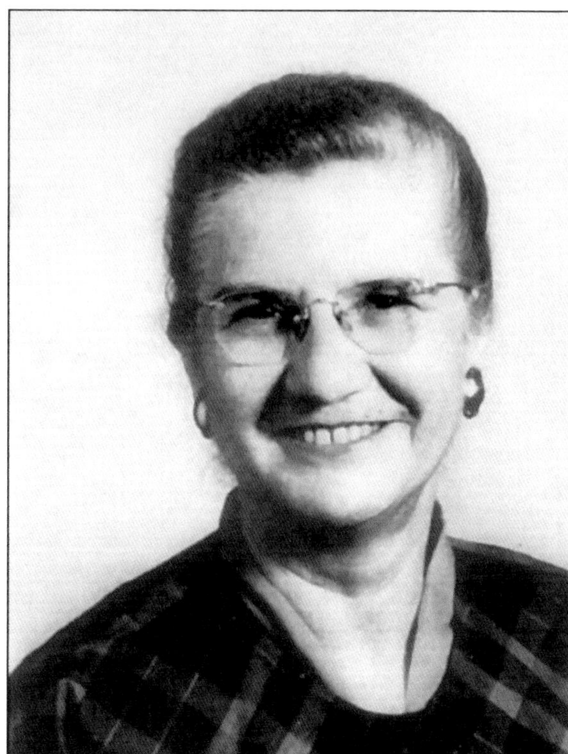

Dora Allison taught mathematics at Union County High School during her career.

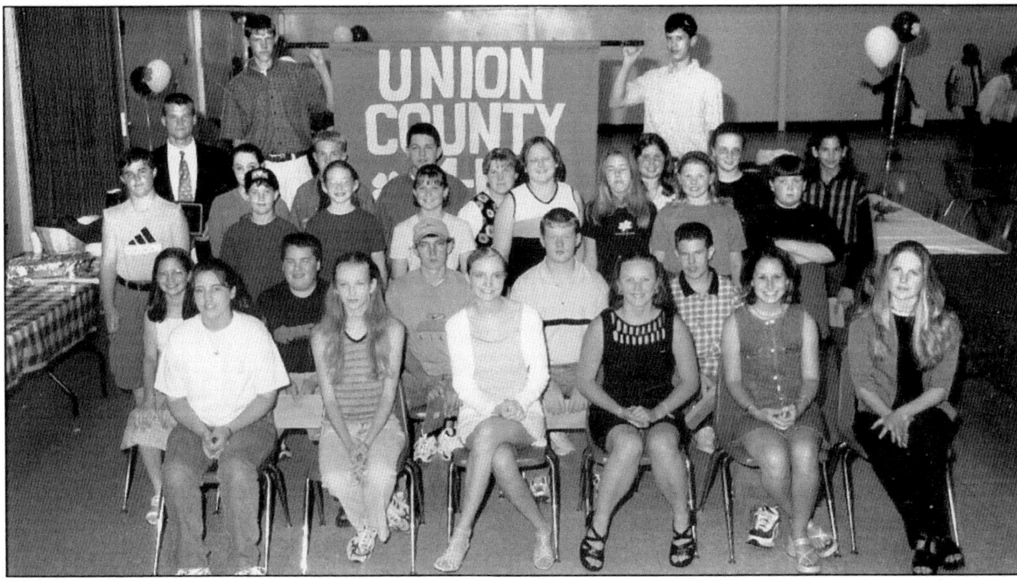

The Union County 4-H Award Banquet is held annually to honor 4-H members. The club's mission is to help youth acquire knowledge, develop life skills, and form attitudes that will enable them to become self-directing, productive, and contributing members of society. The mission is accomplished through hands-on learning experiences focused on agricultural and environmental issues, agriculture awareness, leadership, communication skills, food and nutrition, health, energy conservation, and citizenship. (Photo by Norman Cooper.)

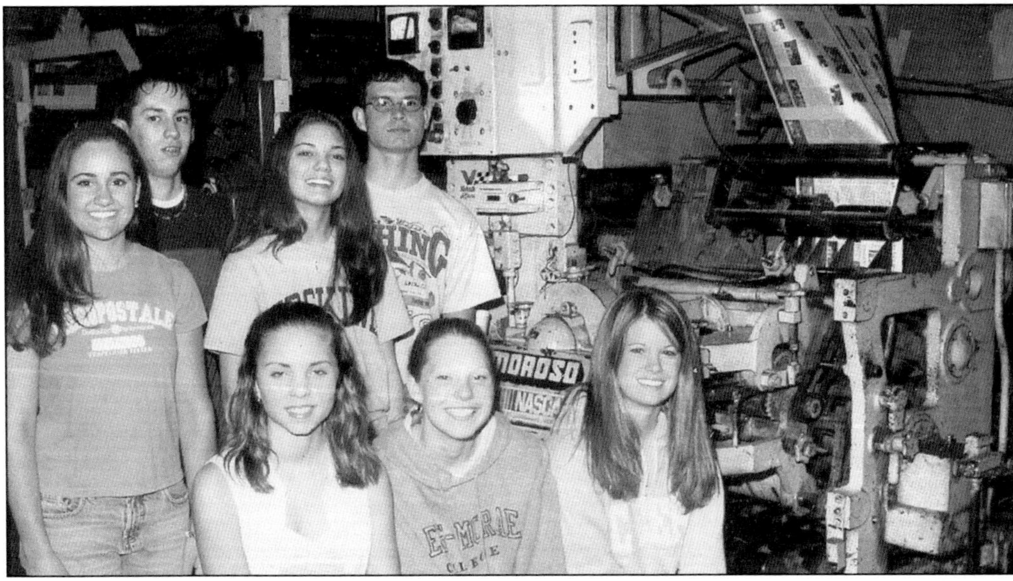

The Prowler, Union County High's school paper, began in the late 1990s. Jackie Hughes and Rhonda Payne have served as teachers, and Norman Cooper serves as journalism advisor. Students produce several issues in each semester. Once per semester the students take a trip to the printing press to see how their work is transformed into a newspaper. On the trip to the press plant in May 2003 were, from left to right (front row) Holly Walker, Rebecca Johnson, and Jillian Thomas; (second row) Emily Knight, Jeremy Smith, Dana Johnson, and Kevin Collins. (Photo by Norman Cooper.)

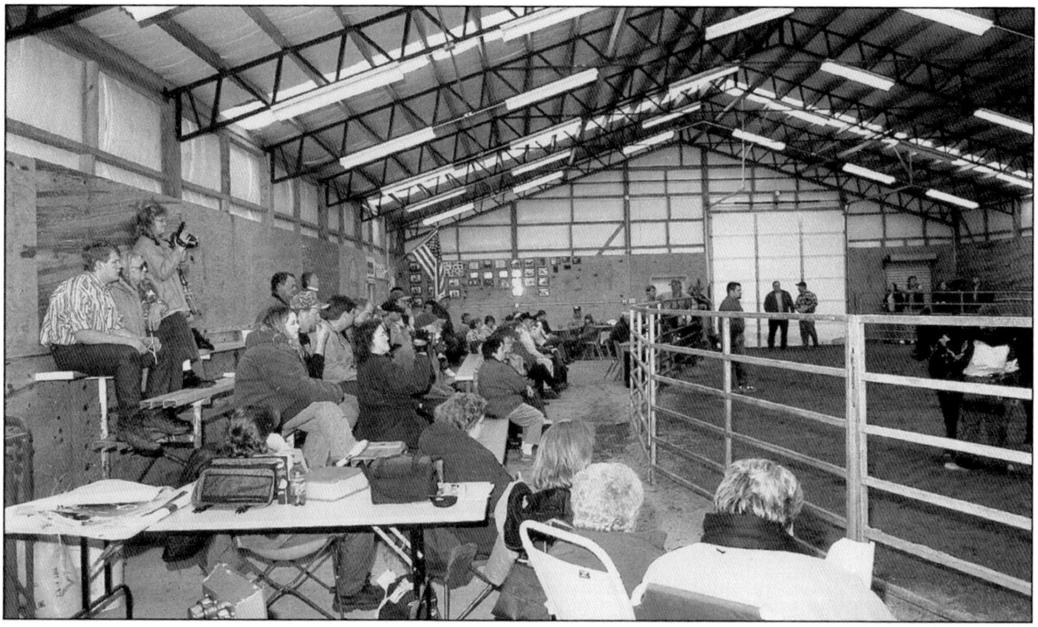

The Union County 4-H and F.F.A. livestock barn was built in the mid-1990s to accommodate the growing number of students showing beef cattle. The facility features a show ring, spectator seating, judging area, and staging area. Near this building is a housing barn where livestock are prepared for showing.

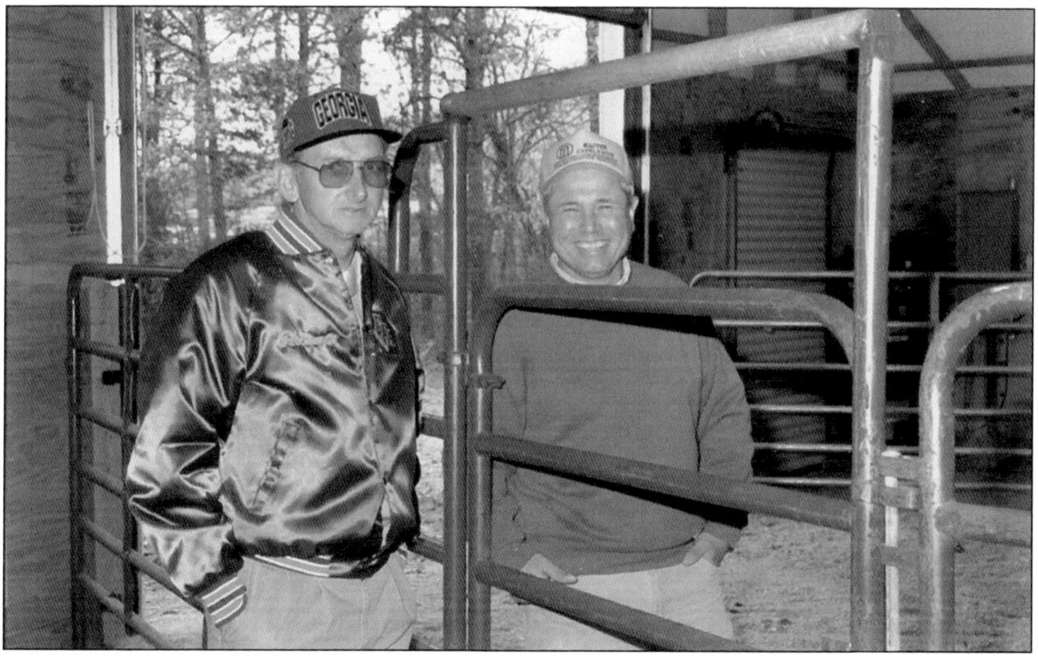

Junior Burnette (left), F.F.A. advisor at Union County High School for many years, was the horticulture teacher in the Union County School System for more than 30 years. Mickey Cummings (right), Union County Extension agent from the University of Georgia, came to Union County in 1990 and has overseen 4-H programs, adult agricultural programs, adult leadership programs, vegetable research, and forage research.

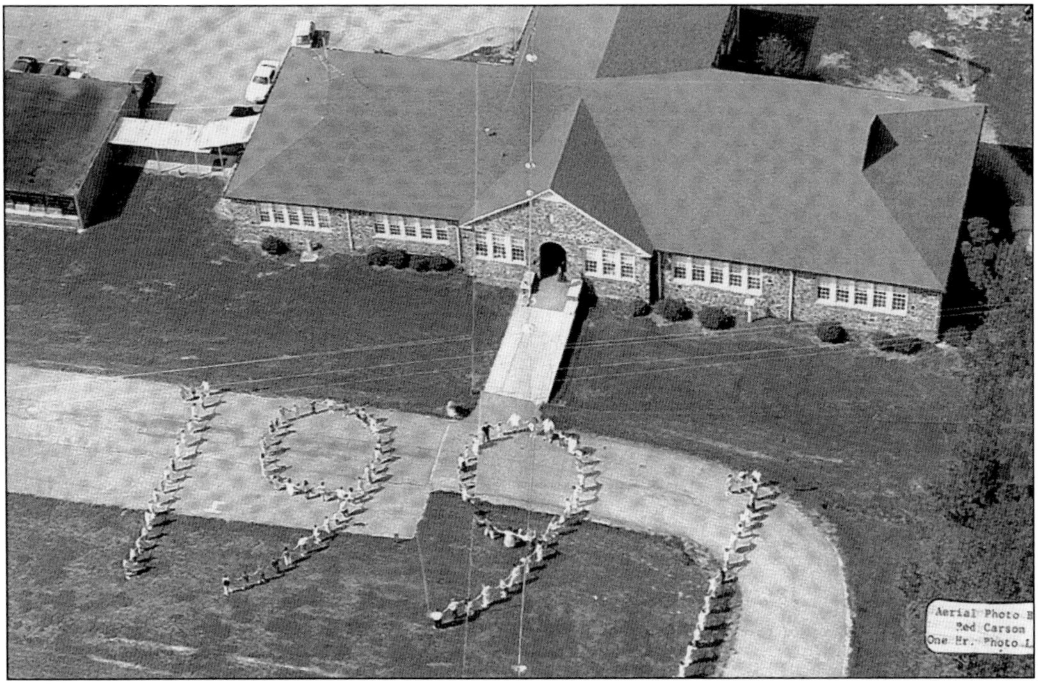

Shown is the Woody Gap School in Suches *c.* 1991. Woody Gap School contains all grade levels.

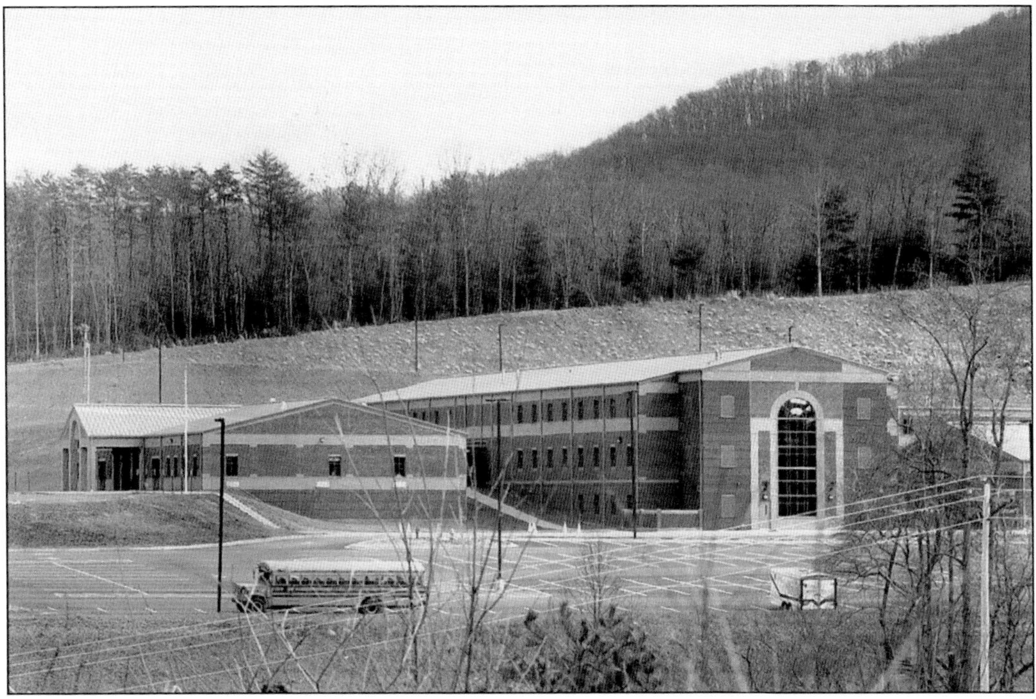

Shown is Union County High School *c.* 2003, built after voters approved a special tax to fund construction. The new facility for the high school features an administration building, multiple education wings, a vocational building, and a new gym. Thousands attended the dedication on August 18, 2002, which featured keynote speaker Sen. Zell Miller. (Photo by Norman Cooper.)

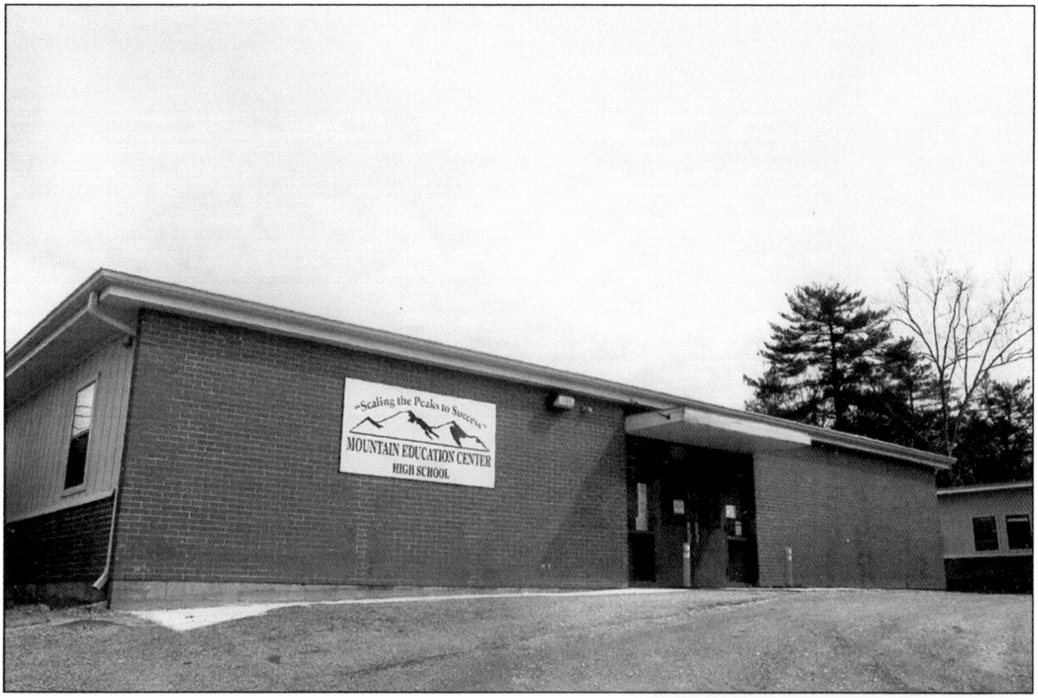

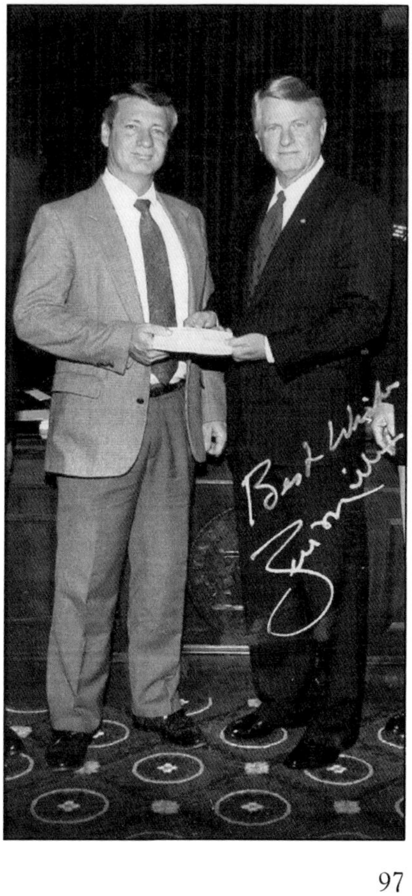

The Mountain Education Center High School serves nontraditional students who wish to receive a high school diploma. In the early 1990s, Union County School superintendent Tommy Stephens was concerned about the high dropout rate of the high school in Union County. He developed an alternative school that served those unable to complete their education in a traditional setting. The Mountain Education Center High School is available to anyone, teenagers through senior citizens. Stephens expected 40–60 students when the school opened in 1994; the first year the school served 329 students, ranging in age from 15 to 63. The school includes several surrounding counties in a collaborative effort. The course of study is self-paced, allowing students to advance at their level of learning. Gov. Zell Miller and Georgia state senator Guy Middleton supported the idea and provided funding through a grant. Superintendent Tommy Stephens, left, is presented the grant from Gov. Zell Miller.

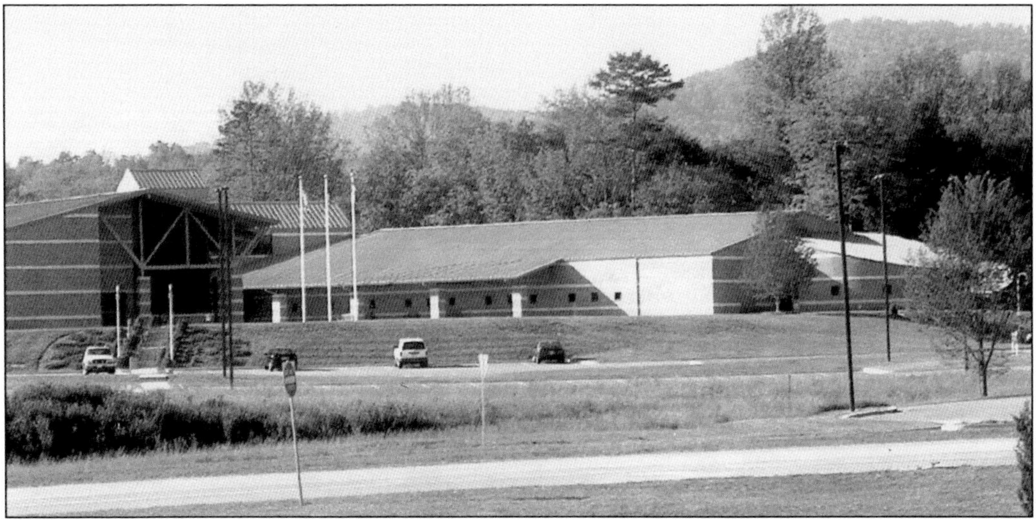

North Georgia Technical College, formerly North Georgia Technical Institute, opened a Blairsville campus focused on quality technical education and business and industry training to individuals. These efforts improve the quality of life of individuals by preparing them to succeed in the workforce and promoting the economic development of North Georgia. The college offers traditional and distance learning courses leading to the certificate, the diploma, and the associate degree. Instruction in work ethics is emphasized and lifelong learning is promoted.

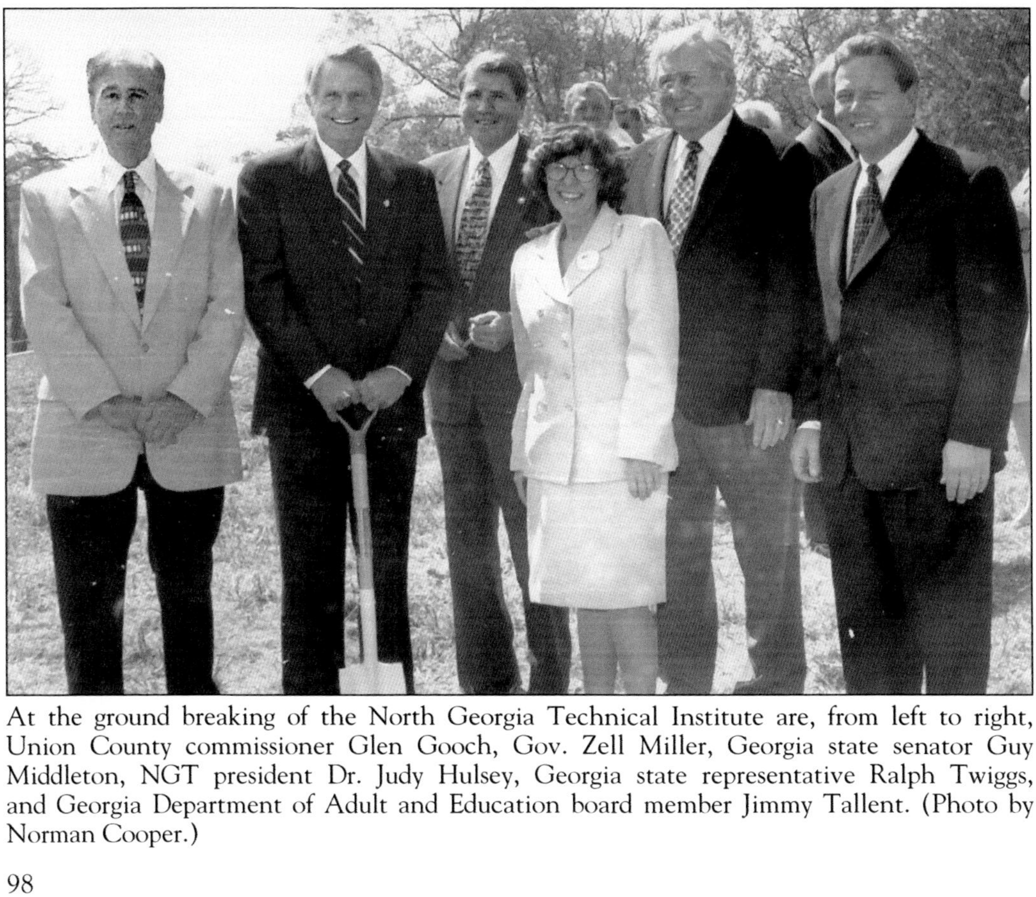

At the ground breaking of the North Georgia Technical Institute are, from left to right, Union County commissioner Glen Gooch, Gov. Zell Miller, Georgia state senator Guy Middleton, NGT president Dr. Judy Hulsey, Georgia state representative Ralph Twiggs, and Georgia Department of Adult and Education board member Jimmy Tallent. (Photo by Norman Cooper.)

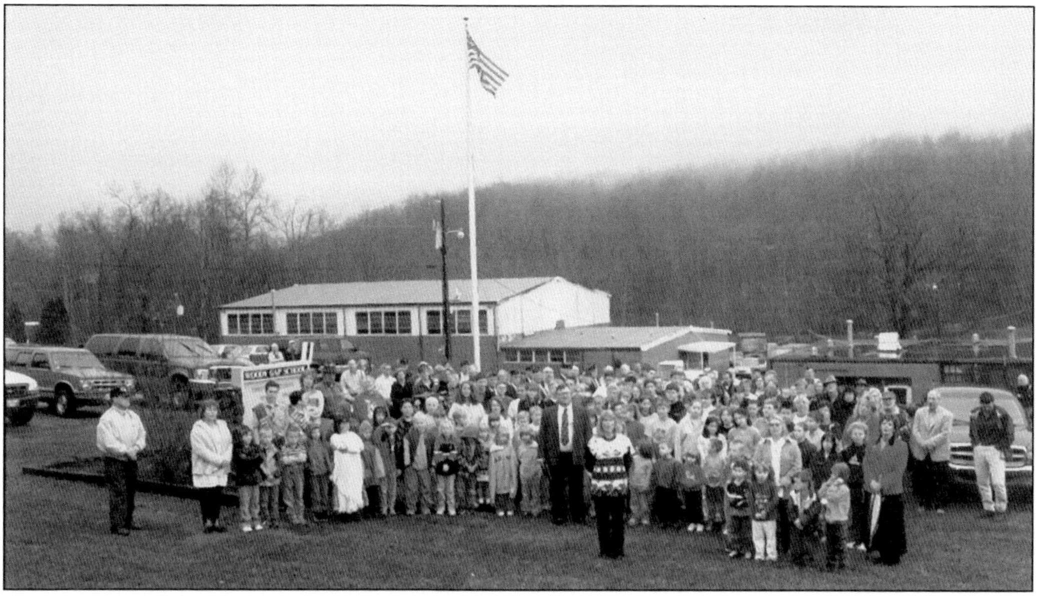

Woody Gap School has traditionally been the smallest public school in Georgia, with most graduating classes in the single digits. The school is in Suches, in the area known as the Valley Above the Clouds. Most of the grades meet in the historic rock structure. In the background on the right is the lunchroom, and the tall building is the gym. The Indian Summer Festival is held on this campus. (Photo by Norman Cooper.)

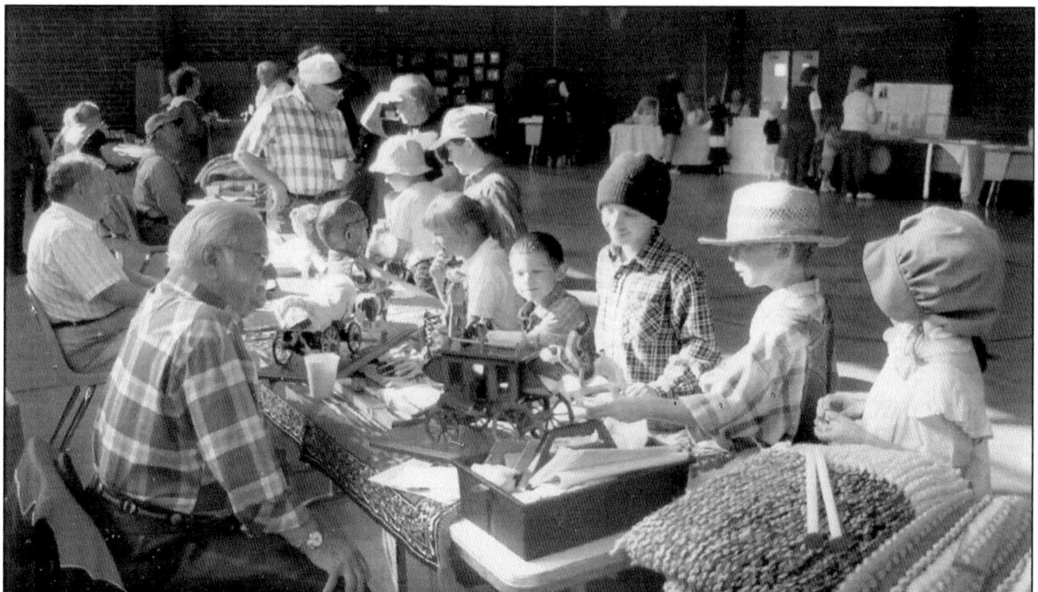

Woody Gap School holds an Old Fashion Day annually, where students and faculty are encouraged to dress in the style students would have worn decades ago. Exhibits are set up by local residents so students can see what life in the area was like in the past. Crafts, churning butter, sawing logs, petting animals, spinning yarn, and grinding corn are just a few of the activities that take place. Bluegrass music is played on period instruments. (Photo by Norman Cooper.)

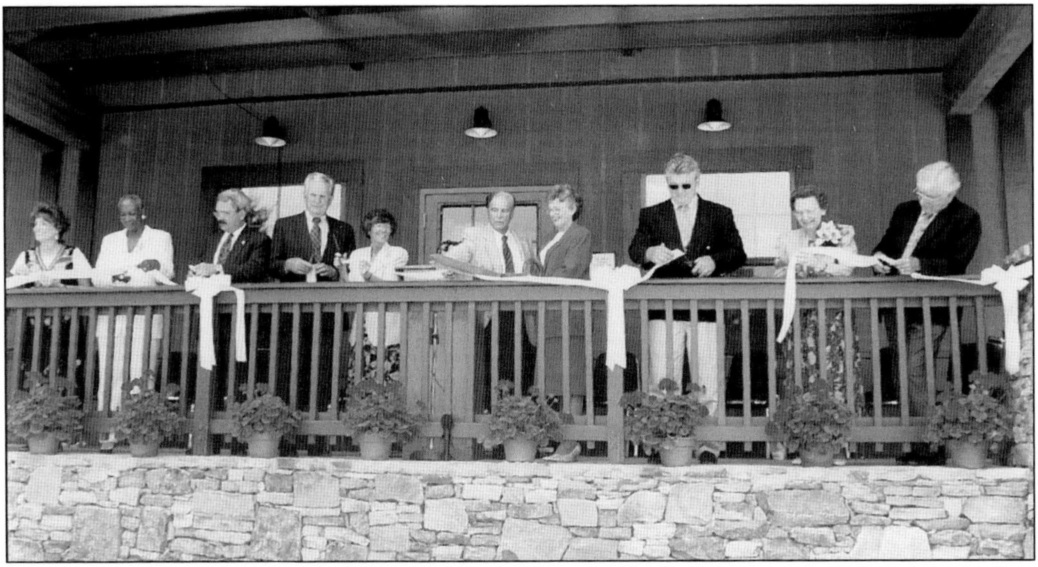

The Shirley Miller Building is home to the Lifelong Learning Center. Shirley Carver Miller, First Lady of Georgia, made improving adult literacy a top priority when Gov. Zell Miller was in office. Participating in the ribbon-cutting ceremony in June 1996 are, from left to right, Dr. Ruth Nichols, Dr. Jean DeVard-Kemp, Dr. Kenneth Breaden, Rep. Carlton Colwell, Dr. Judy Hulsey, Commissioner Glenn Gooch, Shirley Miller, Curtis Colwell, Renva Acree, and Rep. Ralph Twiggs. Each year, hundreds of students use the facility. Teachers have included Pattie Hamilton, Cathy Wheeler, and Kathy Rich. (Photo by Norman Cooper.)

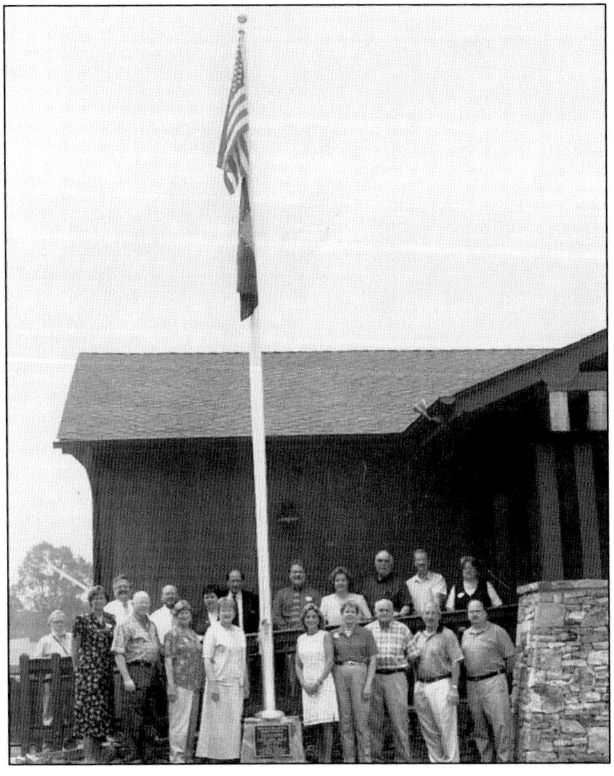

The dedication ceremony for the new flagpole at the LLLC took place in 2001. Attending the dedication are, from left to right (front row) Cathy Wheeler, Roy Hamby, Martha Cone, Carol Head, Dr. Ruth Nichols, Dr. Barbara Melichar, Bob Head, Lamar Paris, and Norman Cooper; (second row) Toby Laster, Dr. Michael King, Dr. Mark Ivester, Joanne Greer, Dr. Jim Watkins, Bobby Nash, Jean Easterling, Tom Murphy, Charles Sowers, and Jerri Allen.

Five

Sports

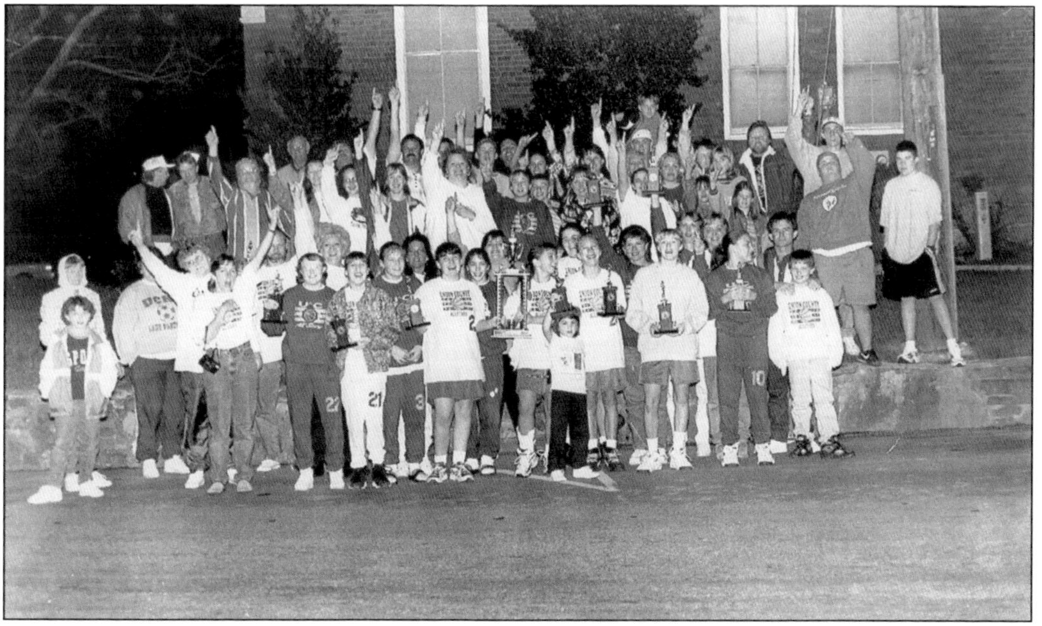

Union County Recreation Department 11–12 Girls Basketball All-Stars captured the Georgia Recreation and Parks State Basketball Championship in 1998. Members of the team included Natasha Wallace, Kelly Panter, Leah Prince, Stacy Garrett, Kellie Hughes, Nakeshia Stepp, Shay Farrell, Miranda Ingram, Tiffany Lee, and Christa Beeler. Coaches were Michelle Ingram and Terry Barrett. This photo was taken on the downtown Blairsville around midnight after the team returned from the game. (Photo by Norman Cooper.)

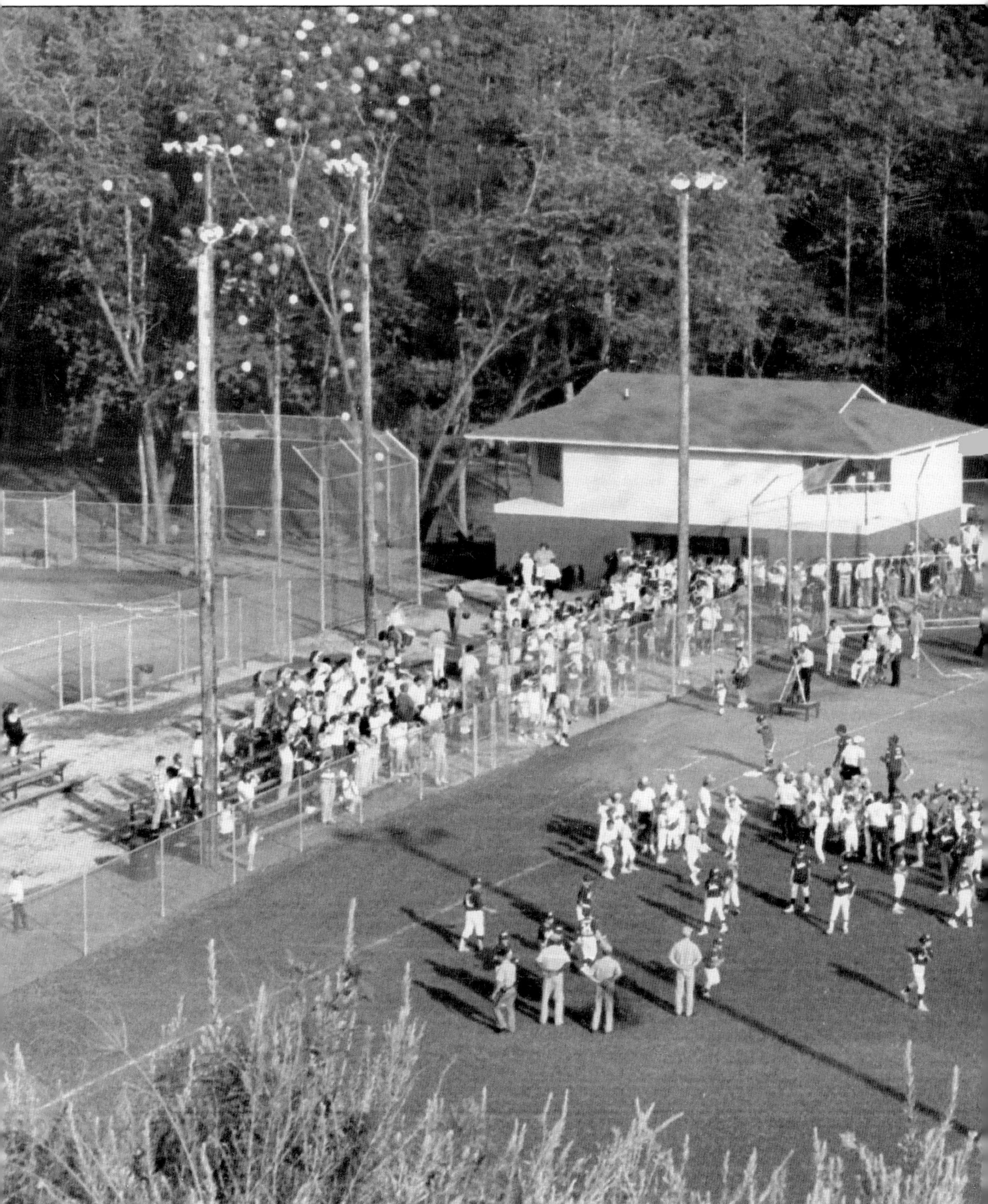

The dedication of Meeks Park in 1991 began a new era of recreational opportunities in Union County. Ball games were played on the new fields. The park featured a kids'

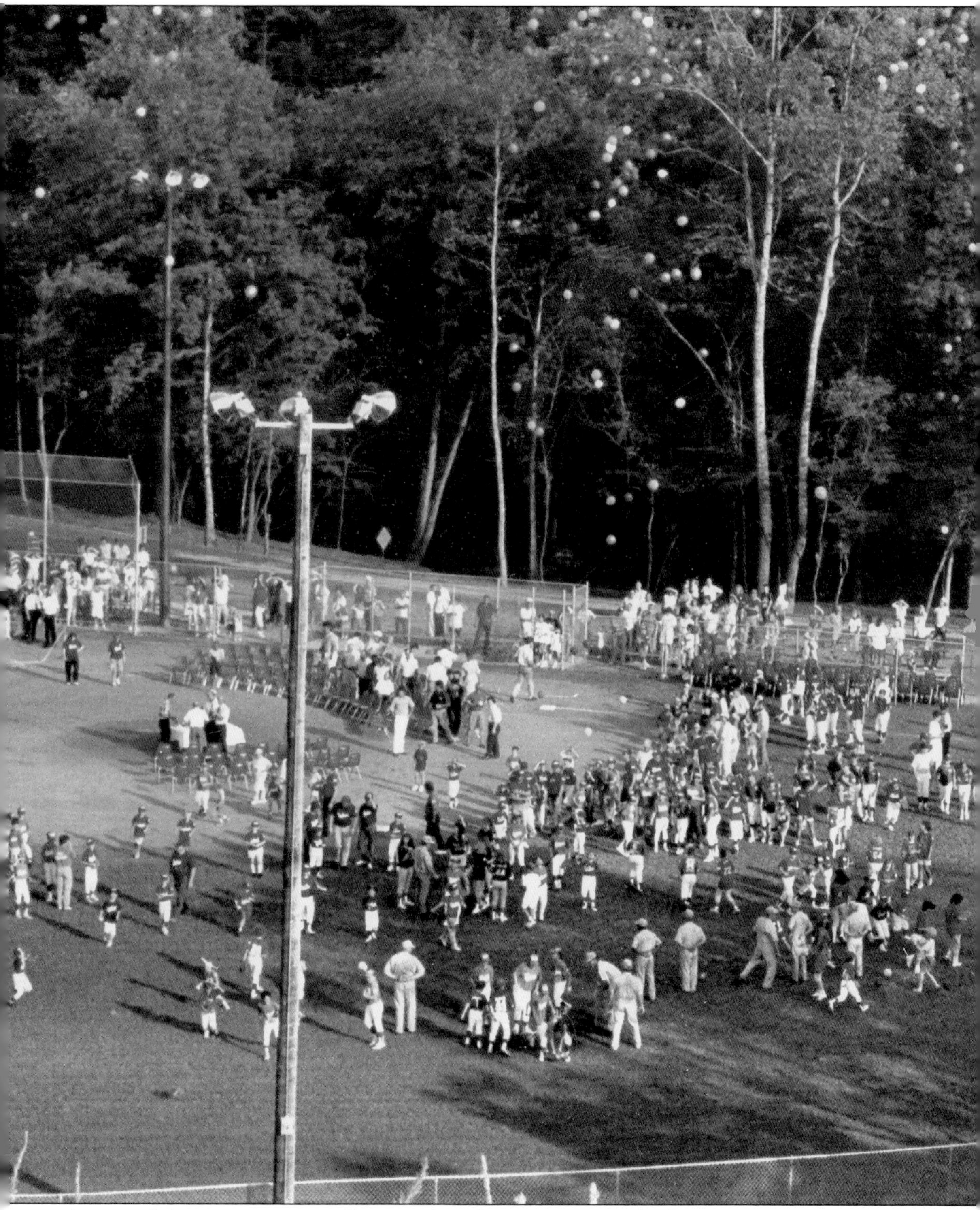

playground, batting cages, a walking trail, and concession stands. (Courtesy Union County Recreation Department.)

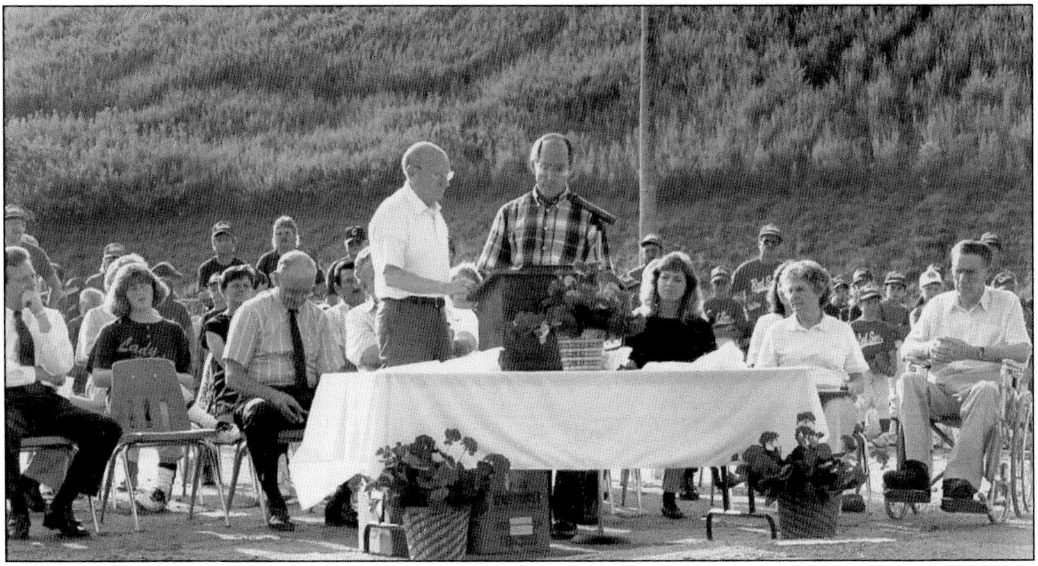

The creation of Meeks Park was made possible when Bill Meeks gifted land along Butternut Creek to Union County. Members of the recreation boards in the 1980s and early 1990s were instrumental in helping the county acquire the land. These boards included Lamar Paris, Jimmy Tallent, Sharon Devereaux, Peggy Callaway, and many others. The dedication ceremony took place in 1991. Bill Meeks, standing at left, is presented a plaque by Union County Recreation Board chairman Lamar Paris. (Photo courtesy Union County Recreation Department.)

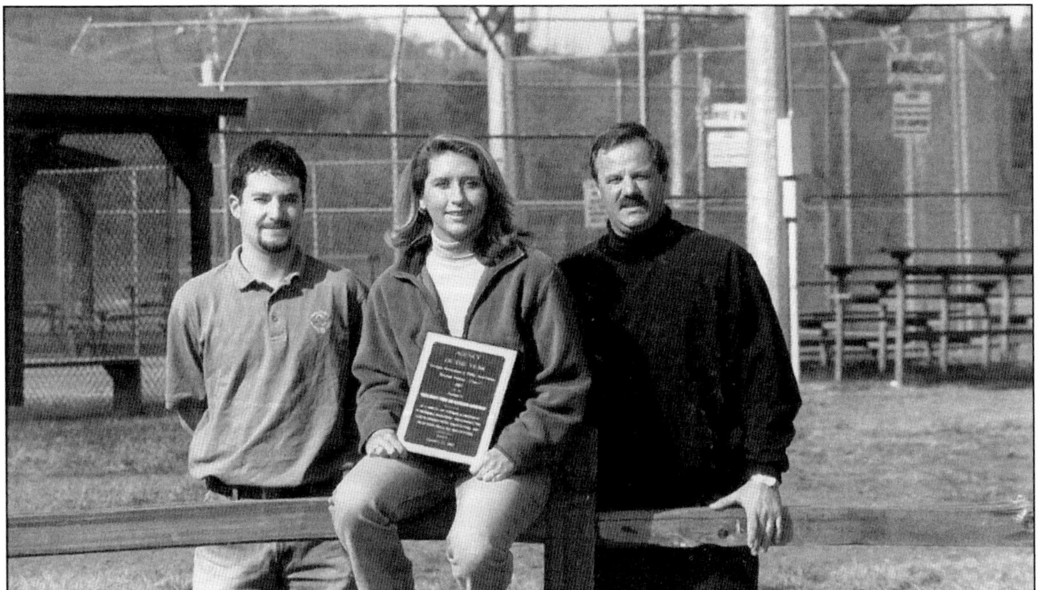

The Union County Recreation Department was named Agency of the Year for District 7 Class C by the Georgia Recreation and Parks Association in October 2002. Shown with the plaque are athletic director Brad Ballard, Meeks Park director Missy Brown, and recreation director Larry Garrett. Garrett took over as Union County recreation director in the early 1990s, when he also assumed the duties of head golf professional and manager of Butternut Creek Golf Course (Photo by Norman Cooper.)

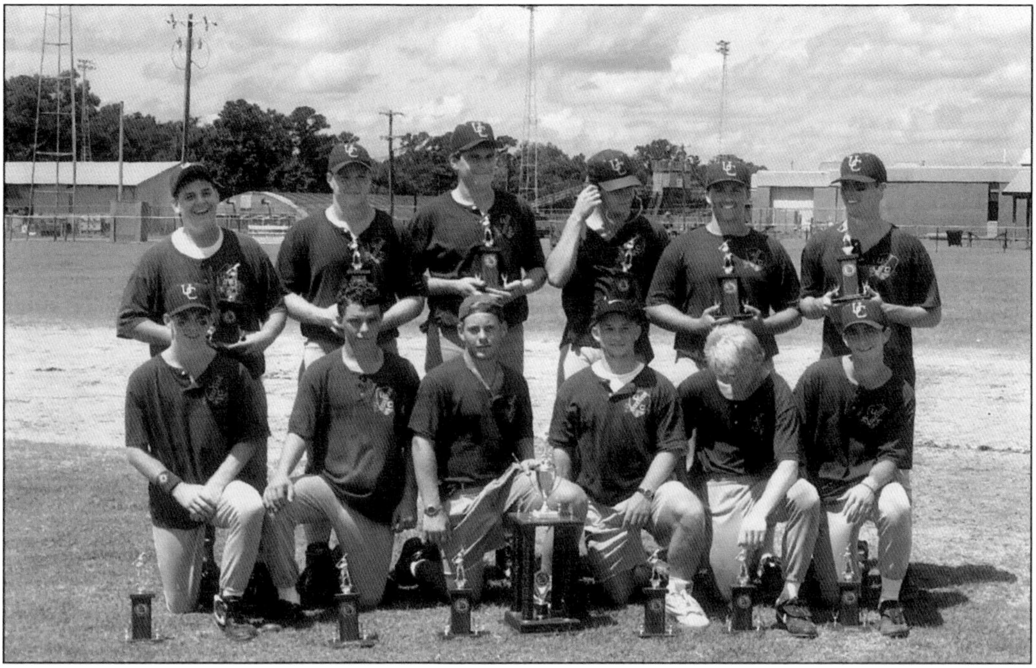

The 1995 U-18 GRPA State Champions included, from left to right, (front row) Chad Rich, Jason Helton, Chad Spiva, John Davis, Wesley Garrett, Cory Conley; (back row) Davey Murray, Kyle Yound, Coach Robert Harkins, Coach Andrew Burks, Jared Henson, and Nathan Helton. (Courtesy Judy Spiva.)

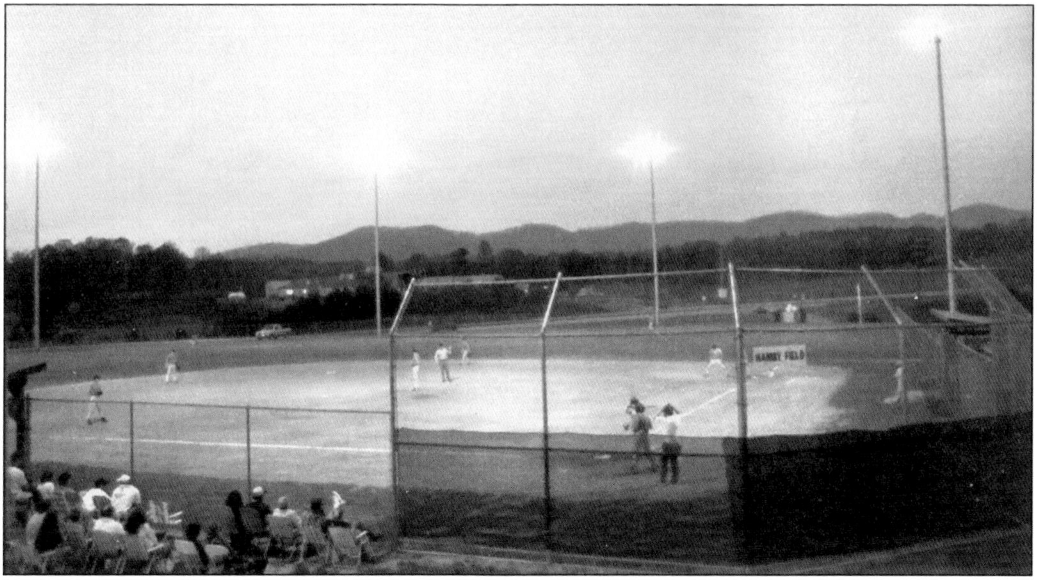

Three new fields opened in 1995 were named in honor of Lamar Paris, Glenn Hamby, and Arthur McAfee. Two fields at Meeks Park are named in honor of Georgia state representative Carlton Colwell. Two fields are named in memory of Barry Bryant and Mike Rich. The Colwell Fields were home to the Union County Recreation Baseball U-18 All-Stars, who won the Georgia Parks and Recreation State Championship in 1995. Seen above is a night game at Meeks Park. (Photo by Norman Cooper.)

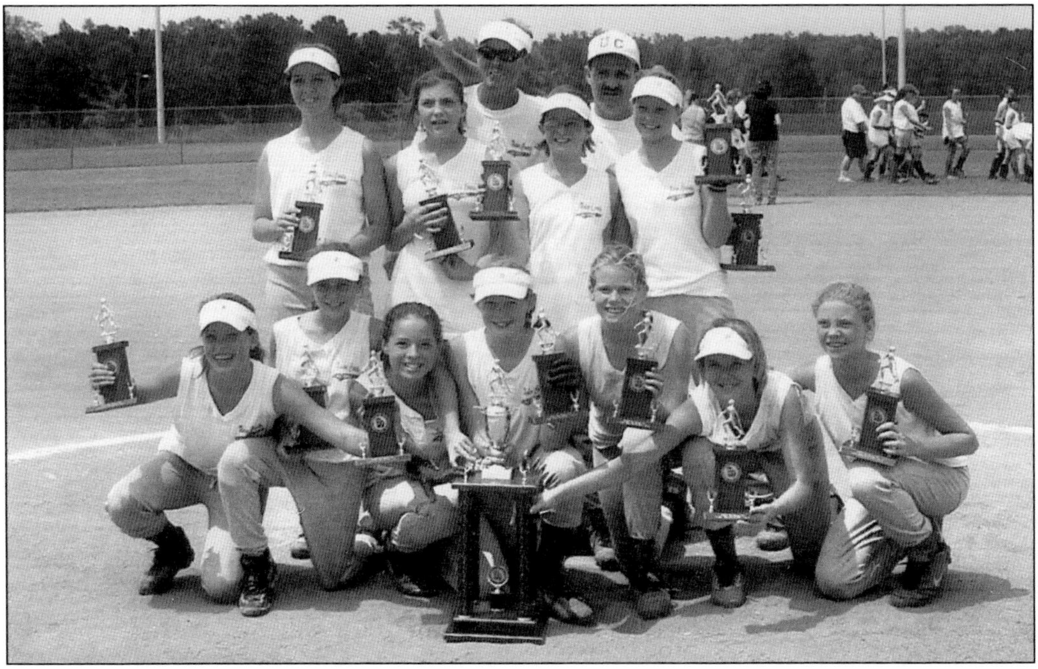

The 2001 State Champs Union County Recreation Department U-12 fast-pitch softball team is, from left to right, (kneeling) Kaley Sullivan, Dana Seabolt, Lauren Dyer, Jennifer Wheeler, C.J. Penland, and Abigail Williams; (standing) Laura Stewart, Alicia Morrow, coach Ralph Beattie, Jess Seabolt, coach David Seabolt, and Amanda Mason.

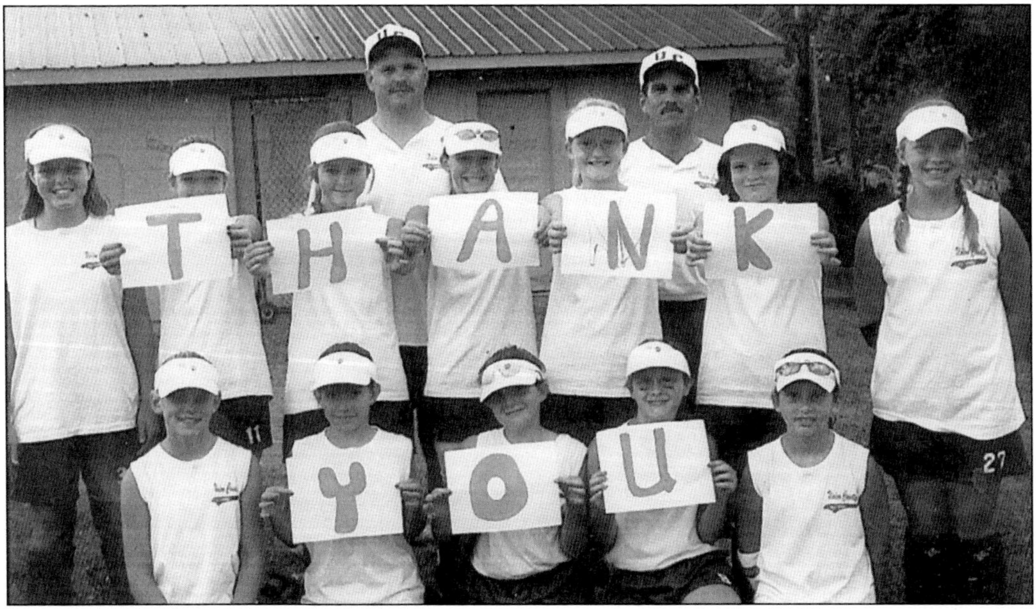

The 2001 State Champs Union County Recreation Department U-10 fast-pitch softball team is, from left to right, (kneeling) Lorianne Huggins, Jessie Payne, Courtney Seabolt, Heather Chastain, and Ashley Wimpey; (standing) April Harper, Brittany Lentz, Laurie Owenby, coach Travis Swartz, Brooklyn Swartz, Laren Brown, coach Doug Harper, Courtney Watts, and Kayla Gowder.

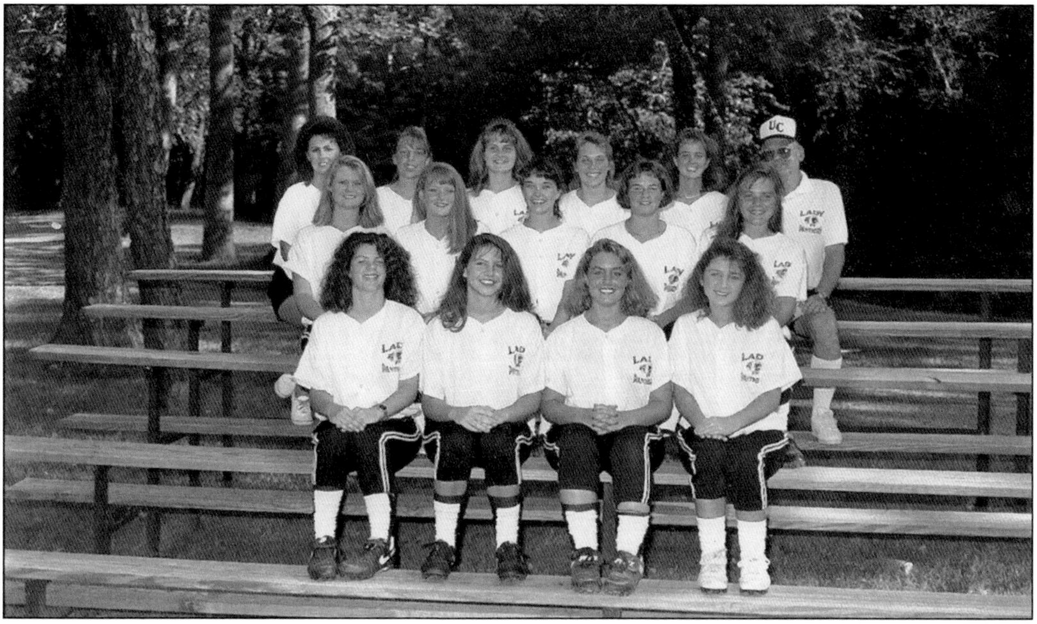

Jacque Devereaux Sr. was an umpire and coach of Pony League baseball and traveling softball teams and was instrumental in establishing softball in Union County. Devereaux was president of the Umpire Association for 16 years. He coached until his death in 2001. This team included, from left to right, (front row) Laura Conley, Haley Colwell, Jennifer Dillinger, and Angie Shubert; (middle row) Laura McCook, Dana Devereux, Megan Collins, Mandy Bradley, and Pam Turner; (back row) coach Jeanne Tallent, Lori Brackett, Christy Queen, Kelley Queen, Jana Tallent, and coach Jacque Devereaux Sr. (Courtesy Dana Devereaux.)

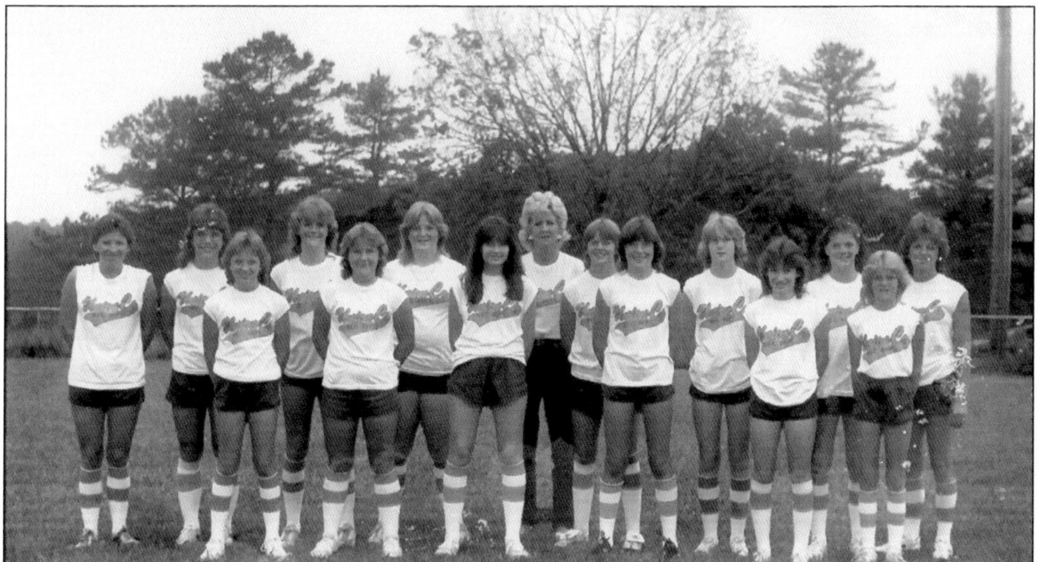

The Recreation Department Slow-Pitch Softball team includes, from left to right, Vicki Lance, Shelia Rose, Karla Rowan, Jamesa Dobbs, Candi Bergen, Marcia Devereaux, Cynthia Brendle, Pat Dobbs, Kim Wilson, Wendy Moss, Ona Crawford, Joanna Dyer, Jennifer Dyer, Tracy Ledford, and Janie Rowan. (Photo courtesy Judy Spiva,)

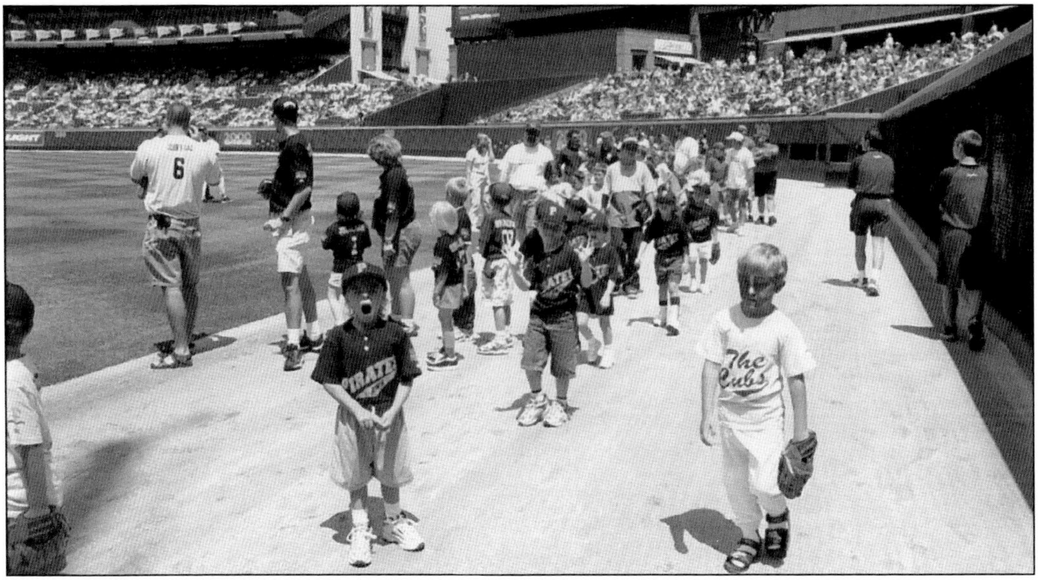

Nearly 1,000 citizens from Union County attended the first Union County Night at Turner Field in the late 1990s. Uniformed players and coaches walked the field before the Braves game, treading on the turf where one of major league baseball's favorite teams plays. The event was co-sponsored by the Union County Recreation Department and the *North Georgia News*.

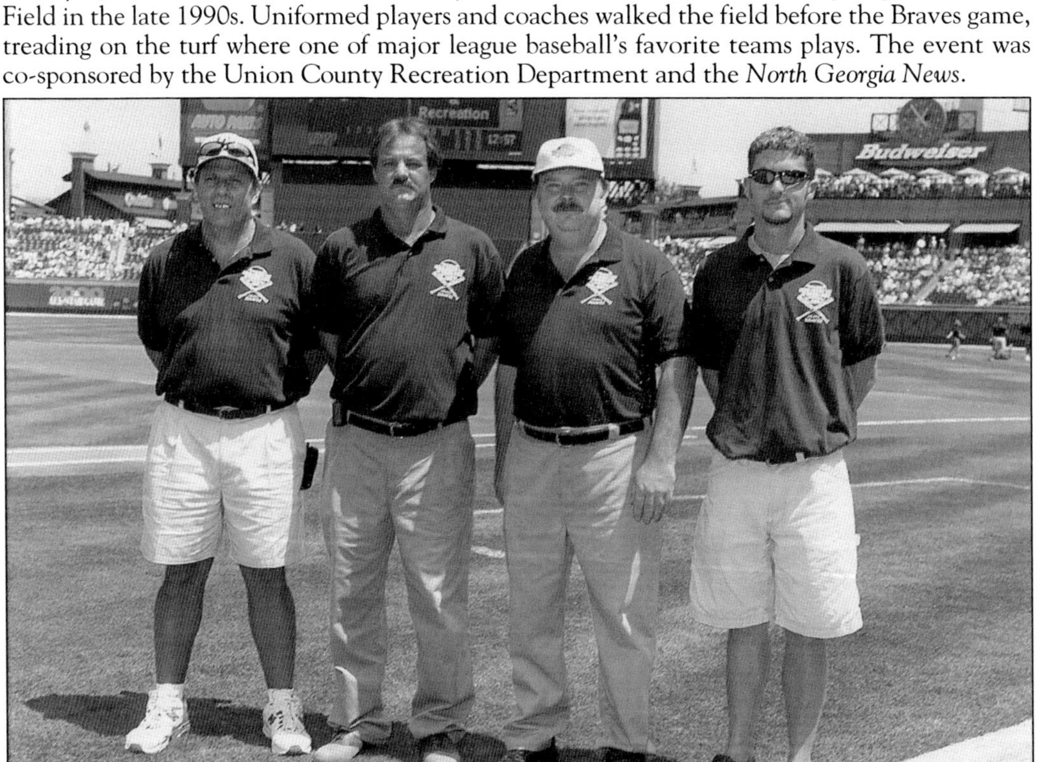

Coordinating the Union County Night at Turner Field event were Andy Ladd of the Union County Recreation Department, Union County recreation director Larry Garrett, *North Georgia News* editor/sports editor Norman Cooper, and Brad Ballard of the Union County Recreation Department. Cooper and Ladd served as masters of ceremonies, addressing the more than 40,000 fans in pre-game ceremonies.

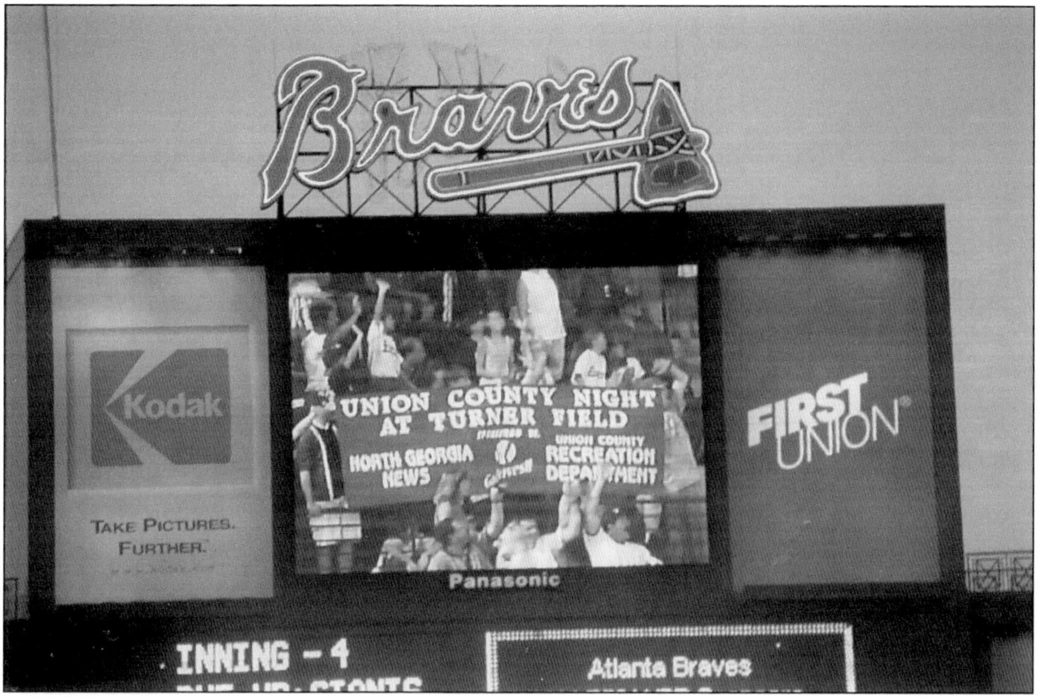

A large banner used in the pre-game ceremonies leading the parade of hundreds of players was held high between innings during the game. Here the banner is being shown on the huge board in centerfield at Turner Field.

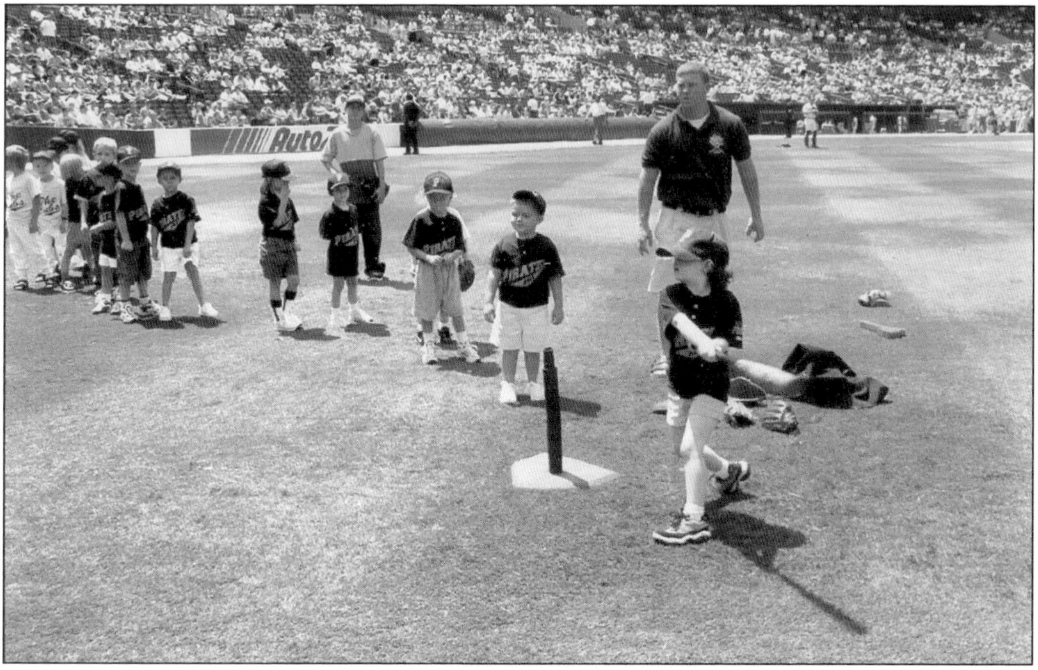

During pre-game activities on Union County Night at Turner Field, t-ball players from the Union County Recreation Department had the chance to hit and run in the Atlanta Braves' outfield.

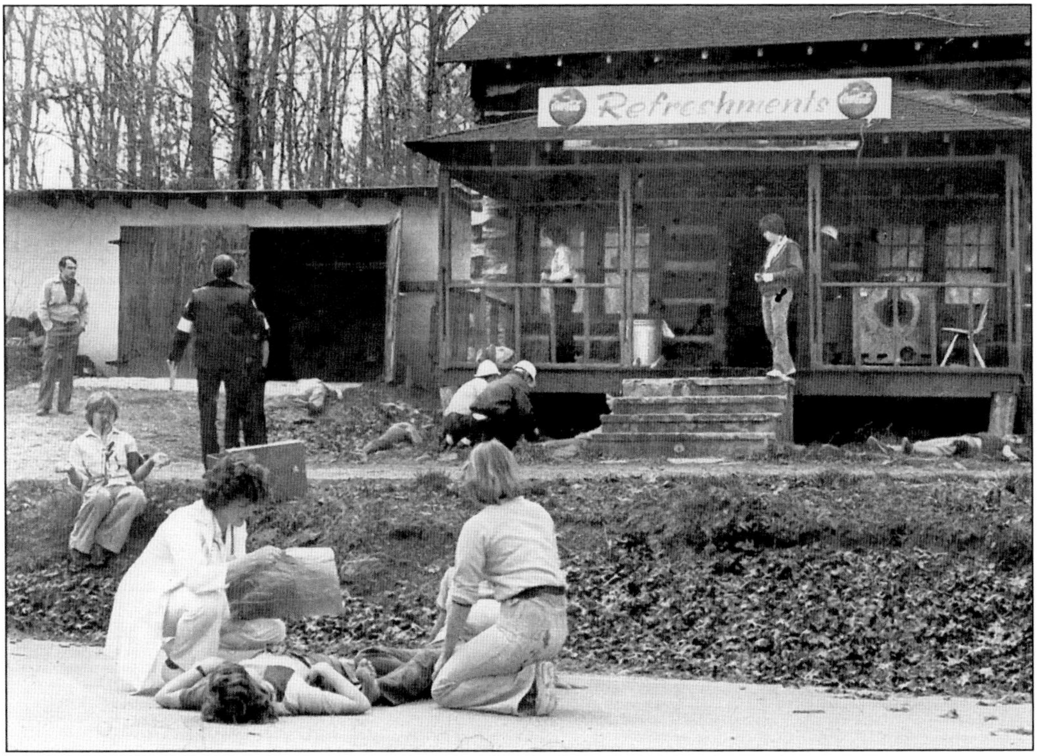

The original clubhouse for the golf course was located on Golf Course Road, just off Highway 515. (Courtesy Union County Recreation Department.)

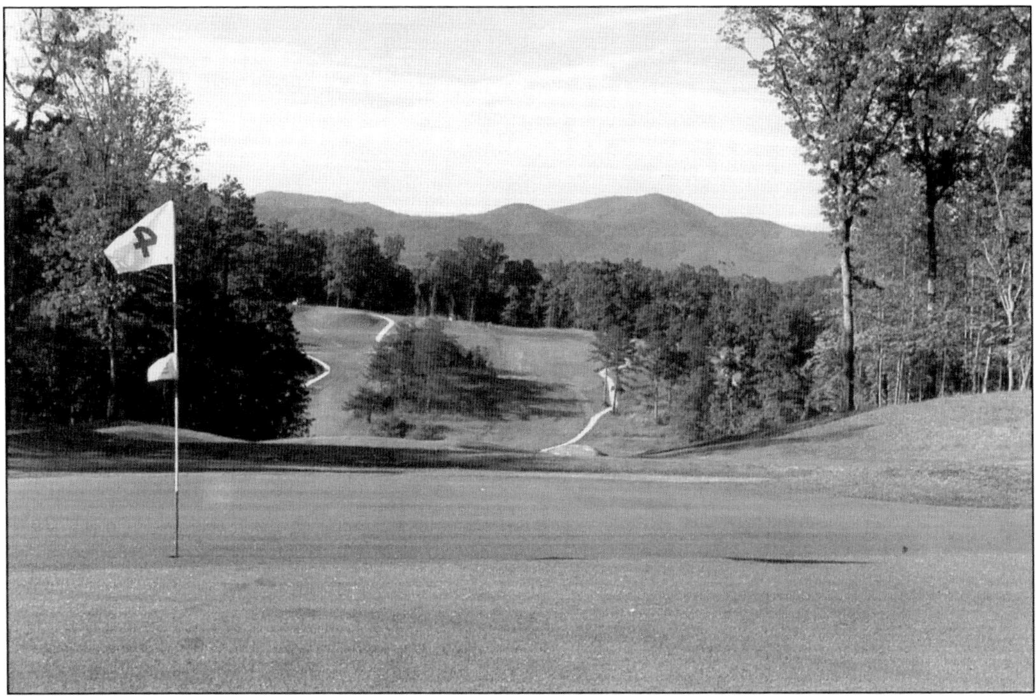

Pictured here is hole number 16 at Butternut Creek Golf Course.

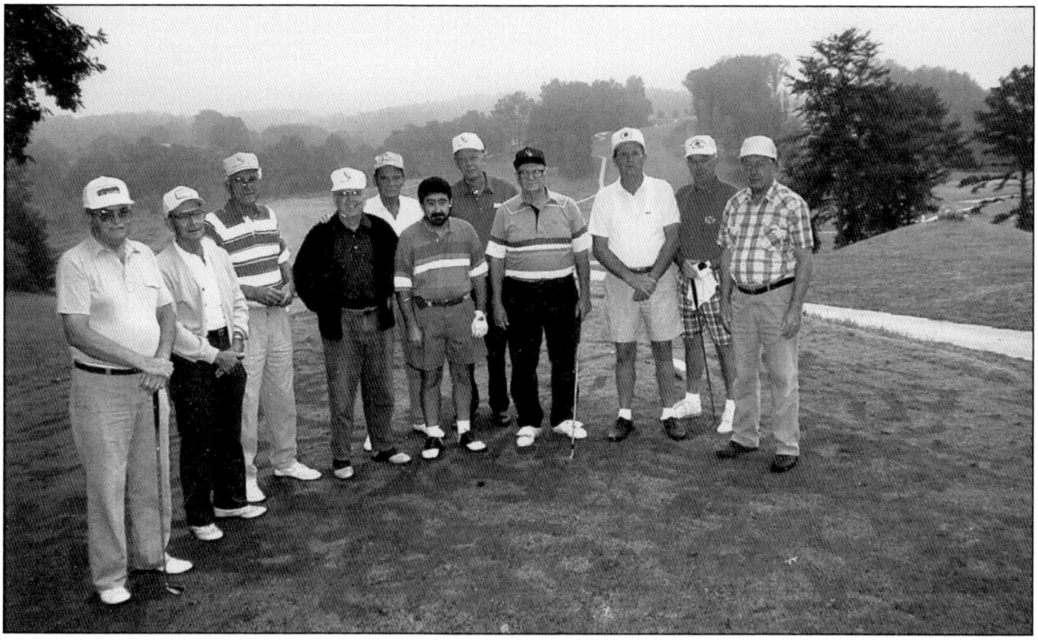

The first golfers to play on the new 18 holes on September 7, 1994, are from left to right, Ray Rhoten, Hoyt Cunningham, Jim Poe, Tommy Dolar, Leroy Cunningham, Clinton Patterson, Earl Odom, Earl Bonnette, Harold Plott, Reid Gillis, and John Ledford. (Courtesy Butternut Creek Golf Course.)

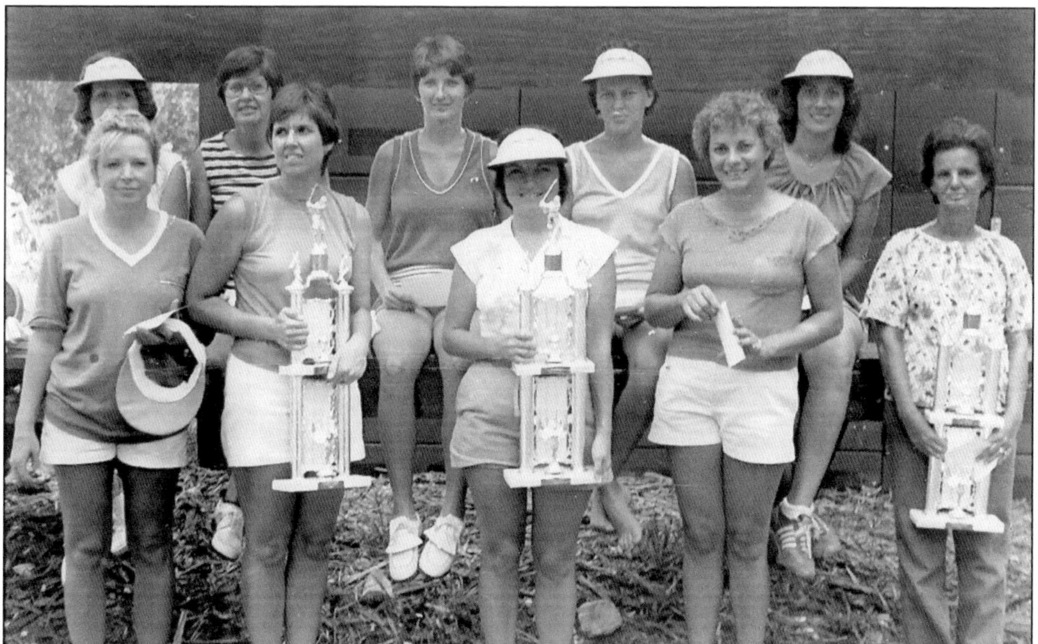

Pictured at the Ladies' Golf Tournament at Butternut Creek Golf Course in the late 1970s are, from left to right, (front row) Jackie White, Eva Decker, Kathy McAfee, Peggy Fair Shuler, and Sally Thomas; (back row) Sandy Birchfield, Patricia Plott, Peggy Wells, Judy Spiva, and Janey Dyer. (Courtesy Butternut Creek Golf Course.)

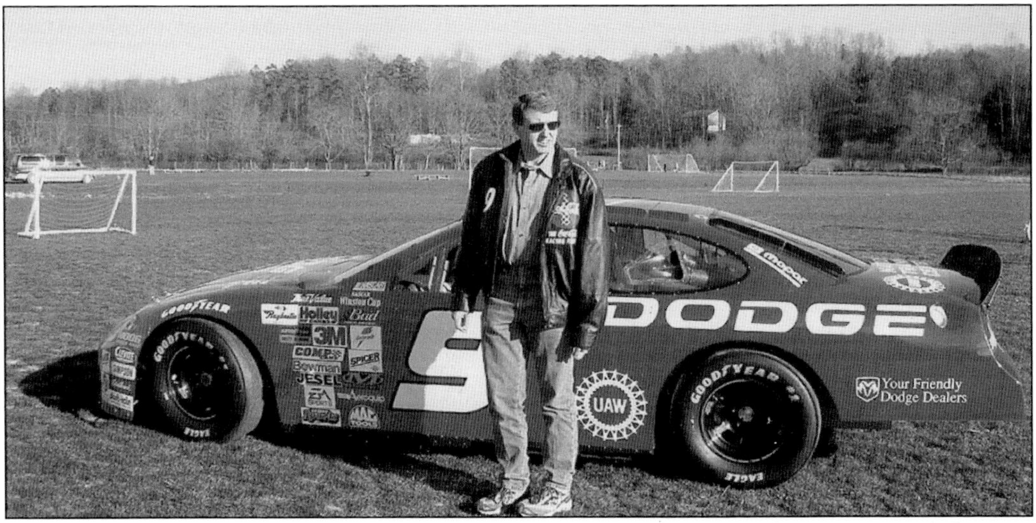

Bill Elliott, a resident of Union County, is known as "Awesome Bill" for his accomplishments in racing. Elliott quietly, generously supports community programs and national charities. In the 26 years since his first Winston Cup race, Bill Elliott has seen and done it all. In that time, he has amassed 659 starts, 41 wins, 51 poles, 160 top-5 finishes, and 294 top-10 finishes. During the 1985 season he won a record 11 races. He won the NASCAR Winston Cup Championship in 1988 and the National Motorsports Press Association's most popular driver award 15 times. Elliott is one of only seven drivers to top $20 million in career winnings. He was named one of NASCAR's 50 Greatest Drivers of All Time in 1998. (Photo by Norman Cooper.)

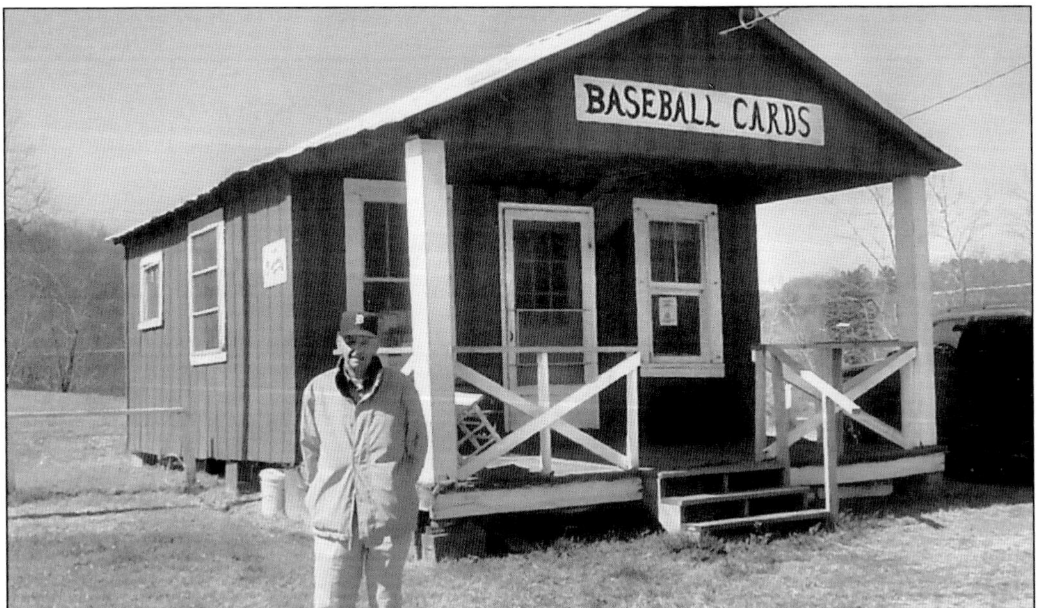

Glenn Hamby played minor league baseball for the Chicago Cubs and California Angels with a batting average of .323 and 11 home runs. Coaching in the Union County Recreation Department, he had a record of 211 wins and only 9 losses in 13 years. Hamby umpired for 35 years in various levels. He also served on the original recreation board in the county. Hamby opened his baseball card shop in 1990. (Photo by Norman Cooper.)

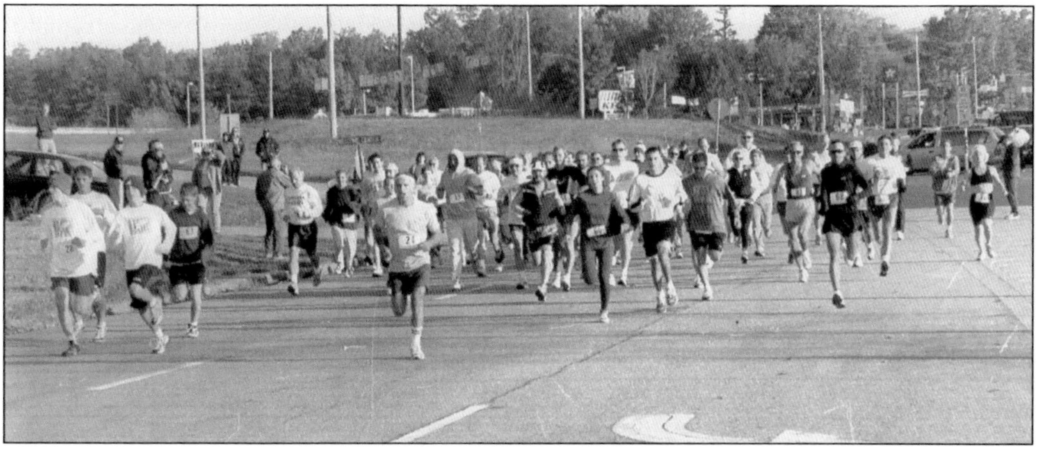

Union County hosted a road race on Independence Day for many years, sponsored by the Blairsville–Union County Chamber of Commerce and coordinated by President Scott Carter and Executive Director Jean Easterling. Overall winners were awarded, and awards were given to runners in various age and gender divisions. The event featured a race through downtown Blairsville. Those who wanted a short jog or a brisk walk over a short distance participated in the fun run. (Photo by Norman Cooper.)

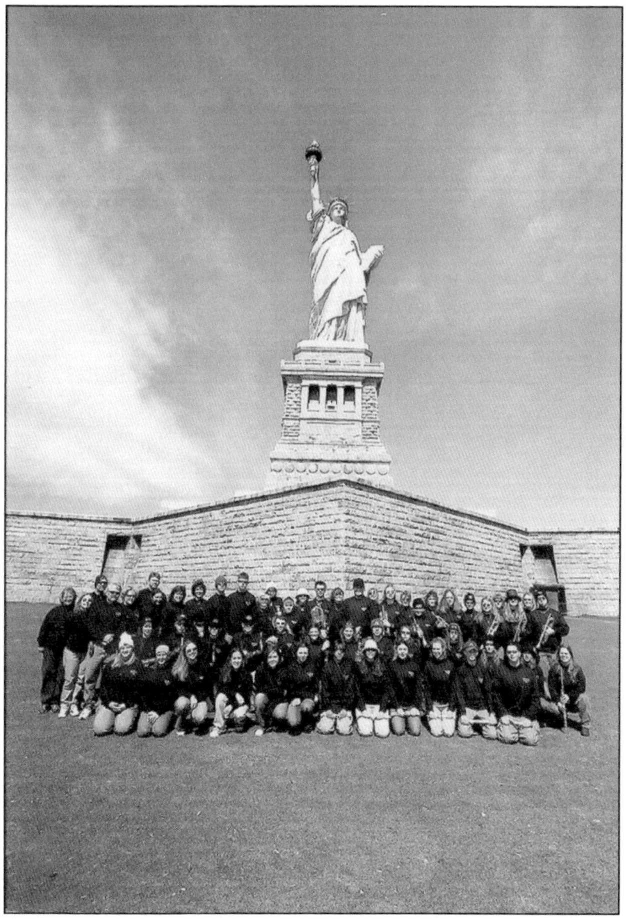

The Union County High School Marching Band is featured during the football season at halftime. The band has been under the direction of Alan Denmon twice. They perform in the Christmas, Sorghum Festival, and Memorial Day parades. They provide music at various functions, including the Memorial Day ceremony at the Union County War Memorial. In 2003, the band performed at the Statue of Liberty in New York.

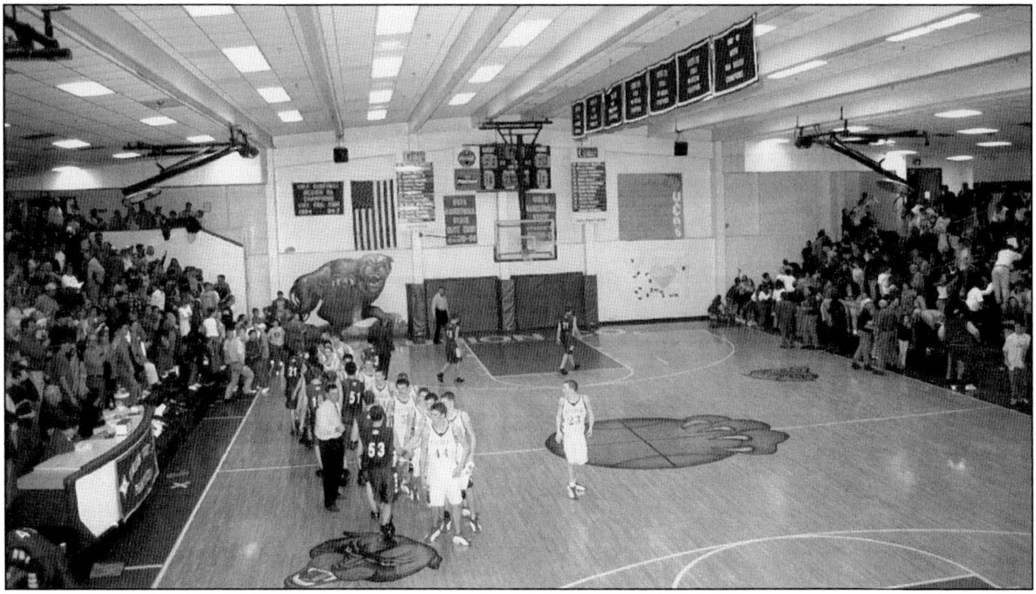

Union County High School said farewell to the Pit in spring 2002. Seen here is the last basketball game to be played in the gym that opened decades earlier. Panthers teams playing here included the 1970–1971 region champions and state runners-up, 1971–1972 region champions and final four, and 1972–1973 region champions. Lady Panthers teams included the 1972–1973 region champions, 1973–1974 region champions and final four, 1993–1994 region champions and state elite eight, and 2000–2001 state runners-up. (Photo by Norman Cooper.)

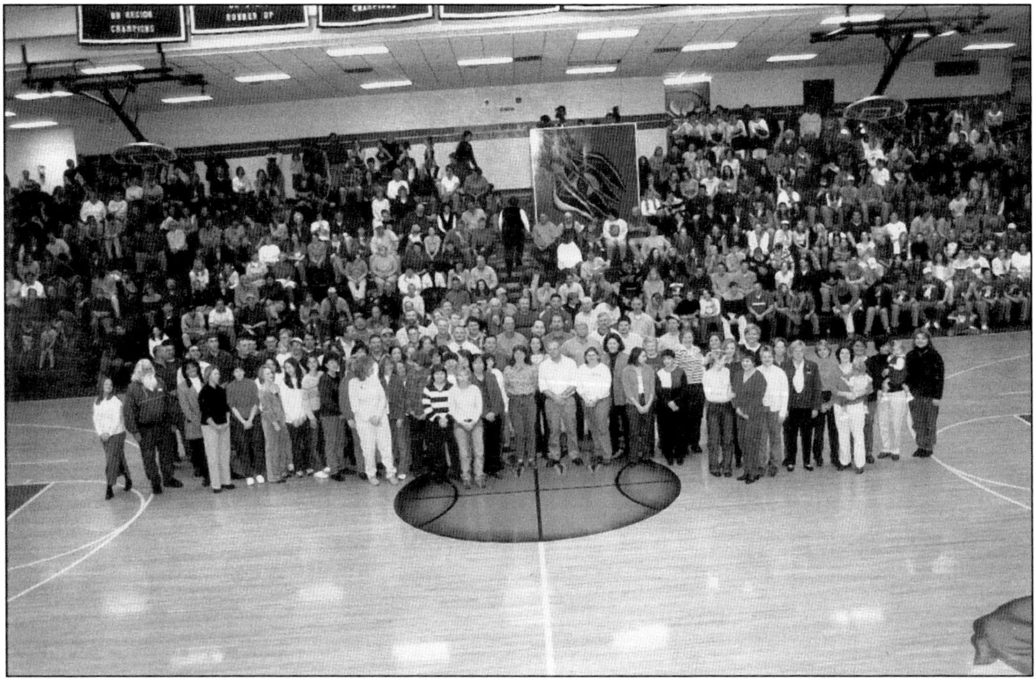

When Union County High School said farewell to the old gym, all those who had played, coached, or been an active part of teams in the gym were asked to come to center court. (Photo by Norman Cooper.)

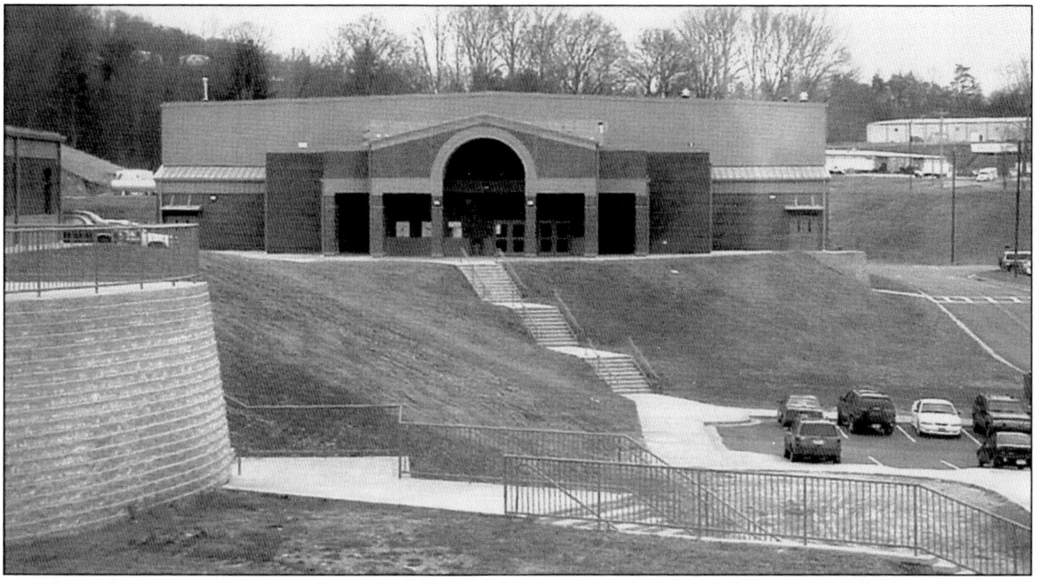

As the school system grew dramatically in the 1990s, the need for new facilities increased. When the new high school was constructed, a new gymnasium was also built. With an estimated seating capacity of 1,600, the facility includes a spacious concession area, adequate restrooms for large crowds, ample parking, classrooms, exceptionally nice locker rooms, coaches' offices, large practice room, and a well-equipped weight room. (Photo by Norman Cooper.)

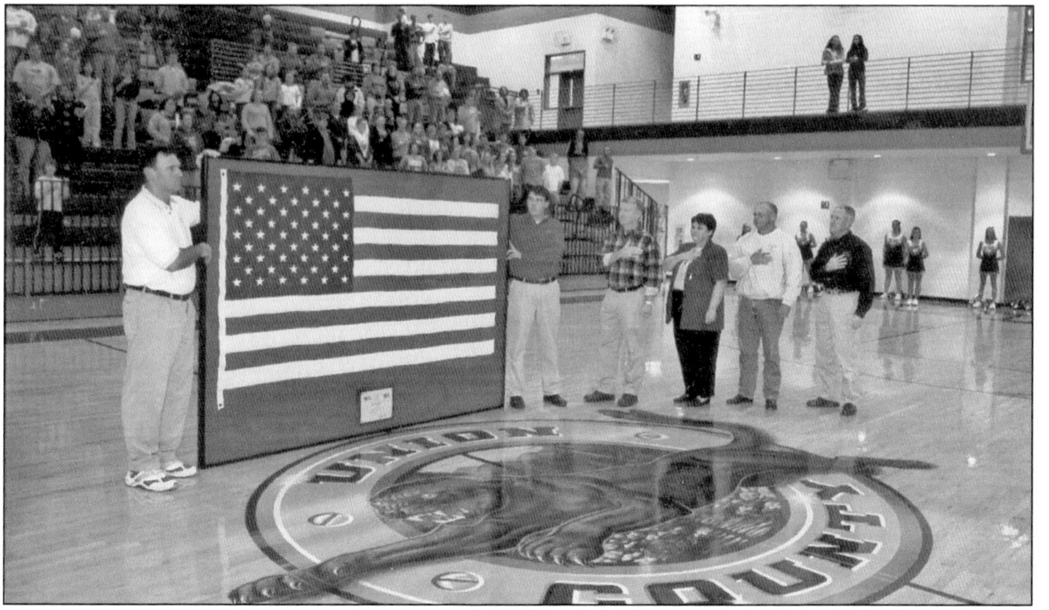

The dedication of the new gym included a large American flag framed behind glass. The flag and frame were donated by United Community Bank. Jim Hughes, far left, and Jimmy Nichols hold the frame during the Pledge of Allegiance. Joining in the pledge were Union County superintendent Tommy Stephens, Union County High principal Dr. Marty Hale, Union County High athletic director Terry Rogers, and United Community Bank president Andy Williams. Note the remarkable painting on the floor at center court. (Photo by Norman Cooper.)

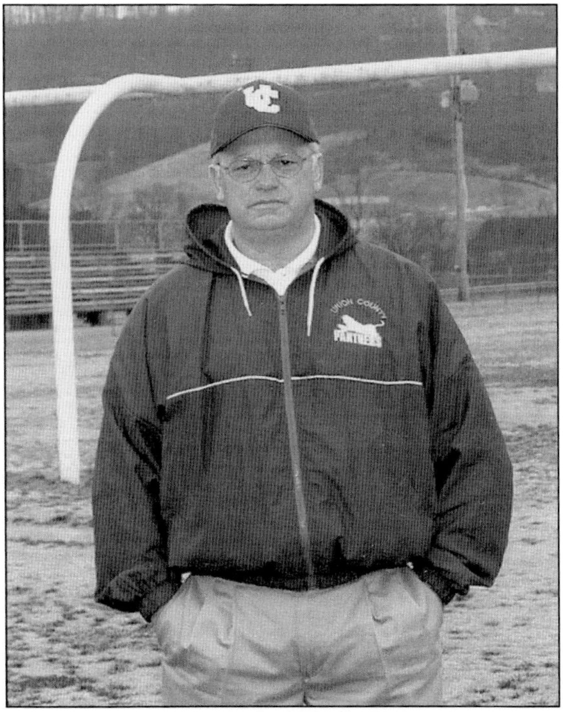

Terry Rogers has been a coach and/or athletic director at Union County High for more than three decades. Rogers coached in the GACA North/South Football Game on the North staff in 1986 and 1994. Rogers' football teams in 1983, 1984, and 1985 were ranked in the state top 10; his girls' basketball teams were in the state top 10 in 1979, 1980, and 1981; and his boys' basketball team was in the state top 10 in 1998. His 1974 girls softball team was undefeated. Rogers has been in the Georgia Athletic Coaches Association for 34 years. He has served as third vice president, second vice president, and president. He is an executive committee member of the Georgia High School Association.

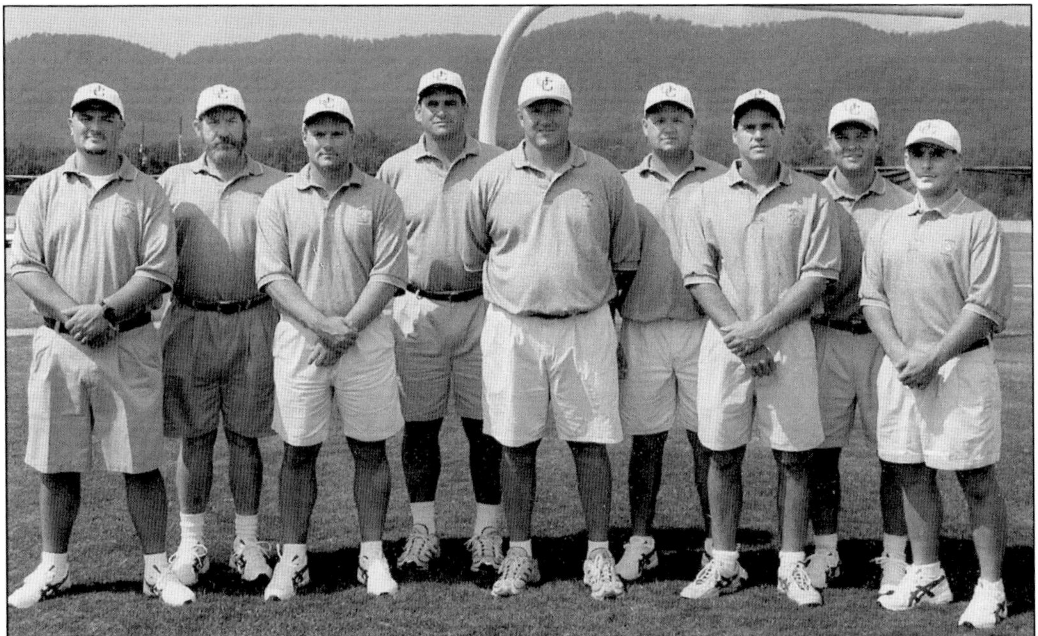

The football staff in the early 2000s has several coaches who attended Union County High. Pictured are Tim Hunter, Richard Long, Mark Donahue, Jim Hughes, Brian Allison, Shaun Conley, Howard McCombs, Ben Corley, and Robert Harkins. Hunter, Donahue, Allison, Conley, McCombs, Harkins, and Long all attended Union County High. Allison, Donahue, Conley, and McCombs played on the 1983 team that went 9–1 and went to postseason play. The 2001 team started a record 9–0 and advanced to postseason play.

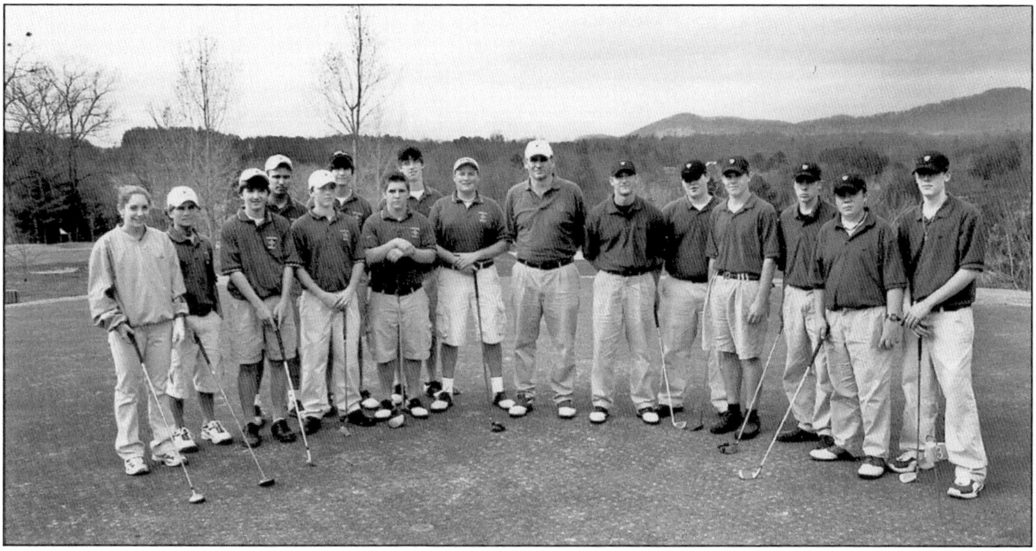

Golf teams from Union County High, on left, and Woody Gap High use Butternut Creek Golf Course. Union County coach Jim Hughes, center, has coached at Union County High for nearly two decades, taking over as head golf coach in 1997. He had 200 wins as a head varsity coach of girls' and boys' basketball. His girls' basketball team, which he coached for 12 years, had one region championship and two state top 10 finishes. Coach Hughes has also coached football and girls' track. Coach Hughes's daughter Kellie, on the girls' golf team, is seen at the far left. (Photo by Norman Cooper.)

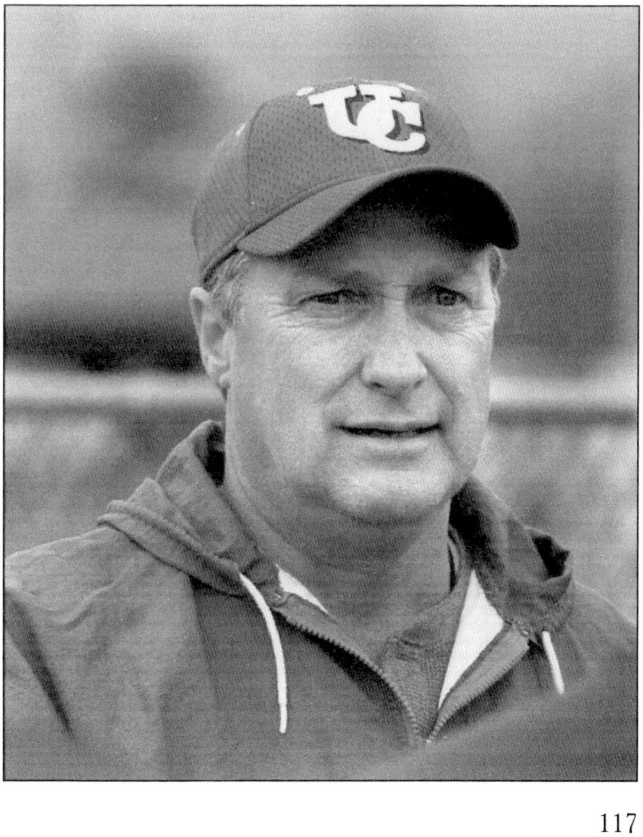

Larry Turner made his mark as a student and as a coach at Union County High. In 1971, Turner won first place with a state of Georgia record triple-jump distance of 43 feet, 3.5 inches. He played football, basketball, and baseball for four years. Coach Turner has skippered the baseball team for 26 years, winning 393 games. His team played in the state championships series in 1996, placing number two overall. He has three region championships and five sub-region championships.

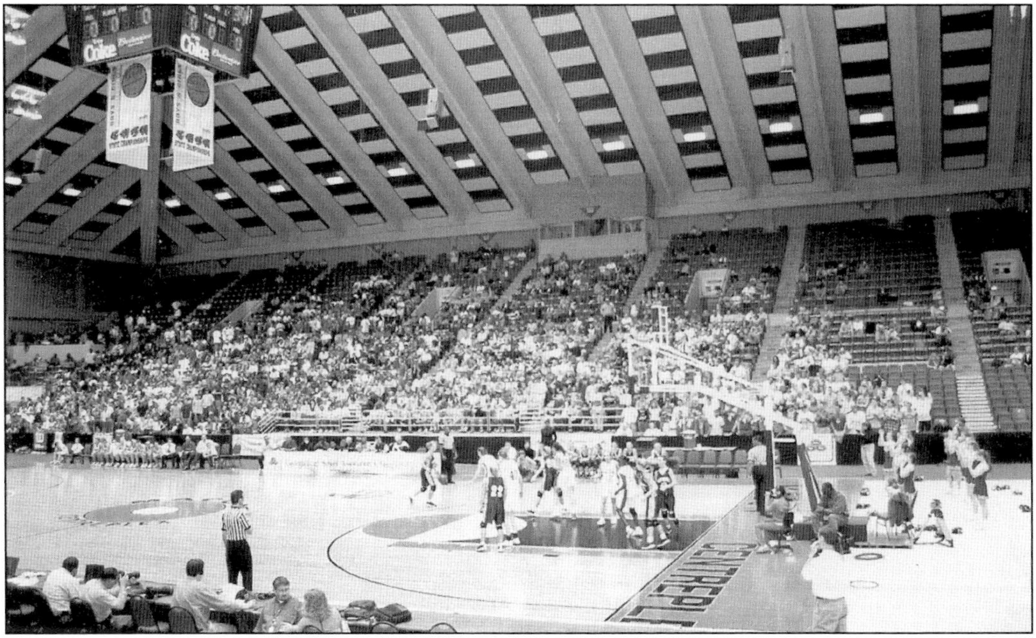

The Lady Panthers basketball team was the best team among public schools in Division AA and number two in the state, including private schools, after advancing to the state finals in the 2000–2001 season. They played in the state championship in the Macon Coliseum, seen above. (Photo by Norman Cooper.)

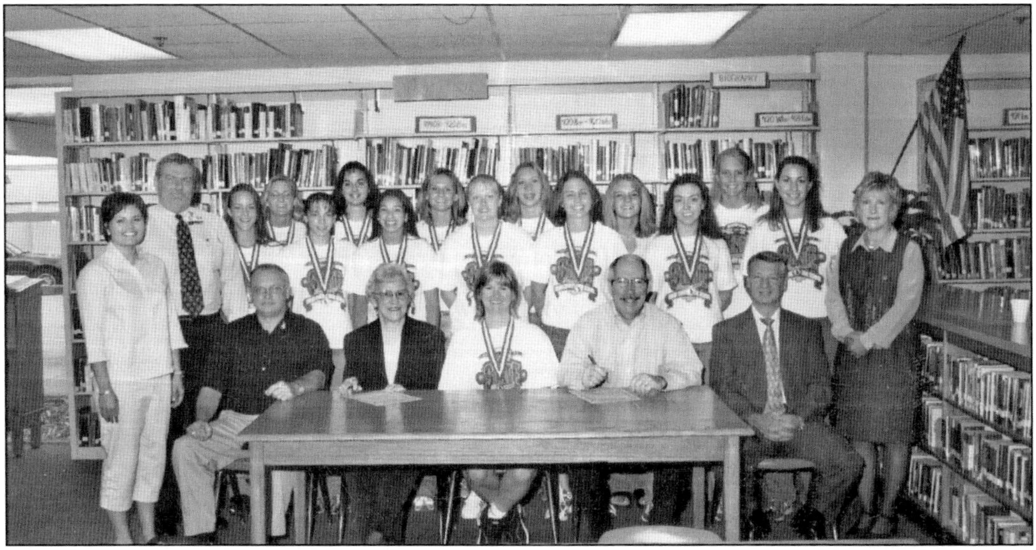

The Lady Panthers basketball team was honored by local officials after finishing second in the state in 2000–2001. The ceremony was attended by, from left to right, (seated) athletic director Terry Rogers, Blairsville mayor Doris Colwell, head coach Robbie Stancil, Union County commissioner Lamar Paris, and Union County superintendent Tommy Stephens; (standing) assistant coach Beth Crawford, principal Jim Clark, Nikki Gurley, Lauren Henderson, Kellie Hughes, Tali Patterson, Brittany Greene, Joanna Day-Lewis, Kelly Panter, Nakeisha Stepp, Nicki Patterson, Christa Beeler, Dana Barnes, Andrea Neely, Georgia Adams, and assistant principal Karen Roxbury. (Photo by Norman Cooper.)

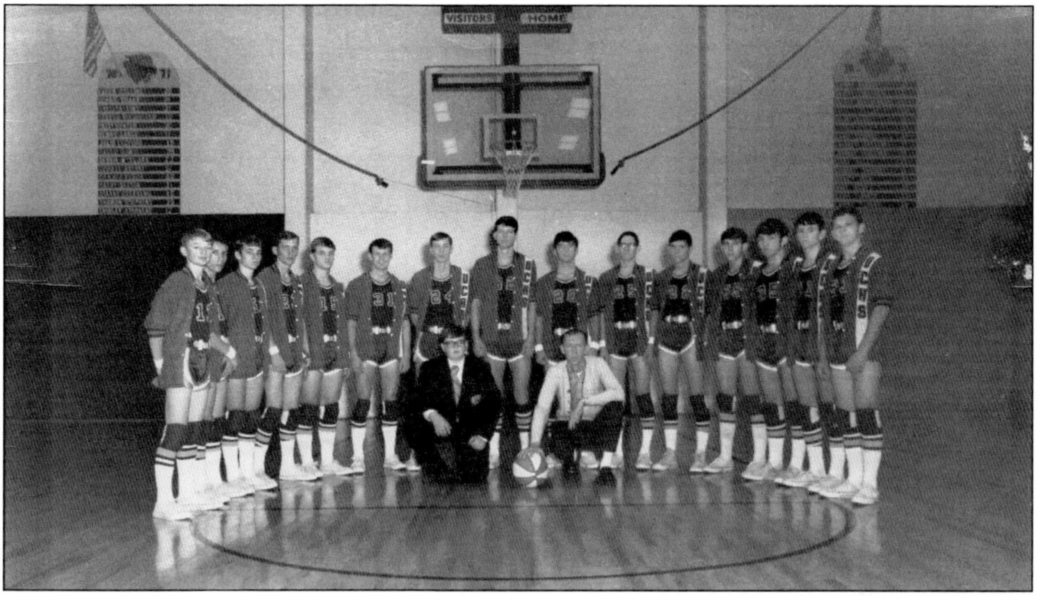

The Panthers advanced to the state basketball tournament in the 1971–1972 season. The team included, from left to right, (kneeling) team manager Rusty McClure and head coach Earl Odom, (standing) Johnny Huggins, Denny Bridges, Sammy Owenby, Gary Turner, Barry Collins, Lindsey Gregory, Larry Turner, Danny Arron, Mike Scott, Gary Kelly, Donald Kelley, Troy Collins, Ricky Rich, David Buchannan, and Gary George. Ray Sneed is not pictured. (Courtesy of Sharon Rohrbaugh.)

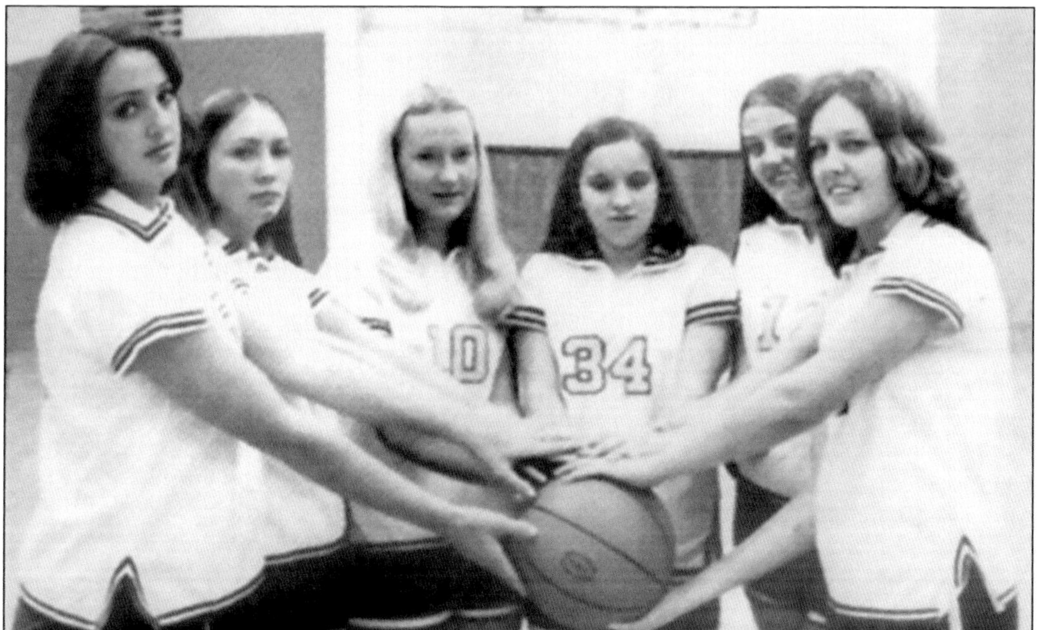

The Lady Panthers 1973–1974 basketball team was region champion and was in the state final four. Seniors on the team were, from left to right, Teresa Nicholson, Sandy Turner, Rosemary Merritt, Vickie Lance, Jamie Nichols, and Judy Burrell (not pictured Judy Rogers). (Courtesy UCHS Yearbook.)

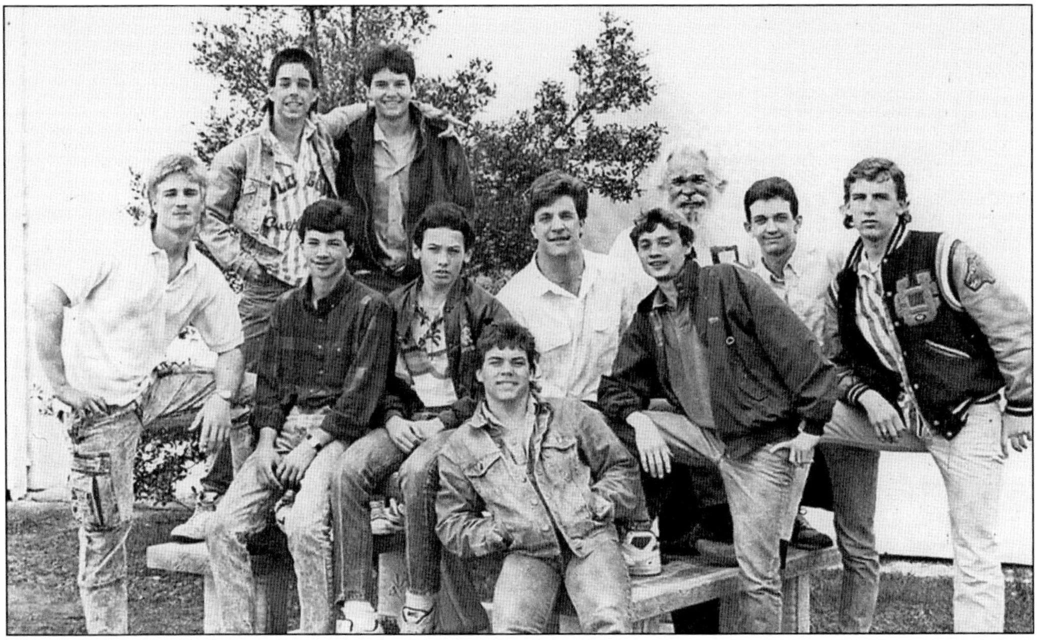

The Union County 1988 golf team finished second in the state championship. The team included Russell Bryer, Greg Baggett, Jamie Gibson, Barry Turner, Bill Burnette, Chuck Kersher, Brad Wildes, Scotty Thompson, Coach Joe White, Steve Adams, and Tim Strickland. (Courtesy UCHS Yearbook.)

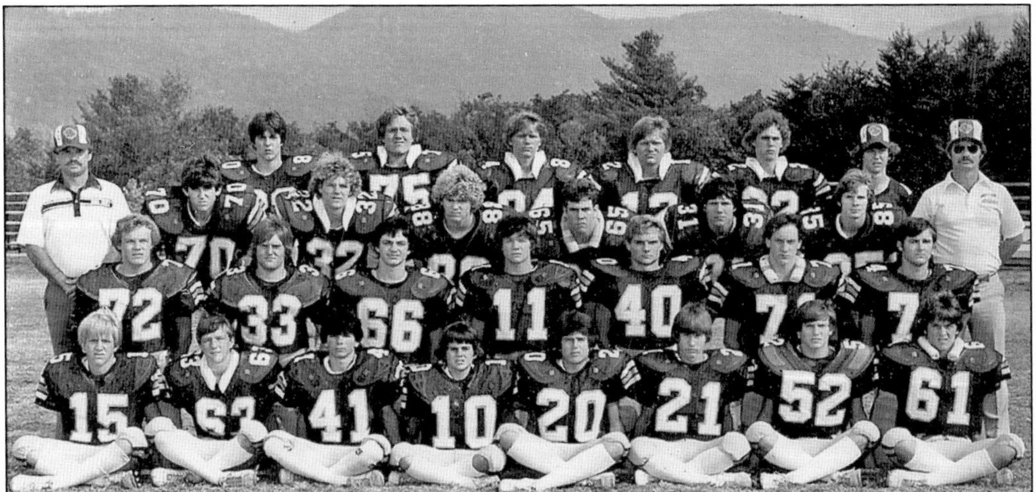

The Panthers 1983 football team went 9–1 and were crowned region 8AA North champions. The team included, from left to right (first row) Daryl Allison, Scott Loyd, David Hand, Howard McCombs, Daniel Griffin, Jay Burks, Travis Swartz, and Bobby Bradley; (second row) Chris Bergen, Jacque Devereaux, Franklin Brown, Shaun Conley, Mark Donahue, Mike Hudson, and Craig Davenport; (third row) head coach Terry Rogers, Mark Rogers, Terry Kelley, Sean Hughes, Mike Kiernan, Doug Hubbard, George Thompson, and coach Tommy Stephens; (fourth row) Jeff Crawford, Brian Allison, Donald Jones, Ronald Jones, Jeff Gooch, and manager Tommy Townsend. Not pictured is coach Ron Byers. (Courtesy Terry Rogers.)

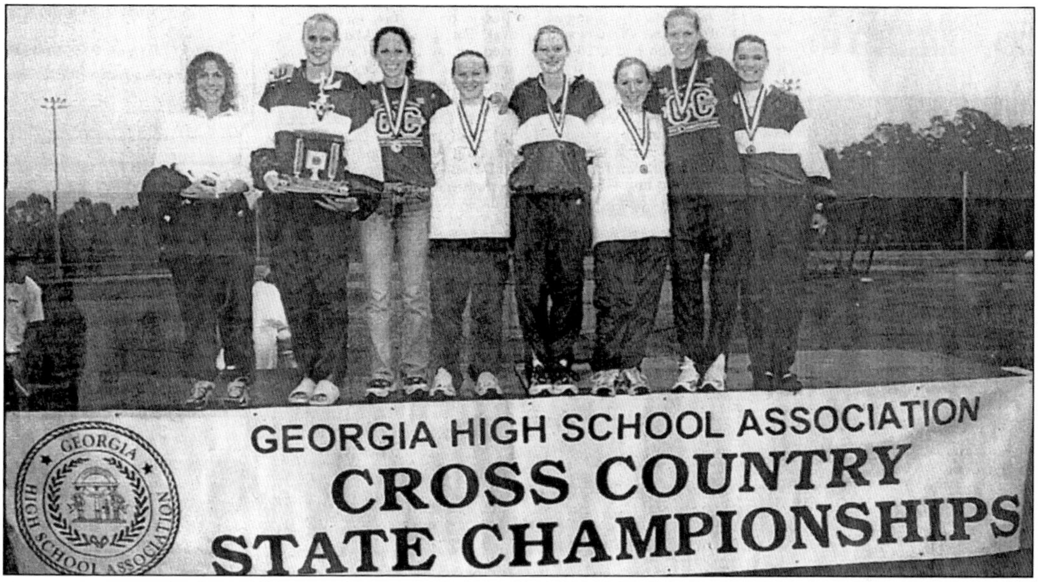

Cross-country began at Union County High School in the late 1990s. Either the boys' team or the girls' team made an appearance in the state championships for six consecutive years. Under Coach Jackie Hughes in 2000, the girls' team was region 8-AA champions and finished fourth in the state. The team included, from left to right, coach Jackie Hughes and runners Andrea Neely, Katie Baribault, Molly Coker, Becky Johnson, Jaime Hansen, Megan Kirkpatrick, and Leah Dove. (Photo by Norman Cooper.)

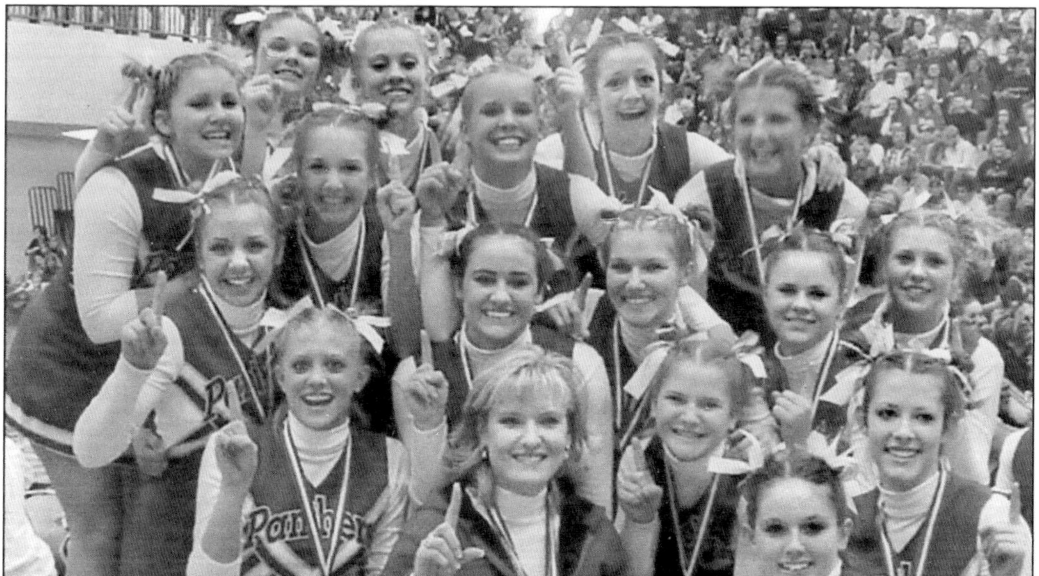

Union County High Competitive Cheerleaders won the region championship and finished seventh in the state championships in only their second year as a team. Shown with the region championship trophy are sponsor Tiffany Winkler (front center), Brittany Crowder, Ashley Snyder, Abigail Williams, Jenna Thomas, Maria Thomas, Emily Knight, Hannah Chapman, Catherine Jarrett, Christina Collins, Brittany Parks, Laura Gowder, Hannah Rollins, Courtney Stephens, Blair Groves, Leila Partin, and Brittany Swautz. (Photo by Norman Cooper.)

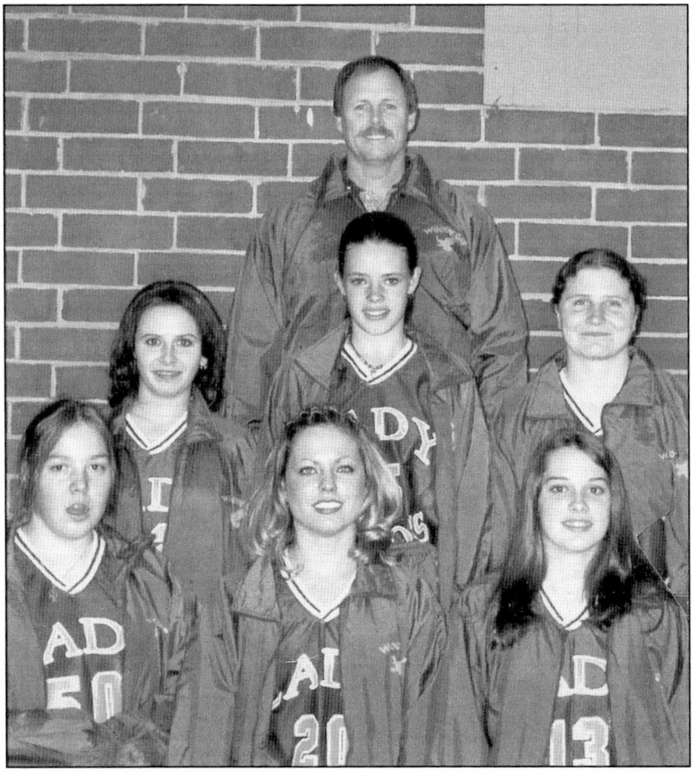

Woody Gap High Lady Falcons basketball team won 38 games from 1996 to 2000. Sabrina Pickelsimer, Laci Burger, and Jesse Corbin were 13–3 in their senior year. Sabrina scored 1,010 points, blocked 42 shots, and had 593 rebounds, 148 assists, and 271 steals in four years. This team in the late 1990s included, from left to right, (front row) Candace Jordan, Laci Burger, and Ashley Reagin; (middle row) Jessie Corbin, Jessica Pierce, and Sabrina Pickelsimer; (back row) coach Glenn Kough. Glenn Kough coached basketball for nine years and tennis for more than a decade, and was athletic director for eight years.

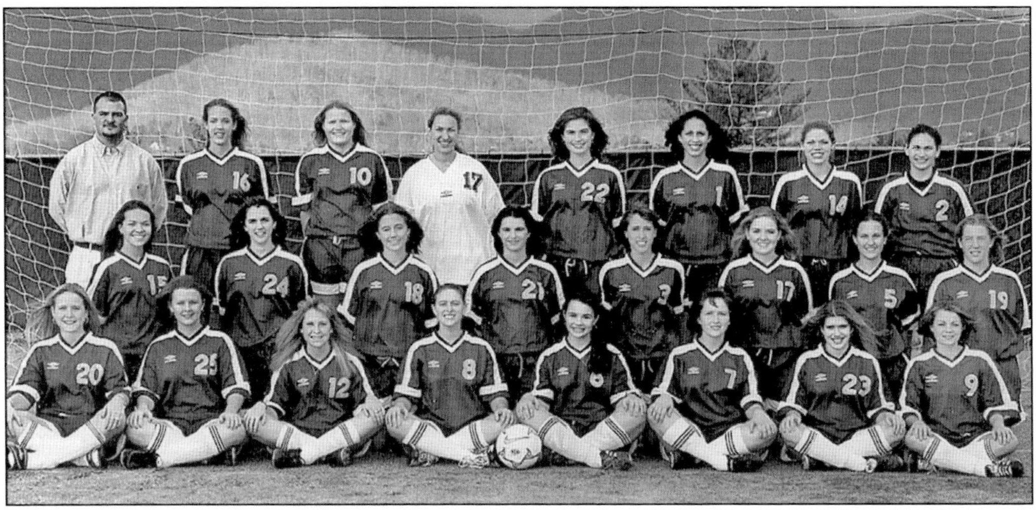

Soccer became a sport at Union County High in the late 1990s. Coach Ed Rohrbaugh skippered the first boys' team. In the boys' second and third year they advanced to state. Tim Hunter's Lady Panthers team in 2000 won a region championship and berth in the state playoffs. Pictured are, from left to right, (front row) Jennifer Morse, Amanda Goyne, Jeni Christensen, Henrietta Dyer, Susan Bailey, Charlie Dyer, Shawnee Matthews, and Katie Rybka; (middle row) Stacy Mellendorf, Tali Patterson, Nicki Patterson, Danielle Romine, Callie Baribault, Lindsay Nelson, Rebecca Day-Lewis, and Nicole Belton; (back row) Coach Tim Hunter, Jamie Weldon, Jodi Tholen, Georgia Adams, Wendy Dwyer, Katie Baribault, Tiffany Stephens, and Caroline Thomas.

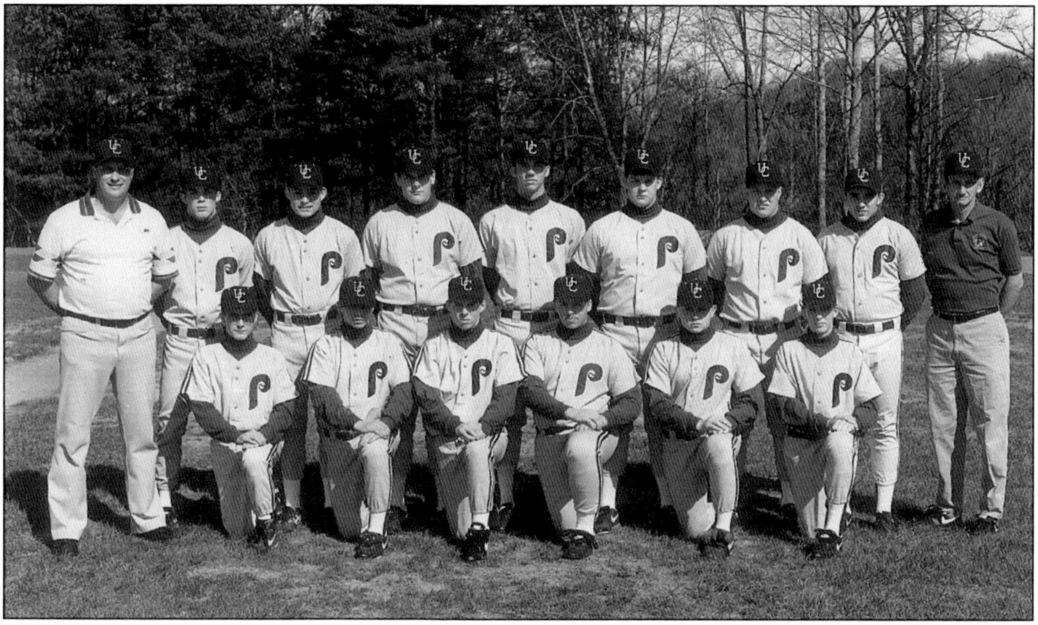

The 1995 Union County Panthers were the best baseball team in the state in their division and the number two team in the state overall, as they played in the state championship series. Coaches Larry Turner and Junior Burnette skippered the team of Keith Banks, Kyle Young, Davy Murray, Wesley Garrett, Mitchell Ingram, Levin MacDougald, Cory Conley, John Davis, Chad Spiva, Chris Adams, Kevin Hutson, Jason Helton, and Chad Farrell. Todd Forrest is not pictured. (Courtesy Judy Spiva.)

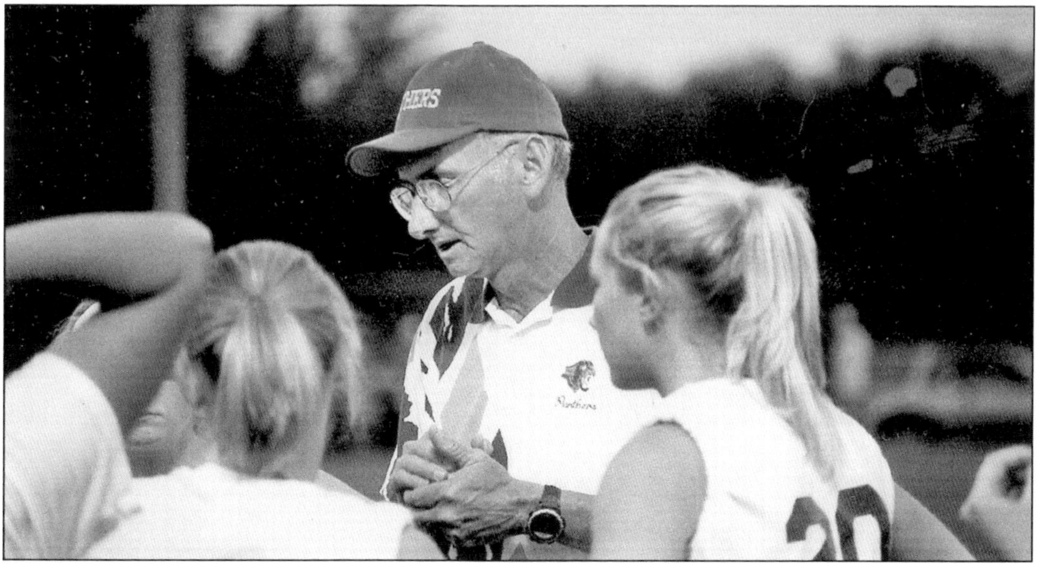

Coach Junior Burnette served as assistant baseball coach for many years at Union County High and was the head girls' softball coach for 16 years. As head softball coach, he and his Lady Panthers advanced to the state tournament four times. In 1994 his team was third in Georgia. In 2000, his team was ranked in the top eight. Coach Burnette was Region Coach of the Year in 1994 and 1995. He had four sub-region championships and two region championships. (Photo by Norman Cooper.)

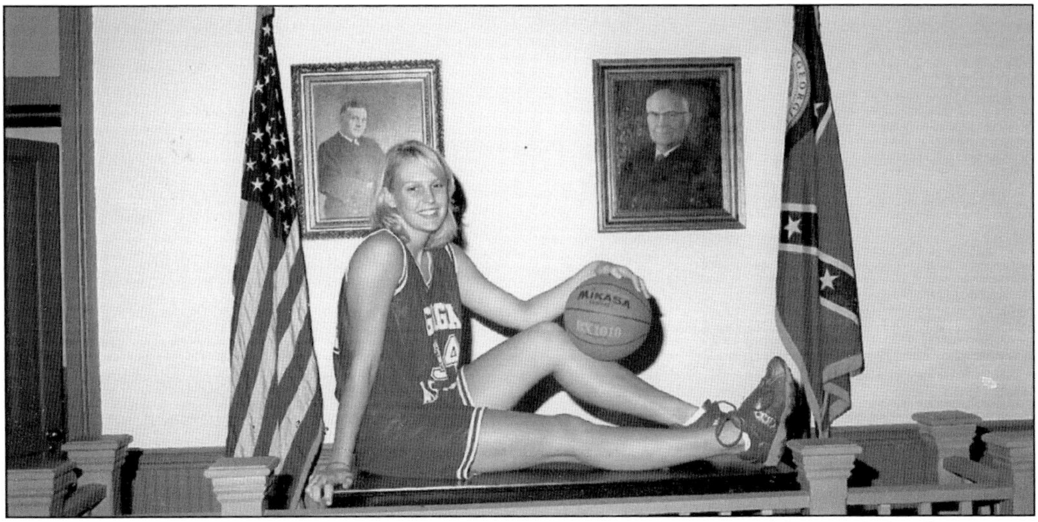

Numerous Union County High athletes have attended college on athletic scholarships since the 1980s. Andrea Neely, seen here, was the first to sign with a Division I school. She played in two NCAA Basketball Tournaments on the Georgia State Panthers basketball team. Robby Brown, a non-scholarship player at Georgia Tech, played in the Humanitarian Bowl. Players attending college on athletic scholarships since the 1980s include (football) Craig Young, Mike Kiernan, Brian Allison, Brad Wildes, Ryan Fitzgerald, Trent Dyer, Ben Arndt; (girls' basketball) Jamesa Dobbs, Annette Colwell, Angie Akins, Amy Rice, Mandy Bradley, Jana Tallent, Angie Garland, Andrea Neely, Joanna Day-Lewis, Nikki Gurley; (boys' basketball) Chris Guthery, Rim Pauley, Chris Adams; (girls' softball) Brandy Dyer, Beth Kelley, Christy Queen; (soccer) Jamie Weldon, Amanda Goyne; (baseball) Todd Cone, Scott Cone, Craig Young, Tommy Rogers, Bobby Pattee, Ivan Phillips, Travis Stalcup, Chris Robbins, Tracey Bracken, Chad Spiva, Jason Helton, Joel Gooch; (golf) Greg Young, Jamey Gibson, and Scott Thompson. (Photo by Norman Cooper.)

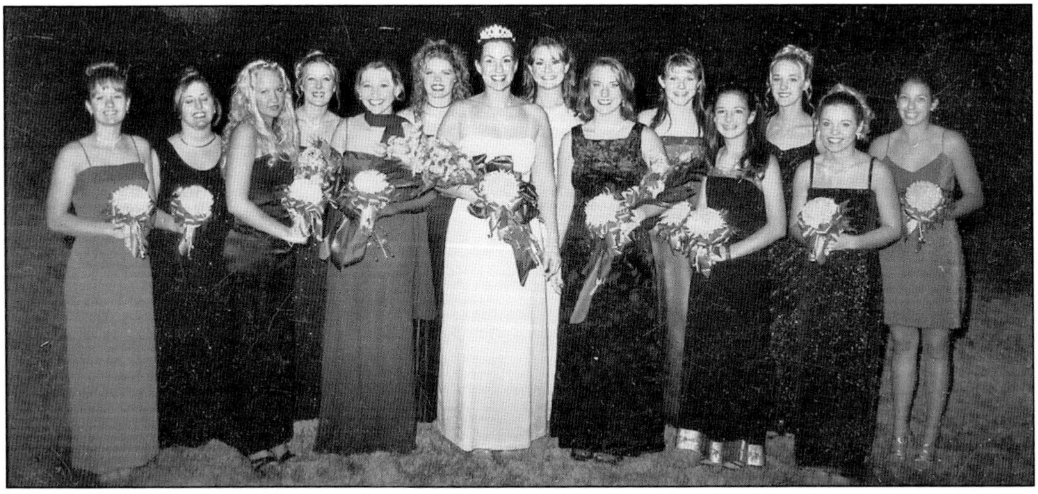

Homecoming is a big tradition at Union County High School and at Woody Gap High School. The Union County High 2000–2001 football homecoming court, shown above, included Jessica Collins, Codie Griggs, Dru Ann Sullivan, Andrea Trandell, Holly Weber, Tiffany Stephens, Georgia Adams, Holly Wright, Alison McAfee, Courtney Stephens, Laura Gowder, Rebecca Brackett, Jessica Logston, and Brittney Green. (Photo by Norman Cooper)

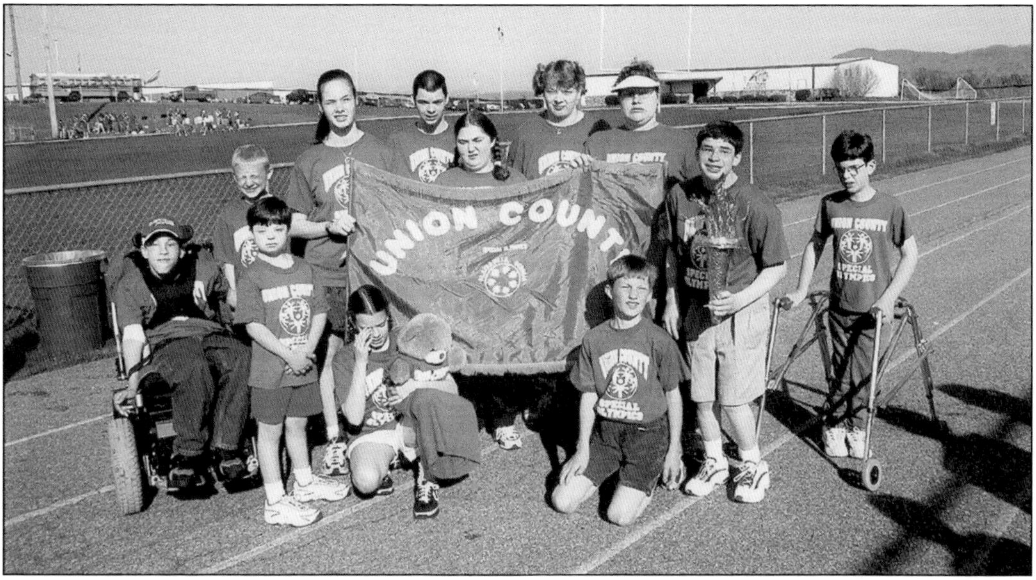

The Special Olympics mission is to provide training and competition in a variety of Olympic sports by helping individuals develop physical fitness, demonstrate courage, experience joy, and participate in a sharing of gifts, skills, and friendship with their families, other Special Olympics athletes, and the community. Every year, Special Olympics are held at the football field in Blairsville. Hundreds of students fill the stands to watch the event, which includes a parade of athletes, competition, and an awards ceremony. (Photo by Norman Cooper.)

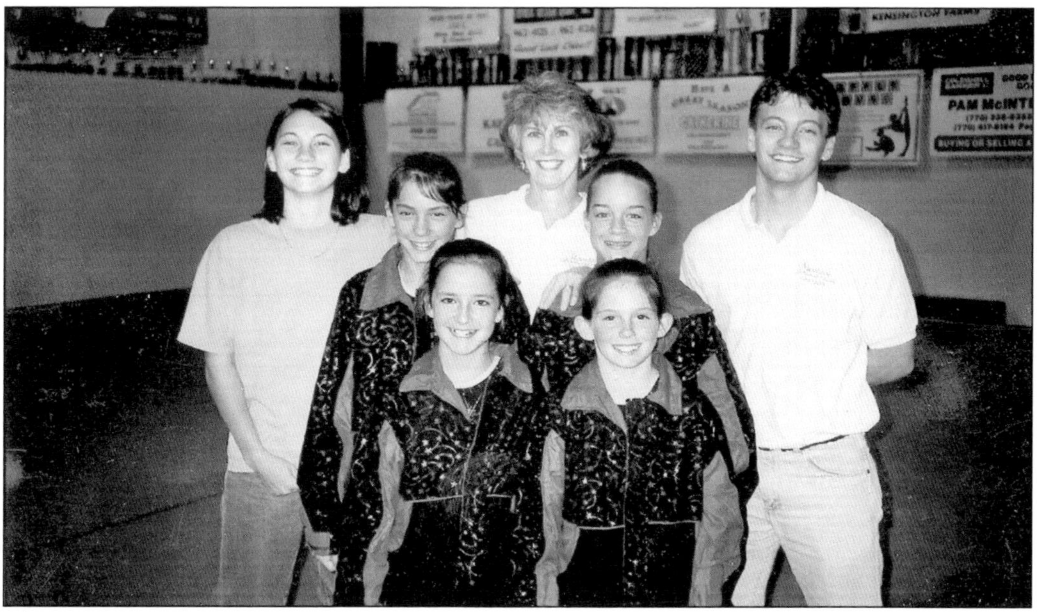

The Mountain Gymnastics Center was founded by Shelley Thomas, back center, and has operated in Blairsville for nearly two decades. Shelley was a member of the University of Georgia gymnastics team from 1973 to 1975, competing in bars and vault. She is assisted by Caroline Thomas, left back, and Patrick Thomas, right back. Gymnasts in the mid-1990s seen here are, from left to right, (front row) Laura Gowder and Jenna Thomas; (middle row) Nikki Gurley and Kellie Hughes.

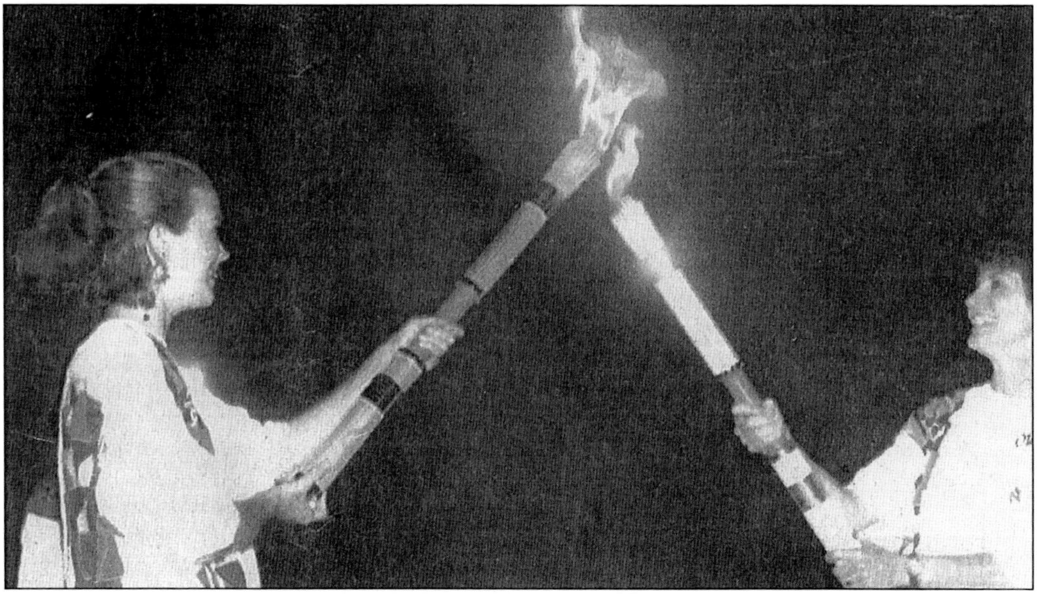

The Olympics came to Atlanta in 1996 and Union County was part of that historic event. The torch came through the county, and an Olympic team chose the county as a pre-Olympic training site. Steve Cockerham, Sandy Bell, Melissa Breedlove, above at left, and Shelly Thomas, at right, carried the torch through Blairsville. Thousands filled the stadium at the Union County High before dawn to welcome the torch as it headed to Atlanta. (Photo by Norman Cooper.)

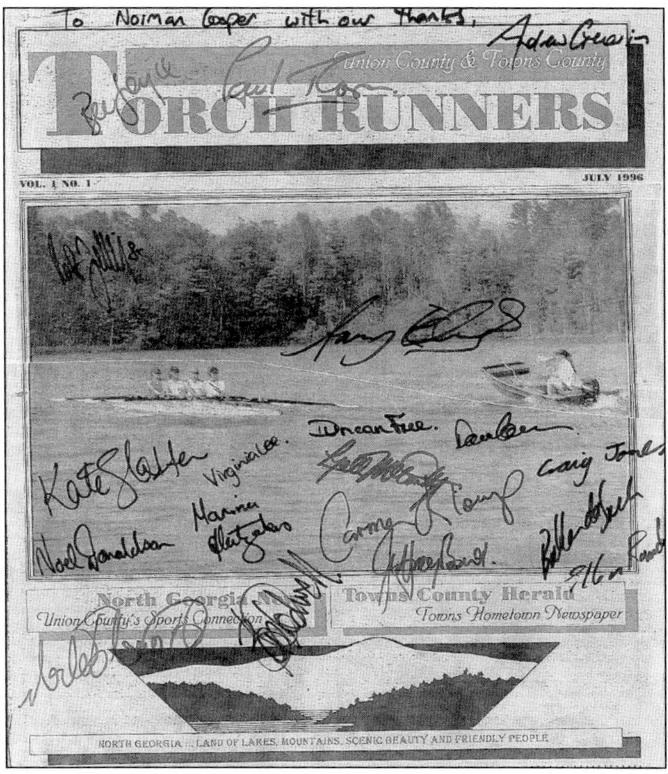

To Norman Cooper with our thanks,

Union County & Towns County

TORCH RUNNERS

VOL. 1 NO. 1 JULY 1996

North Georgia News
Union County's Sports Connection

Towns County Herald
Towns Hometown Newspaper

NORTH GEORGIA ... LAND OF LAKES, MOUNTAINS, SCENIC BEAUTY AND FRIENDLY PEOPLE

TorchRunners was a publication created by *North Georgia News* editor/sports editor Norman Cooper, featuring photos and articles that recorded the story of Union County's involvement in the Olympics. Members of the 1996 Australian Olympic rowing team signed one of the issues, and most of those signing earned gold medals in the Olympics. Scores of the publications were sent to Australia.

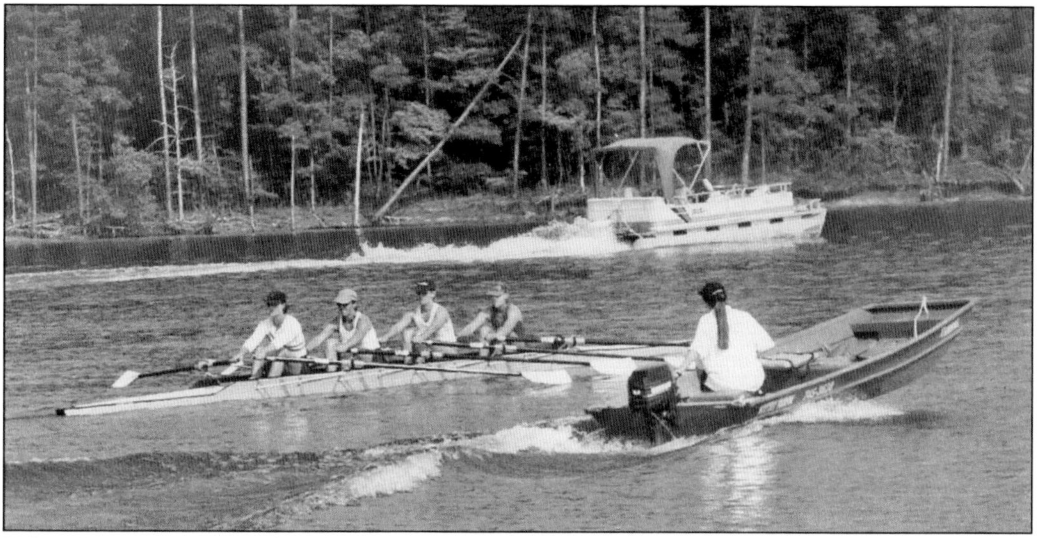

When Union County Chamber of Commerce president Steve Cockerham, Australian team manager Andy Guerin, surveyor Jimmy Alexander, and Norman Cooper scouted for a practice venue on Lake Nottely, the temperature was below freezing with wind and snow. The local Olympic Committee was headed by Blairsville-Union County Chamber of Commerce president Steve Cockerham, Chamber Executive Director Libby Freeman, and future Chamber Executive Director Jean Easterling. Local students chosen as part of the Dream Team, designed to promote the Olympic spirit, included Wesley Burnette, Carvel Wood, Pam Turner, Bretney Turner, Jody Bridges, and Kyle Young. Ray Ashurst was the Dream Team advisor. The Garden Club of Georgia installed 50 banners featuring the Olympics in Union County. The photo shows some members of the rowing team training on Lake Nottely. (Photo by Norman Cooper.)

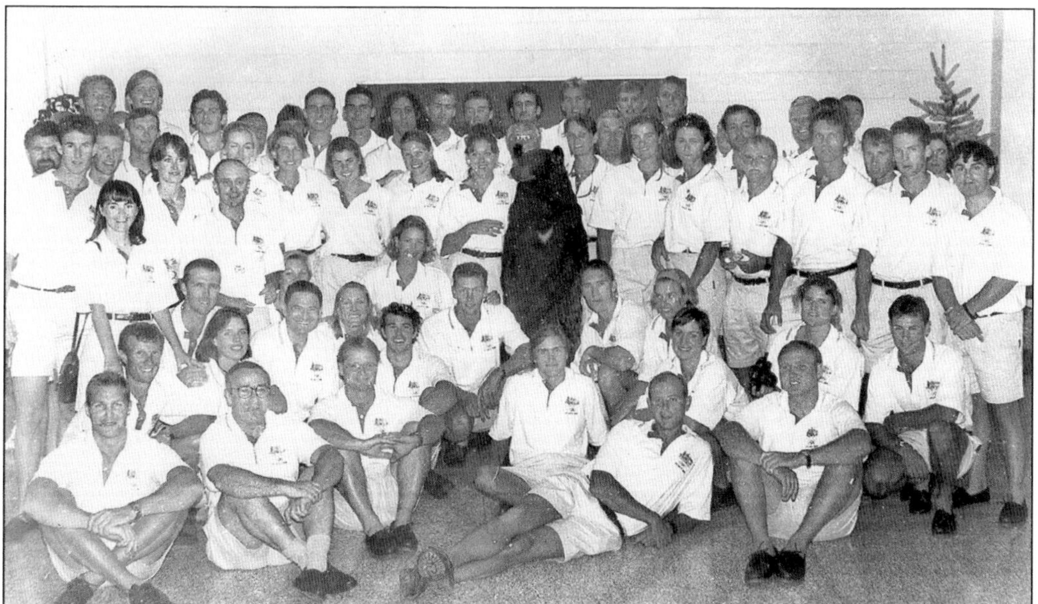

The Australian Olympic rowing team gathers for a group photo after their reception at the Union County Middle School cafeteria. (Photo by Norman Cooper.)

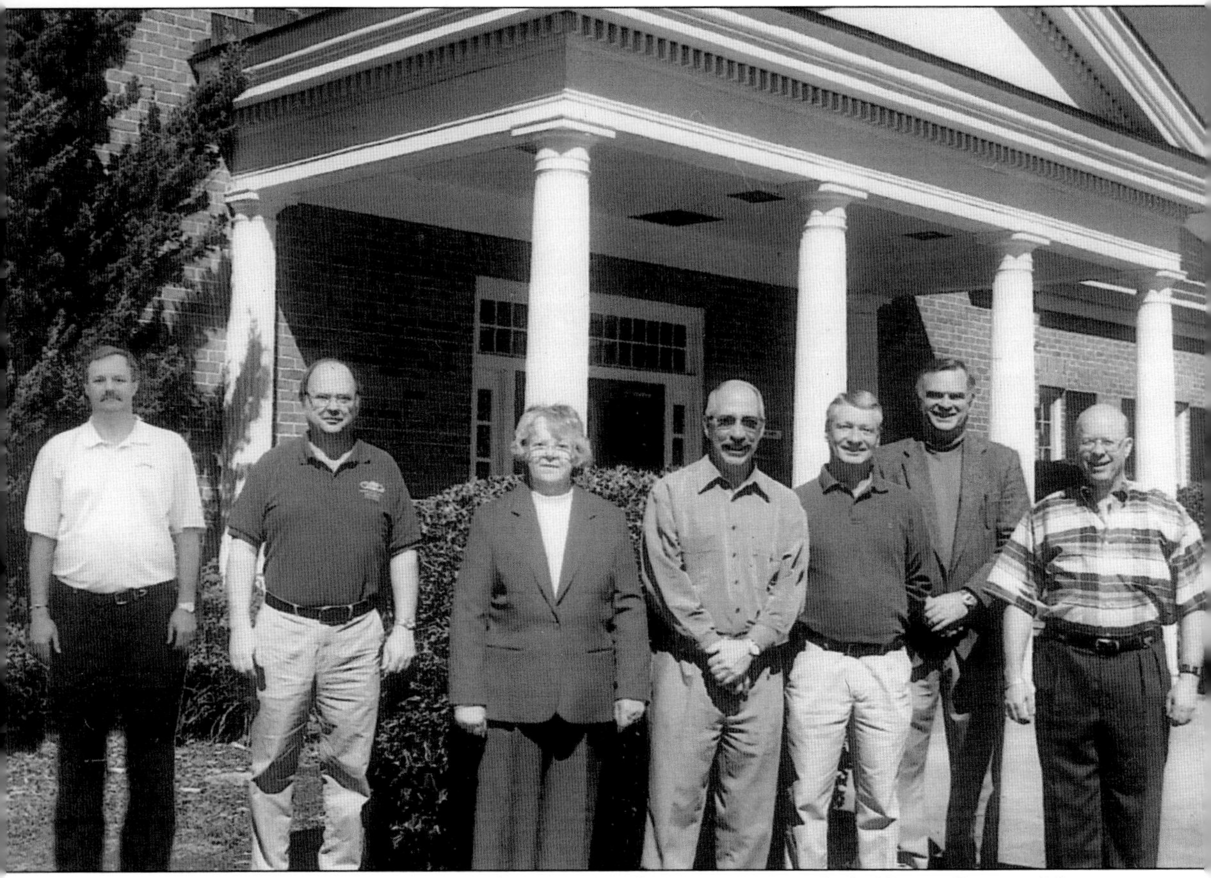

The Union County Georgia Pictorial History Book Committee included Larry Garrett, Norman Cooper, Martyne Jokela, Lamar Paris, Tommy Stephens, Ron Byers, and Roy Hamby.

Presenting this rich history—which spans 33 years and could be shown in thousands of photographs—in one pictorial book was no easy task. The goal of the committee was to include as much variety and uniqueness as possible. It is our sincere desire that you have enjoyed reading this hook as much as we enjoyed creating it.

—Norman, Martyne, Ron, Tommy, Lamar, Roy, Larry